ANNE BRONTË was born on 17 January 1820 at Thornton, Yorkshire, the youngest of the six children of the Rev. Patrick Brontë and his wife, Maria. Anne lived with the family at Haworth on the Yorkshire moors until the age of nineteen when she left to become governess to the Inghams at Blake Hall. In 1841 she left to take up a similar post with the Robinson family at Thorp Green, where she remained until 1845. Her first novel, *Agnes Grey*, based upon her experiences as a governess, was published in 1847. She also published poetry under the name of Acton Bell in collaboration with her sisters, Charlotte and Emily. Her second novel, *The Tenant of Wildfell Hall*, appeared in 1848. A year later, on 28 May 1849, she died from tuberculosis, and was buried at Scarborough.

ANNE SMITH is a freelance writer, journalist and reviewer. She has published a number of critical essays on nineteenth-century fiction, and edited and contributed to books of essays on the period. She was founder-editor of *The Literary Review*. Her first novel, *The Magic Glass*, won Authors' Club and Arts Council awards.

JULIET R. V. BARKER has edited and introduced *The Brontës: Selected Poems* for the Everyman's Library.

# ANNE BRONTË

# *Agnes Grey*
# *and*
# *Poems*

Introduction by Anne Smith
Poems selected by
Juliet R. V. Barker

J. M. Dent & Sons Ltd
London
Charles E. Tuttle Co., Inc.
Rutland, Vermont

EVERYMAN'S LIBRARY

© Introduction, David Campbell Publishers Ltd,
1985
All rights reserved

Phototypeset in 10/11½pt Linotron Sabon by
The Word Factory Ltd, Rossendale
Made in Great Britain by
The Guernsey Press Co. Ltd, Guernsey, C.I. for
J. M. Dent & Sons Ltd
91 Clapham High Street, London SW4 7TA
and
Charles E. Tuttle Co., Inc.
28, South Main Street,
Rutland, Vermont
05701, U.S.A.

First published in Everyman's Library with
*The Tenant of Wildfell Hall* in 1914
Reprinted, *Agnes Grey* only, as an
Everyman Classic, 1982
Reset edition, 1985
Reprinted 1987, 1989
Reissued with *Poems* 1991

ISBN 0 460 87121 8

Everyman's Library
Reg. U.S. Patent Office

# Introduction

Mrs Gaskell's description of the Brontë children as their mother lay dying must be one of the most haunting passages in literature:

> . . . the six little creatures used to walk out, hand in hand, towards the glorious wild moors, which in after days they loved so passionately; the elder ones taking thoughtful care for the toddling wee things.

She went on to say that they 'were grave and silent beyond their years; subdued, probably, by the presence of serious illness in the house'. A servant commented more frankly, ' . . . there never were such good children. I used to think them spiritless, they were so different to any children I had ever seen.'

Mrs Brontë was married in 1812; between 1813 and 1820 she had six children, of whom Anne was the youngest, born just twenty months before her mother died, at thirty-nine, of stomach cancer. It was shortly after Anne's first birthday that Mrs Brontë's illness confined her to bed. An informant told Mrs Gaskell that she 'was not very anxious to see much of her children, probably because the sight of them, knowing how soon they were to be left motherless, would have agitated her too much'.

Elizabeth Branwell, Mrs Brontë's elder sister, came then from her native Cornwall to take charge of the household, which Winifred Gérin described thus:

> Haworth Parsonage is a dignified, finely proportioned Georgian house, built in the seventeen-seventies, but it contained only five bedrooms, of which one was a narrow slip without a fireplace over the entrance-hall, and another little more than a box-room over the back. Into these five rooms Mr and Mrs Brontë, their six children, Miss Branwell, the two servants and Mrs Brontë's nurse had to be packed. In the worst room of all from the point of view of hygiene the four eldest girls slept in little camp-beds that were collapsed by day, when it was converted into the children's nursery. Here, until long after they were into their teens, the survivors slept, played, wrote and enjoyed unchallenged liberty. The dimensions of the room are 9 ft by 5 ft 7½ in.

Miss Branwell's feelings about Haworth, and the children's feelings about her, are admirably summed up in the Gaskell *Life*:

> Miss Branwell ... had strong prejudices, and soon took a distaste to Yorkshire ... She missed the small round of cheerful, social visiting perpetually going on in a country town; she missed the friends she had known from her childhood, some of whom had been her parents' friends before they were hers; she disliked many of the customs of the place, and particularly dreaded the cold damp arising from the flag floors in the passages and parlours of Haworth Parsonage. ... The children respected her, and had that sort of affection for her which is generated by esteem; but I do not think they ever freely loved her. It was a severe trial for any one at her time of life to change neighbourhood and habitation so entirely as she did ...

She had had no intention of remaining at Haworth as a substitute mother to her nieces, but since all Mr Brontë's efforts at finding a new wife failed, remain there she did.

Although she took to little Anne, Miss Branwell's attitude to her seems to have been that of the Victorian spinster of limited experience suddenly presented with the opportunity to put her theories of child-moulding into practice. Anne, for her part, had the loving, clinging sort of nature that no doubt encouraged her aunt in this. But the main element in Miss Branwell's system of upbringing seems to have been a dour, hellfire brand of Methodism. 'With all the dogmatism of an arid temperament,' Winifred Gérin comments, 'Miss Branwell expounded the tenets of a religion of love as though it were first and foremost a religion of fear.' She brainwashed Anne with a sense of sin and guilt that she had to struggle with all her life.

Maria, the eldest of the Brontë children and the fondly remembered Helen Burns of Charlotte's *Jane Eyre*, was much more of a mother to her sisters and brother than Elizabeth Branwell could ever be. For a start, she was their intellectual equal, which their aunt plainly was not. At seven years old, Maria would 'shut herself up with a newspaper and be able to tell one everything when she came out'. Miss Branwell's literary tastes ran to light literature like the *Ladies' Magazine* and to the sensational *Methodist Magazine*, all dreams and apparitions calculated to appeal to the morbid sensibilities of menopausal Victorian maiden aunts.

Since Anne was the youngest and often laid low with asthma, she came most directly under her aunt's influence. That influence would have increased immeasurably when, three years after Mrs Brontë's death, Maria was sent with Elizabeth and Charlotte to The Clergy Daughters' School at Cowan Bridge (the Lowood of *Jane Eyre*). It was then that the bond between Anne and Emily, left at home to their own devices, was first formed. But three months later Emily was also packed off to school at Cowan Bridge, and her departure coincided with the dismissal of the two young sisters, Nancy and Sarah Garrs, who had been the children's nursemaids since the Brontës' arrival in Haworth. Eight months later Maria and Elizabeth were dead, and the remaining sisters were together at home again.

Anne's early childhood therefore was fraught with traumatic events – deaths, separations and illness, with no constant mother-figure to sustain her. She never knew stability. The counterpart of Mrs Brontë's avoiding her children in her illness must be Patrick Brontë's decision to take his main meals separately from them. Mrs Gaskell tactfully explains that he was 'obliged' to dine alone, 'to have the quiet necessary for digestion'. Miss Branwell, too, took her meals on a tray in her room when she could. The children were therefore thrown on to their own resources and company. The parsonage and the moors were their whole world. They appear to have had little or no social intercourse outside their own immediate circle:

> . . . owing to Mrs Brontë's death so soon after her husband had removed into the district, and also to the distances, and the bleak country to be traversed, the wives of these clerical friends did not accompany their husbands; and the daughters grew up out of childhood into girlhood bereft, in a singular manner, of all such society as would have been natural to their age, sex, and station.

In such circumstances, it is little wonder that the Brontë sisters grew up to be pathologically shy, with a deep conviction of their own personal lack of worth and a corresponding need to feel independent at any cost, not to be a burden, financially or emotionally, upon anyone.

The Clergy Daughters' School was a charitable institution. In other ways, too, the sisters had to accept charity: Charlotte's stiff little letters of gratitude to kindly god-parents for their gifts of cast-off clothing are painful to read. Already marked out by their social timidity and eccentricity, they were also marked out from their peers by their dress. Charlotte's friend Mary Taylor recalled that Charlotte arrived at Roe Head School in 'a covered cart, in very old-fashioned clothes . . . When she appeared in the schoolroom, her dress was changed, but just as old. She looked a little old woman . . .' Her hair, according to Ellen Nussey, was in 'an unbecoming tight frizz'.

None of the Brontë sisters was equipped to cope with the social life of school. The only kindred spirits they had encountered were one another, and there was no adult female who could provide them with a congenial role-model. On the one hand they had Miss Branwell with her melancholy Methodism and a mind and habits more suited to the bygone days of social trivia in genteel Penzance, on the other hand the beloved servant Tabby, who perhaps provided them with the only example of normality in their immediate environment, but who was nonetheless a spinster and a peasant.

Their childhood lives were divided between the absolute freedom of the moors and the claustrophobic little parsonage. The freedom they enjoyed had its basis in benign neglect: they could do what they liked as long as they did their chores and did not impinge on the lives of the adults around them. When Charlotte described Anne in a letter to her friend Ellen Nussey as 'a patient, persecuted stranger' she might equally well have been describing herself or Emily outside their native heath.


As an infant, Anne Brontë was the darling of the family, the more so perhaps because she was the only one who was weak at birth, and whose survival often seemed to hang in the balance – the dampness of the climate at Haworth, and Miss Branwell's suffocating efforts to hold it at bay, did not offer the best conditions in which an asthmatic infant might thrive. The grip this exerted on her sisters' imaginations, no doubt fed by their aunt's readings of inspiring death-bed scenes from the *Methodist Magazine*, is evident in an anecdote from Nancy Garrs. When

Anne was a baby, 'Charlotte rushed into her Papa's study to say there was an angel standing beside Anne's cradle, but when they returned it was gone, though Charlotte was sure she had seen it.'

Anne grew up to be the best-looking of the Brontë sisters, like Emily taller than the then average height for a woman. Ellen Nussey described her in her 'Reminiscences' (1871): 'Her hair was very pretty, light brown, and fell on her neck in graceful curls. She had lovely violet-blue eyes, fine pencilled eyebrows, and a clear, almost transparent complexion.' But Ellen was very fond of Anne and hers might have been a partial eye.

The more sophisticated, objective view of Anne was given by George Smith, of Smith, Elder & Co., Charlotte's publisher: 'She was a gentle, quiet, rather subdued person, by no means pretty, yet of pleasing appearance . . . Her manner was curiously expressive of a wish for protection and encouragement, a kind of constant appeal, which invited sympathy.' Winifred Gérin adds that Anne 'was not persecuted with the sense of her plainness, as Charlotte was'.

Since Victorian biographers and memoirists of the Brontë sisters found the quiet, low-key Anne of little interest compared to the passionate Charlotte and the enigmatic, mystical Emily, they have not offered and did not seek much information about her. We know that she remained at home until she was fifteen, when Charlotte undertook to work as a governess at Roe Head School to pay her fees. Anne attended Roe Head from 1835 to Christmas 1837, when a severe bout of gastric 'flu alarmed Charlotte about her health, and led to her withdrawal from the school. During her illness at Roe Head Anne underwent a religious crisis. At her request a Moravian bishop from a nearby village was called in to give her spiritual comfort. In a letter to a friend after the publication of Mrs Gaskell's *Life*, the Rev. La Trobe explained the crux of the problem: 'I found her well acquainted with the main truths of the Bible respecting her salvation, but seeing them more through the law than the Gospel, more as a requirement from God than His Gift in His Son.' This seems to have been the first open manifestation of the religious dilemmas that worried Anne all her life, and stemmed from her inability to accept her aunt's Calvinistic doctrine of election.

Put simply, Anne's problem was that if she believed in Miss Branwell's God, and accepted that those whom He had not chosen were destined for eternal damnation, she could not bring herself to love Him as she had been taught she should; if she believed in a more personal, loving God, she had to fear the artificial comfort of self-delusion. With La Trobe's guidance, he says, she became 'conscious more of her not loving the Lord her God than of acts of enmity to Him'. This implies that the gentle Anne, still in her teens, must have been fretting about her supposed sins ('acts of enmity') and finding it very hard, if not impossible, to love the God her aunt had described to her. The problem recurred, as is evident in her poetry.

For long stretches at a time, Anne had been the only daughter left at the parsonage to keep Miss Branwell company. She shared her mother's bedroom with her aunt, which meant that she could not join in Charlotte and Emily's 'secret plays' in the little bedroom at night. In short, she had had to endure the full blast of Miss Branwell's religious melancholy, and it had affected her deeply – Charlotte wrote that it 'communicated a sad shade to her brief, blameless life'.

It is this that underpins the exchanges between Agnes and Nancy Brown in Chapter 11 of *Agnes Grey*. Indeed, it is not too fanciful to see correspondences between the Rev. Mr Hatfield in the novel and Aunt Branwell. Ellen Nussey's diplomatic remarks on Miss Branwell show her to be somewhat vain of her appearance – she always wore silk dresses, shawls and lace; she owned some valuable jewellery, and took snuff 'out of a very pretty gold snuff box' – none of which was at all compatible with the Methodism she professed. There is a similar disparity between Mr Hatfield's narcissistic behaviour and the censorious intolerance which he preached. Such ambivalence would disturb and depress the mind of Anne Brontë in her childhood every bit as much as it did Nancy Brown in the novel.

Mrs Gaskell, no doubt taking her cue from Charlotte, describes Anne as 'docile, pensive ... always patient and tractable'. Charlotte herself wrote of her in a Preface to *Wuthering Heights and Agnes Grey*, a year after Anne's death, as 'Long-suffering, self-denying, reflective and intelligent, a constitutional reserve and taciturnity placed and kept her in the shade, and covered her mind, and especially her feelings, with a sort of nun-like veil, which was rarely lifted ... hers was naturally a sensitive, reserved and dejected nature.' But the eldest sister's interpretation of the youngest's nature should not be accepted without serious reservations. Other evidence modifies this image of Anne.

It is tempting, and not inappropriate, to believe that we might be seeing through Anne's own eyes something of her relationship with Charlotte and Aunt Branwell in Agnes Grey's description of herself in the opening pages of the novel:

> I, being the younger by five or six years, was always regarded as the *child*, and the pet of the family: father, mother, and sister all combined to spoil me – not by foolish indulgence to render me fractious and ungovernable, but by ceaseless kindness to make me too helpless and dependent – too unfit for buffeting with the cares and turmoils of life.

> . . . . though a woman in my own estimation, I was still a child in theirs; and my mother, like most active, managing women, was not gifted with very active daughters: for this reason – that being so clever and diligent herself, she was never tempted to trust her affairs to a deputy, but on the contrary, was willing to act and think for others as well as for number one; and whatever was the business in hand, she was apt to think that no one could do it so well as herself.

> How delightful it would be to be a governess! To go out into the world; to enter upon a new life; to act for myself; to exercise my unused faculties; to try my unknown powers; to earn my own maintenance, and something to comfort and help my father, mother, and sister, besides exonerating them from the provision of my food and clothing . . .

The well-meant patronage that the youngest has to endure in most families is as implicit in these passages as it is apparent in Charlotte's letter to Ellen Nussey about Anne's taking up her first post as a governess, in 1839, a year after she left Roe Head:

> Poor child! she left us last Monday; no one went with her; it was her own wish that she might be allowed to go alone, as she thought she could manage better, and summon more courage, if thrown entirely upon her own resources. We have had one letter from her since she went. She expresses herself very well satisfied, and says that Mrs—— is extremely kind; the two eldest children alone are under her care, the

rest are confined to the nursery, with which and its occupants she has nothing to do . . . I hope she'll do. You would be astonished what a sensible, clever letter she writes; it is only the talking part that I fear. But I do seriously apprehend that Mrs—— will sometimes conclude that she has a natural impediment in her speech.

The saintly, self-effacing and rather insipid image of Anne does not quite chime with the fact that she was dismissed from this post for tying two of the children to a table-leg to restrain them while she got on with her work. Nor does it chime with the Victorian critics' interpretation of the outspoken diatribe against modern notions of education in *Agnes Grey* and of her bold description of the cruelty and savagery of the children in Agnes's charge as 'eccentric and unpleasant'; nor, indeed, with the courageous stand she took against these critics in her Preface to the second edition of *The Tenant of Wildfell Hall*. It is just possible that Charlotte – and incidentally Branwell, who had dismissed her as 'nothing, absolutely nothing' when she was fourteen – did not understand her at all. Just in passing we might note, too, how close was the affinity between Anne's fiction and Jane Austen's: Charlotte never could bring herself to like 'Miss Austen's "mild eyes"'. Anne was emphatically not the washed-out version of her older sisters and brother we have been led to imagine. But that is to anticipate.

At the beginning of 1840 she was back at the parsonage, looking out for another post. Charlotte and Emily were also there, and it was then that they conceived the idea of starting their own school at home. Both Charlotte and Emily had suffered and felt themselves exploited as governesses. The sisters knew they could only be happy together, at Haworth.

In the summer of 1840 Anne became governess to the family of Mr and Mrs Edmund Robinson of Thorp Green Hall near York. The worldly Murrays in *Agnes Grey* are based on the Robinsons. Anne was not happy there. She wrote in her 'birthday note' for 1841, 'I dislike the situation and wish to change it for another.' In Emily's birthday note for the same year she described Anne as 'exiled and harrassed' (*sic*), and in Charlotte's letter to Ellen Nussey, in which she described Anne as 'a patient, persecuted stranger', she said, 'I have one aching feeling at my heart . . . it is about Anne; she has so much to endure: far, far more than I ever had . . . She is more lonely – less gifted with the power of making friends, even than I am.' In another letter she described Anne's return to Thorp Hall as going 'back to Egypt and the house of bondage'.

Not long after she arrived at the Robinsons', Anne's poem, 'Lines Written at Thorp Green', expressed her sense of exile and misery naively and feelingly:

> O! I am very weary
>> Though tears no longer flow;
> My eyes are tired of weeping,
>> My heart is sick of woe
>
> My life is very lonely,
>> My days pass heavily . . .

She endured her exile with the Robinsons for the better part of five years, in which time Charlotte and Emily had gone to Brussels to polish up their French and German with a view to presenting more attractive qualifications on the curriculum of the projected school.

Branwell came to Thorp Green as a tutor in 1843. At the beginning of 1845, Anne seems to have discovered something of his furtive relationship with Mrs Robinson. She gave up the position in June that year and in her 'birthday note' for July 1845 she writes, looking back to the 1841 note,

How many things have happened since it was written – some pleasant, some far otherwise. Yet I was then at Thorp Green, and now I am only just escaped from it. I was wishing to leave it then, and if I had known that I had four years longer to stay how wretched I should have been; but during my stay I have had some very unpleasant and un-dreamt-of experiences of human nature.

In a corresponding diary note, Emily describes the failure of the school project:

I should have mentioned that last summer the School Scheme was revived in full vigour – We had prospectuses printed, despatched letters to all acquaintances imparting our plans, and did our little all but it was found no go –

> now I don't desire a school at all, and none of us have any
> great longing for it.

Aunt Branwell had died when Charlotte and Emily were in
Brussels in 1842, leaving the sisters her money so that they had,
according to Emily, 'cash enough' for their needs, 'with a prospect of accumulation'.

Not enough has been made by Brontë critics and biographers
of Anne's prolonged and intimate contact with such a sociable,
worldly family as the Robinsons; they have tended to con-
centrate rather on the trauma of her discovery of Branwell's
liaison with Mrs Robinson, and the effect of his subsequent
course of self-destruction on his sisters. Yet surely this experience would have been the formative influence on Anne's
fiction, predisposing her to write Austenish novels of manners
rather than the novels of solitary, passionate and embattled
consciousnesses that her sisters wrote from their own very
different experiences. Mrs Gaskell describes Charlotte and Emily
at the Pensionnat Heger, for example, thus:

> During the hours of recreation, which were always spent in
> the garden, they invariably walked together, and generally
> kept a profound silence; Emily, though so much the taller,
> leaning on her sister. Charlotte would always answer when
> spoken to, taking the lead in replying to any remark
> addressed to both; Emily rarely spoke to anyone.

This was typical, and there is no reason to suppose that even
Charlotte ever came very far out of her shell of shyness and
humility. But after a break in the Robinson sisters'
correspondence with Anne following Branwell's dismissal, it was
renewed and went on for a long time almost on a daily basis,
showing that she had formed close ties with them in her five
years at Thorp Green, and that they turned to her for advice.

This aspect of Anne's experience is worth stressing, because it
demonstrates the difference between her and her sisters: for
whatever reason, she appears to have had greater stamina than
either Emily or Charlotte; during her five years at Thorp Green
she was much less often at home than they; she had lived
continuously with an English family who differed in every respect from her own. Usually Anne's fiction is measured against
Charlotte's and Emily's and dismissed out of hand as insipid in

the comparison. Yet one might venture to claim that if she had been Jane Austen's younger sister, the assessment and interpretation of her two novels, written when she was only twenty-six and twenty-eight years old, would have been much nearer the mark than it is. If Charlotte had left only *The Professor*, she would with greater justice have been assigned the role that is now assigned to Anne. The English do not, on the whole, find the low key attractive – witness the history of Barbara Pym.

That is not to claim that *Agnes Grey* or *The Tenant of Wildfell Hall* are better novels than *Jane Eyre, Villette* or *Wuthering Heights*, though a case could certainly be made for their superiority to *The Professor* and *Shirley*. It is to say that the novel of manners is a difficult genre for the young inexperienced author and that Anne's work had more in common with Jane Austen's or Mrs Gaskell's than with either of her sisters'.

It may have been the marked difference in their characters, as well as the simple fact that the two younger sisters in a family are always closer to each other than either is to the oldest sister, that drew Anne and Emily together, so closely that Ellen Nussey said they were 'like twins – inseparable companions and in the very closest sympathy, which never had any interruption'. In many ways their natures appear to have been complementary. Emily was the mystic, inclined to pantheism, physically as well as spiritually brave – capable of cauterizing her own arm with a red-hot fire-iron when her dog bit it – and altogether eccentric, solitary, unworldly, fading like a wild flower in a hot-house when transplanted from Haworth for any length of time. Anne was the gentle, reserved, earnest and intelligent Christian constantly seeking the God she believed in; physically weak, asthmatic – with tremendous courage and moral determination, but sweet where Emily was strong. Emily's imagination was pagan, romantic, even Gothic. Anne's was constricted by the realities she observed and by her religious beliefs. Both loved music. The masculine was as strong in Emily as the feminine in Anne.

While Charlotte and Branwell wrote about Angria, Anne and Emily collaborated on the Gondal saga. In Emily's diary note for 1845 when she was twenty-seven and Anne twenty-five, she wrote of their 'first long journey' by themselves, by train to York:

.... during our excursions we were, Ronald Macalpin, Henry Angora, Juliet Angusteena, Rosabella Esmalden, Ella and Julian Egremont, Catharine Navarre, and Cordelia Fitzaphnold, escaping from the palaces of instruction to join the Royalists who are hard driven at present by the victorious Republicans. The Gondals still flourish bright as ever. I am at present writing a work on the First Wars – Anne has been writing some articles on this, and a book by Henry Sophona – We intend sticking firm by the rascals as long as they delight us which I am glad to say they do at present.

Anne was seven and Emily nine when the Gondal saga began. Eighteen years later, long after Branwell and Charlotte had given up the Angria fantasy, Gondal was still going forward. There is in fact some evidence that Anne felt herself to have outgrown it, though Emily never did, but after she left Thorp Green and with the growing evidence of Branwell's ruin, Anne seems to have needed it again, as a kind of reassuring regression. Yet it is strange to think that while Emily was writing *Wuthering Heights* and Anne *Agnes Grey*, the two sisters still kept up this childish (but for the poetry it inspired) literary activity.

One possible explanation for their continuing collaboration may lie in the fact that much of the inspiration for Gondal derived from the other world of the moors, the free, wild and private world, which they shared. Anne's and Emily's love of nature was absolute. Ellen Nussey recalled a walk over the moors with the Brontë sisters and Branwell on her first visit to Haworth:

> One long ramble made in those early days was far away over the moors to a spot familiar to Emily and Anne, which they called 'The Meeting of the Waters'. It was a small oasis of emerald green turf, broken here and there by small clear springs; a few large stones served as resting-places; seated here, we were hidden from all the world, nothing appearing in view but miles and miles of heather, a glorious blue sky, and brightening sun.

Plainly the moors were their spiritual home, the only place on earth where they might be fully and unselfconsciously themselves. To be away from there, even within the same county, was intolerable exile.

Agnes's discovery of the primroses in Chapter 12 of *Agnes Grey* is a simple forerunner of the infinitely more sophisticated episode of Proust with the madeleine. As she walked from church, Agnes 'longed intensely for some familiar flower ... the brown moorlands, of course, were out of the question', and was overwhelmed to find three primroses growing together out of her reach. This has a poignant echo in Mrs Gaskell's account of Emily's death in December 1848:

> I remember Miss Brontë's shiver at recalling the pang she felt when, after having searched in the little hollows and sheltered crevices of the moors for a lingering spray of heather – just one spray, however withered – to take in to Emily, she saw that the flower was not recognized by the dim and indifferent eyes.

Next to the moors, it was the sea at Scarborough, where she went with the Robinsons every year, that Anne loved. When she knew she was dying, she determined to go there, and persuaded Charlotte and Ellen Nussey to take her. The town of A— in *Agnes Grey* is based on Scarborough, and it is easy to discern the relief of the asthmatic girl by the sea in summer in Agnes Grey's description of a walk on the shore:

> Refreshed, delighted, invigorated, I walked along, forgetting all my cares, feeling as if I had wings to my feet, and could go at least forty miles without fatigue, and experiencing a sense of exhilaration to which I had been an entire stranger since the days of early youth.

It is on this walk that Agnes again meets Mr Weston, the curate, often suggested to be another of Anne's characters based on a real person.

William Weightman was Mr Brontë's curate from 1839 till his death, at twenty-five, in 1842. He was a kind, genial young man, not nearly so sober-minded as Mr Weston in *Agnes Grey* and, it seems, much given to falling in love. There is some evidence that Anne had romantic feelings for him, most directly in a letter from Charlotte to Ellen Nussey (20 January 1842), where she describes Weightman as sitting opposite Anne at church, 'sighing softly and looking out of the corners of his eyes to win her attention – and Anne is so quiet, her looks so downcast – they are a picture'.

In the introduction to his edition of *The Poems of Anne Brontë* (London, 1979) Edward Chitham analyses the poems by Anne that may refer to her love for Weightman and her sense of loss on his death, but concludes, very reasonably, that 'while it seems likely that Weightman was the origin of Anne's "love poems", Edward Weston of *Agnes Grey* seems to have little in common with him but an interest in the poor'. Indeed, Weston would seem to have a great deal more in common with Charlotte's Professor – stern, remote, self-disciplined and virtuous. It would be misleading to read too much into Charlotte's amused, elder-sisterly remark, and wrong to underestimate the power of Anne's imagination.

In April 1846, when Anne had been home for a year, and just before the *Poems by Currer, Ellis and Acton Bell*, were published, Charlotte wrote to the publishers Aylott & Jones that 'C., E. and A. Bell are now preparing for the press a work of fiction, consisting of three distinct and unconnected tales'. These were *The Professor, Wuthering Heights* and *Agnes Grey*, the latter two of which were published in one volume in 1847.

Since they were published together, they were reviewed together, and since *Wuthering Heights* was by far the more dramatic production, *Agnes Grey* tended to be mentioned only as an afterthought, and usually in terms of the similarity of its sensational content to that of *Wuthering Heights*. The *Athenaeum's* reviewer (probably H.F. Chorley) commented disapprovingly that the Bells 'do not turn away from dwelling on those physical acts of cruelty which we know to have their warrant in the real annals of vice and suffering, – but the contemplation of which taste rejects'.

As far as this refers to the Bloomfield children, there can be little doubt that Anne was speaking out of her own experiences with the Inghams of Blake Hall, where she first went as a governess. Mrs Gaskell records a conversation she had with Charlotte:

> I was once speaking to her about 'Agnes Grey' – the novel in which her sister Anne pretty literally describes her own experience as a governess – and alluding more particularly to the account of the stoning of the little nestlings in the presence of the parent birds. She said that none but those who had been in the position of a governess could ever realize the dark side of 'respectable' human nature; under

no great temptation to crime, but daily giving way to selfishness and ill-temper, till its conduct towards those dependent on it sometimes amounts to a tyranny of which one would rather be the victim than the inflicter.

The Inghams really were *enfants terribles*. Charlotte wrote to Ellen Nussey a week after Anne became their governess:

Both her pupils are desperate little dunces; neither of them can read, and sometimes they profess a profound ignorance of their alphabet. The worst of it is they are excessively indulged, and she is not empowered to inflict any punishment.

Charlotte's own experience, and her knowledge of Anne, ensured that she never doubted the truth of her descriptions.

As her Preface to the second edition of *The Tenant of Wildfell Hall* explains, Anne Brontë would put her hand in the fire before she would compromise the truth: 'I shall not limit my ambition . . . to producing "a perfect work of art" . . . when I feel it my duty to speak an unpalatable truth . . . I *will* speak it, though it be to the prejudice of my name . . .' She also takes a side-swipe at the critics of *Agnes Grey* for accusing her 'of extravagant over-colouring in those very parts that were carefully copied from the life', and goes on to chide the Victorians for their hypocrisy.

We tend to think of Victorian children as characters in the little moral fables they were encouraged to read in the nursery. Middle- and upper-class Victorian parents might have shared this belief, since they saw their children at their best, at fixed times of the day, presented by their nannies. But it is not difficult to imagine that Thomas Hughes's Flashman and Dickens's Steerforth had just the sort of upbringing Anne Brontë describes in *Agnes Grey*.

The novel contains another powerful critique of contemporary behaviour for which Anne Brontë has been given little credit, except in a back-handed way. In his *The Brontës and Their Background* (London, 1973) Tom Winnifrith writes of 'a little anti-aristocratic propaganda' in *Agnes Grey*. 'Propaganda' is probably the wrong word. In her portrayal of the Murrays' talk and behaviour, Anne Brontë was doing for shallow-minded snobbery exactly what she did for the educational system in her tale of life with the Bloomfields. Charlotte tried to do the same, but with a heavier hand, with Blanche Ingram in *Jane Eyre*.

The basis of the two sisters' attitude is best shown in an anecdote Charlotte told Mrs Gaskell. Once she had been left in charge of two brothers, one her pupil aged three or four, the other eight or nine. When she followed them to get them to come away from the stable-yard, which was forbidden them, the elder incited the younger to throw stones at her. One stone hit Charlotte on the head. The next day their mother asked her what had happened to her head. 'An accident, ma'am,' Charlotte discreetly replied. This gained her the trust and affection of the boys, till one day the younger declared 'I love 'ou, Miss Brontë', in front of his mother, who immediately exclaimed, 'Love the *governess*, my dear!'

Governesses were seen as a life-form little higher than mice and birds. One feels that Mrs Bloomfield's reply to Agnes's protest against Tom's sadism might equally well have been applied to the governess – 'You seem to have forgotten . . . that the creatures were all created for our convenience . . . I think a child's amusement is scarcely to be weighed against the welfare of a soulless brute.' There is not such a very big step from this to Miss Murray's irritation with Agnes for reading her family's letter: '. . . do put away that dull, stupid letter . . . You should tell the good people at home not to bore you with such long letters . . . and above all, do bid them write on proper note-paper, and not on those great vulgar sheets.'

Anne related what she actually saw, which is a far cry from propaganda. From the governess's social limbo, this is how the aristocratic young ladies appeared – smug, superficial, callous and ignorant, as Agnes Grey is at pains to explain:

> . . . . they, chiefly owing to their defective education, com-
> ported themselves towards their inferiors in a manner that
> was highly disagreeable for me to witness. They never, in
> thought, exchanged places with them; and, consequently,
> had no consideration for their feelings, regarding them as
> an order of beings entirely different from themselves. They
> would watch the poor creatures at their meals, making
> uncivil remarks about their food, and their manner of
> eating; they would laugh at their simple notions and pro-
> vincial expressions, till some of them scarcely durst venture
> to speak; they would call the grave elderly men and women
> old fools and silly old blockheads to their faces; and all this

without meaning to offend. I could see that the people were
often hurt and annoyed by such conduct . . .

But the attitude of the Murrays is doubly damned later in the
novel. When Miss Murray is out to impress the curate who is
known to care for the poor, she is made to show a sensitivity that
makes her previous callousness all the more reprehensible: 'The
old woman will like to know when to expect you – you know
such people think more of having their cottages in order when
decent people come to see them than we are apt to suppose.'
When it suits her, Miss Murray is quite capable of exchanging
places, in thought, with the poor. Yet it is likely that Anne
Brontë was not making a political point here, but a religious one.
As much a Tory as her sisters and father, she nonetheless believed that everyone is equal in the eyes of God, and that those
who were born to a privileged family were dutybound not to lose
sight of that fact.

The same motive inspires the brilliant satire on the foppery
and hypocrisy of ambitious clerics in the person of the rector, Mr
Hatfield. When Nancy Brown brings her spiritual problems to
him, she later hears him dismissing her to the curate as 'a canting
old fool'. He never deigns to speak to Agnes, has no sympathy
with his humble parishioners, and makes a complete ass of
himself in aspiring beyond his own social sphere to the affections
of Miss Murray.

In her portrayal of Hatfield Anne Brontë also pokes some fun
at male vanity, as she does in her descriptions of the Bloomfields.
Tom is always shown to be pompous, a fully fledged chauvinist
already. When he is not being a little brute, he is absurdly
comical, as when he insists on showing Agnes his rocking-horse:
'. .. ordering his sister to hold the reins, he mounted, and made
me stand for ten minutes, watching how manfully he used his
whip and spurs'. His uncle's vanity comes out in another direction:

He was a thick-set, strongly-built man, but he had found
some means of compressing his waist into a remarkably
small compass; and that, together with the unnatural
stiffness of his form, showed that the lofty-minded, manly
Mr Robson, the scorner of the female sex, was not above
the foppery of stays.

But uncle and nephew are united in their brutality: 'Uncle Robson had been coming up the walk with his gun, and was just then pausing to kick his dog.' Mr Hatfield shares the characteristic. When Snap the terrier interrupts his wooing of Miss Murray, he delivers 'with his cane . . . a resounding smack upon the animal's skull'.

Agnes is as tender of the animal creation as she is of the cottagers but she is no shrinking violet. She remarks that she 'would have given a sovereign any day' to see one of his dogs bite Mr Robson; she is forced to drop a heavy stone to crush a nest of birds to save them from Tom's torture, and feels that 'a few sound boxes on the ear' would have settled him.

On the surface, hers is a story, as Emile Montégut observed, 'of small unhappinesses suffered without murmur'. He went on, and few have since disagreed with him, 'Resignation is the soul of this little book.' Ostensibly it is, but that resignation is constantly undercut by caustically comic, Austenish asides. When Mrs Murray describes her children, for example, she says of Tom, 'He seems to scorn deception', and Agnes comments, '(this was good news)'. Again, at another point she tells us that Tom 'favoured us with his company and conversation till eight'. Of Matilda Murray she says, 'As an animal, Matilda was all right, full of life, vigour and activity', judging her as she herself might judge a horse. She has Mrs Murray criticize Miss Murray's walking in the lanes 'like some poor neglected girl that has no park to walk in', and lets Mrs Bloomfield senior condemn herself out of her own mouth. Mary Ann Bloomfield is given 'a certain affected simper and a craving for notice', and is described in plain Yorkshire terms as 'bellowing like a bull when her unreasonable desires were not gratified'. Mr Bloomfield himself might be a younger version of Austen's Mr Woodhouse as seen through decidedly unsympathetic eyes.

In short, there is much more to *Agnes Grey* than immediately meets the eye. George Moore, after all, thought it 'the most perfect prose narrative in English literature'. It is not that, but beyond a doubt it has its own unique qualities and attractions and must be considered as a vital part of the great artistic whole that is the life and work of the Brontë sisters.

1985                                                          Anne Smith

# Select Bibliography

FICTION

*Agnes Grey*, 1847.
*The Tenant of Wildfell Hall*, 1848.

POETRY

*Poems by Currer, Ellis and Acton Bell*, 1846.
*The Poems of Anne Brontë. A New Text and Commentary*, ed. Edward Chitham, 1979.

BIOGRAPHY

Charlotte Brontë, 'Biographical Notice of Ellis and Acton Bell', in the posthumous edition of *Wuthering Heights and Agnes Grey*, 1850.
— 'A Memoir of Acton Bell', in the posthumous edition of the poetry, 1850.
S. Brooke, 'Anne Brontë at Blake Hall: An Episode of Courage and Insight', *Transactions of the Brontë Society*, 68, pp. 239–50.
Edward Chitham, 'Almost like Twins', *Transactions of the Brontë Society*, 85, p. 365 ff.
E. M. Delafield, *The Brontës: Their Lives Recorded by their Contemporaries*, 1935.
Christopher Fry, 'Genius, talent and failure', *Transactions of the Brontë Society*, 86, p. 1 ff.
Elizabeth Gaskell, *The Life of Charlotte Brontë*, 1857.
Winifred Gérin, *Anne Brontë. A Biography*, 1959 .
A. Harrison and D. Stanford, *Anne Brontë: Her Life and Work*, 1959.
Guy Schofield, 'The gentle Anne', *Transactions of the Brontë Society*, 81, p. 1 ff.
W. Scruton, 'Reminiscences of the Late Miss Ellen Nussey', *Transactions of the Brontë Society*, 8, pp. 23 – 42.
C. K. Shorter, *The Brontës, Lives and Letters*, 2 vols., 1908.
P. Stone, *The Captive Dove*, 1968.

favouring Anne', *Transactions of the Brontë Society,* 92, p.
143 ff.

CRITICISM

W. L. Andrews, 'A Challenge by Anne Brontë', *Transactions of
the Brontë Society,* 75, pp. 25–30.

Miriam Allott (ed.), *The Brontës: The Critical Heritage,* 1974.

Ian Gregor (ed.), *The Brontës,* 1970.

Elizabeth Langland, *Anne Brontë: The Other One,* 1989.

Robert Liddell, *Twin Spirits: The Novels of Emily and Anne
Brontë,* 1990.

George Moore, *Conversations in Ebury Street,* 1930.

F. B. Pinion, *A Brontë Companion: Literary Assessment,
Background and Reference,* 1975.

Barbara Prentis, *The Brontë Sisters and George Eliot: A Unity
of Difference,* 1988.

F. E. Ratchford, *The Brontës' Web of Childhood,* 1941.

P. M. J. Scott, *Anne Brontë: A New Critical Assessment,* 1983.

Tom Winnifrith, *The Brontës and Their Background,* 1973.

Tom Winnifrith & Edward Chitham (eds.), *Brontë Facts and
Brontë Problems,* 1983.

# Chapter 1

## The Parsonage

All true histories contain instruction; though, in some, the treasure may be hard to find, and, when found, so trivial in quantity, that the dry, shrivelled kernel scarcely compensates for the trouble of cracking the nut. Whether this be the case with my history or not, I am hardly competent to judge. I sometimes think it might prove useful to some, and entertaining to others; but the world may judge for itself. Shielded by my own obscurity, and by the lapse of years, and a few fictitious names, I do not fear to venture; and will candidly lay before the public what I would not disclose to the most intimate friend.

My father was a clergyman of the north of England, who was deservedly respected by all who knew him; and, in his younger days, lived pretty comfortably on the joint income of a small incumbency and a snug little property of his own. My mother, who married him against the wishes of her friends, was a squire's daughter, and a woman of spirit. In vain it was represented to her that, if she became the poor parson's wife, she must relinquish her carriage and her lady's-maid and all the luxuries and elegances of affluence; which to her were little less than the necessaries of life. A carriage and a lady's-maid were great conveniences; but, thank Heaven, she had feet to carry her, and hands to minister to her own necessities. An elegant house and spacious grounds were not to be despised; but she would rather live in a cottage with Richard Grey than in a palace with any other man in the world.

Finding arguments of no avail, her father, at length, told the lovers they might marry if they pleased; but, in so doing, his daughter would forfeit every fraction of her fortune. He expected this would cool the ardour of both; but he was mistaken. My father knew too well my mother's superior worth not to be sensible that she was a valuable fortune in herself: and if she would but consent to embellish his humble hearth, he should be happy to take her on any terms; while she, on her part, would rather labour with her own hands than be divided from the man she loved, whose happiness it would be her joy to make, and who was already one with her in heart and soul. So her fortune went to swell the purse of a wiser sister, who had married a rich nabob; and she, to the wonder and compassionate regret of all who knew her, went to bury herself in the homely village parsonage among the hills of ——. And yet, in spite of all this, and in spite of my mother's high spirit and my father's whims, I believe you might search all England through, and fail to find a happier couple.

Of six children, my sister Mary and myself were the only two that survived the perils of infancy and early childhood. I, being the younger by five or six years, was always regarded as the *child*, and the pet of the family: father, mother, and sister all combined to spoil me – not by foolish indulgence to render me fractious and ungovernable, but by ceaseless kindness to make me too helpless and dependent – too unfit for buffeting with the cares and turmoils of life.

Mary and I were brought up in the strictest seclusion. My mother, being at once highly accomplished, well informed, and fond of employment, took the whole charge of our education on herself, with the exception of Latin – which my father undertook to teach us – so that we never even went to school; and, as there was no society in the neighbourhood, our only intercourse with the world consisted in a stately tea-party, now and then, with the principal farmers and tradespeople of the vicinity (just to avoid being stigmatized as too proud to consort with our neighbours), and an annual visit to our paternal grandfather's; where himself, our kind grandmamma, a maiden aunt, and two or three elderly ladies and gentlemen, were the only persons we ever saw. Sometimes our mother would amuse us with stories and anecdotes of her younger days, which, while they entertained us amazingly, frequently awoke – in *me*, at least – a secret wish to see a little more of the world.

I thought she must have been very happy: but she never seemed to regret past times. My father, however, whose temper was neither tranquil nor cheerful by nature, often unduly vexed himself with thinking of the sacrifices his dear wife had made for him; and troubled his head with revolving endless schemes for the augmentation of his little fortune for her sake and ours. In vain my mother assured him she was quite satisfied; and if he would but lay by a little for the children, we should all have plenty, both for time present and to come: but saving was not my father's forte. He would not run in debt (at least, my mother took good care he should not), but while he had money he must spend it: he liked to see his house comfortable, and his wife and daughters well clothed and well attended; and besides, he was charitably disposed, and liked to give to the poor according to his means: or, as some might think, beyond them.

At length, however, a kind friend suggested to him a means of doubling his private property at one stroke; and further increasing it, hereafter, to an untold amount. This friend was a merchant, a man of enterprising spirit and undoubted talent, who was somewhat straitened in his mercantile pursuits for want of capital; but generously proposed to give my father a fair share of his profits, if he would only entrust him with what he could spare; and he thought he might safely promise that, whatever sum the latter chose to put into his hands, it should bring him in cent. per cent. The small patrimony was speedily sold, and the whole of its price was deposited in the hands of the friendly merchant; who as promptly proceeded to ship his cargo, and prepare for his voyage.

My father was delighted, so were we all, with our brightening prospects. For the present, it is true, we were reduced to the narrow income of the curacy; but my father seemed to think there was no necessity for scrupulously restricting our expenditure to that; so with a standing bill at Mr Jackson's, another at Smith's, and a third at Hobson's, we got along even more comfortably than before: though my mother affirmed we had better keep within bounds, for our prospects of wealth were but precarious, after all; and if my father would only trust everything to her management, he should never feel himself stinted: but he, for once, was incorrigible.

What happy hours Mary and I have passed, while sitting at our work by the fire, or wandering on the heath-clad hills, or idling under the weeping birch (the only considerable tree in the garden), talking of future happiness to ourselves and our parents, of what we would do, and see, and possess; with no firmer foundation for our goodly superstructure than the riches that were expected to flow in upon us from the success of this worthy merchant's speculations. Our father was nearly as bad as ourselves: only that he affected not to be so much in earnest: expressing his bright hopes and sanguine expectations in jests and playful sallies that always struck me as being exceedingly witty and pleasant. Our mother laughed with delight to see him so hopeful and happy: but still she feared he was setting his heart too much upon the matter; and once I heard her whisper as she left the room, 'God grant he be not disappointed! I know not how he would bear it.'

Disappointed he was; and bitterly, too. It came like a thunder-clap on us all, that the vessel which contained our fortune had been wrecked, and gone to the bottom with all its stores, together with several of the crew, and the unfortunate merchant himself. I was grieved for him; I was grieved for the overthrow of all our air-built castles: but, with the elasticity of youth, I soon recovered the shock.

Though riches had charms, poverty had no terrors for an inexperienced girl like me. Indeed, to say the truth, there was something exhilarating in the idea of being driven to straits, and thrown upon our own resources. I only wished papa, mamma, and Mary were all of the same mind as myself; and then, instead of lamenting past calamities, we might all cheerfully set to work to remedy them; and the greater the difficulties, the harder our present privations, the greater should be our cheerfulness to endure the latter, and our vigour to contend against the former.

Mary did not lament, but she brooded continually over the misfortune, and sank into a state of dejection from which no effort of mine could rouse her. I could not possibly bring her to regard the matter on its bright side as I did: and indeed I was so fearful of being charged with childish frivolity, or stupid in-sensibility, that I carefully kept most of my bright ideas and cheering notions to myself, well knowing they could not be appreciated.

My mother thought only of consoling my father, and paying our debts and retrenching our expenditure by every available means; but my father was completely overwhelmed by the calamity: health, strength, and spirits sank beneath the blow, and he never wholly recovered them. In vain my mother strove to cheer him, by appealing to his piety, to his courage, to his affection for herself and us. That very affection was his greatest torment: it was for our sakes he had so ardently longed to increase his fortune – it was our interest that had lent such brightness to his hopes, and that imparted such bitterness to his present distress. He now tormented himself with remorse at having neglected my mother's advice; which would at least have saved him from the additional burden of debt – he vainly reproached himself for having brought her from the dignity, the ease, the luxury of her former station to toil with him through the cares and toils of poverty. It was gall and wormwood to his soul to see that splendid, highly accomplished woman, once so courted and admired, transformed into an active managing housewife, with hands and head continually occupied with household labours and household economy. The very willingness with which she performed these duties, the cheerfulness with which she bore her reverses, and the kindness which withheld her from imputing the smallest blame to him, were all perverted by this ingenious self-tormentor into further aggravations of his sufferings. And thus the mind preyed upon the body, and disordered the system of the nerves, and they in turn increased the troubles of the mind, till by action and reaction his health was seriously impaired; and not one of us could convince him that the aspect of our affairs was not half so gloomy, so utterly hopeless, as his morbid imagination represented it to be.

The useful pony phaeton was sold, together with the stout well-fed pony – the old favourite that we had fully determined should end its days in peace, and never pass from our hands; the little coach-house and stable were let; the servant boy and the more efficient (being the more expensive) of the two maid-servants were dismissed. Our clothes were mended, turned, and darned to the utmost verge of decency; our food, always plain, was now simplified to an unprecedented degree – except my father's favourite dishes; our coals and candles were painfully economized – the pair of candles reduced to one, and that most sparingly used; the coals carefully husbanded in the half-empty grate: especially when my father was out on his parish duties, or confined to bed through illness – then we sat with our feet on the fender, scraping the perishing embers together from time to time, and occasionally adding a slight scattering of the dust and fragments of coal, just to keep them alive. As for our carpets, they in time were worn threadbare, and patched and darned even to a greater extent than our garments. To save the expense of a gardener, Mary and I undertook to keep the garden in order; and all the cooking and household work that could not easily be managed by one servant girl was done by my mother and sister, with a little occasional help from me: only a little, because, though a woman in my own estimation, I was still a child in theirs; and my mother, like most active, managing women, was not gifted with very active daughters: for this reason – that being so clever and diligent herself, she was never tempted to trust her affairs to a deputy, but on the contrary, was willing to act and think for others as well as for number one; and whatever was the business in hand, she was apt to think that no one could do it so well as herself: so that whenever I offered to assist her, I received such an answer as – 'No, love, you cannot indeed – there's nothing here you can do. Go and help your sister, or get her to take a walk with you – tell her she must not sit so much, and stay so constantly in the house as she does – she may well look thin and dejected.'

'Mary, mamma says I'm to help you; or get you to take a walk with me: she says you may well look thin and dejected, if you sit so constantly in the house.'

'Help me you cannot, Agnes; and I cannot go out with *you* – I have far too much to do.'

'Then let me help you.'

'You cannot, indeed, dear child. Go and practise your music, or play with the kitten.'

There was always plenty of sewing on hand; but I had not been taught to cut out a single garment, and, except plain hemming and seaming, there was little I could do even in that line; for they both asserted that it was far easier to do the work themselves than to prepare it for me: and, besides, they liked better to see me prosecuting my studies, or amusing myself – it was time enough for me to sit bending over my work, like a grave matron, when my favourite little pussy was become a steady old cat. Under such circumstances, although I was not many degrees more useful than the kitten, my idleness was not entirely without excuse.

Through all our troubles, I never but once heard my mother

complain of our want of money. As summer was coming on, she observed to Mary and me, 'What a desirable thing it would be for your papa to spend a few weeks at a watering-place. I am convinced the sea-air and the change of scene would be of incalculable service to him. But then, you see, there's no money,' she added, with a sigh. We both wished exceedingly that the thing might be done, and lamented greatly that it could not. 'Well, well!' said she, 'it's no use complaining. Possibly something might be done to further the project after all. Mary, you are a beautiful drawer. What do you say to doing a few more pictures in your best style, and getting them framed, with the water-coloured drawings you have already done, and trying to dispose of them to some liberal picture-dealer, who has the sense to discern their merits?'

'Mamma, I should be delighted if you think they *could* be sold; and for anything worth while.'

'It's worth while trying, however, my dear: do you procure the drawings, and I'll endeavour to find a purchaser.'

'I wish *I* could do something,' said I.

'You, Agnes! well, who knows? You draw pretty well, too: if you choose some simple piece for your subject, I dare say you will be able to produce something we shall all be proud to exhibit.'

'But I have another scheme in my head, mamma, and have had long, only I did not like to mention it.'

'Indeed! pray tell us what it is.'

'I should like to be a governess.'

My mother uttered an exclamation of surprise, and laughed. My sister dropped her work in astonishment, exclaiming, '*You* a governess, Agnes! What *can* you be dreaming of!'

'Well! I don't see anything so *very* extraordinary in it. I do not pretend to be able to instruct great girls; but surely I could teach little ones: and I should like it *so* much: I am so fond of children. Do let me, mamma!'

'But, my love, you have not learned to take care of *yourself* yet: and young children require more judgment and experience to manage than elder ones.'

'But, mamma, I am above eighteen, and quite able to take care of myself, and others too. You do not know half the wisdom and prudence I possess, because I have never been tried.'

'Only think,' said Mary, 'what would you do in a house full of strangers, without me or mamma to speak and act for you – with a parcel of children, besides yourself, to attend to; and no one to look to for advice? You would not even know what clothes to put on.'

'You think, because I always do as you bid me, I have no judgment of my own: but only try me – that is all I ask – and you shall see what I can do.'

At that moment my father entered, and the subject of our discussion was explained to him.

'What, my little Agnes a governess!' cried he, and, in spite of his dejection, he laughed at the idea.

'Yes, papa, don't *you* say anything against it: I should like it *so* much; and I am sure I could manage delightfully.'

'But, my darling, we could not spare you.' And a tear glistened in his eye as he added – 'No, no! afflicted as we are, surely we are not brought to that pass yet.'

'Oh, no!' said my mother. 'There is no necessity whatever for such a step; it is merely a whim of her own. So you must hold your tongue, you naughty girl; for, though you are so ready to leave *us*, you know very well we cannot part with *you*.'

I was silenced for that day, and for many succeeding ones; but still I did not wholly relinquish my darling scheme. Mary got her drawing materials, and steadily set to work. I got mine too; but while I drew, I thought of other things. How delightful it would be to be a governess! To go out into the world; to enter upon a new life; to act for myself; to exercise my unused faculties; to try my unknown powers; to earn my own maintenance, and something to comfort and help my father, mother, and sister, besides exonerating them from the provision of my food and clothing; to show papa what his little Agnes could do; to convince mamma and Mary that I was not quite the helpless, thoughtless being they supposed. And then, how charming to be entrusted with the care and education of children! Whatever others said, I felt I was fully competent to the task: the clear remembrance of my own thoughts in early childhood would be a surer guide than the instructions of the most mature adviser. I had but to turn from my little pupils to myself at their age, and I should know, at once, how to win their confidence and affections: how to waken the contrition of the erring; how to embolden the timid, and console the afflicted; how to make Virtue practicable, Instruction desirable, and Religion lovely and comprehensible.

——Delightful task!
To teach the young idea how to shoot!

To train the tender plants, and watch their buds unfolding day by day!

Influenced by so many inducements, I determined still to persevere; though the fear of displeasing my mother, or distressing my father's feelings, prevented me from resuming the subject for several days. At length, again, I mentioned it to my mother in private; and, with some difficulty, got her to promise to assist me with her endeavours. My father's reluctant consent was next obtained, and then, though Mary still sighed her disapproval, my dear, kind mother began to look out for a situation for me. She wrote to my father's relations, and consulted the newspaper advertisements – her own relations she had long dropped all communication with: a formal interchange of occasional letters was all she had ever had since her marriage, and she would not at any time have applied to them in a case of this nature. But so long and so entire had been my parents' seclusion from the world, that many weeks elapsed before a suitable situation could be procured. At last, to my great joy, it was decreed that I should take charge of the young family of a certain Mrs Bloomfield; whom my kind, prim Aunt Grey had known in her youth, and asserted to be a very nice woman. Her husband was a retired tradesman, who had realised a very comfortable fortune; but could not be prevailed upon to give a greater salary than twenty-five pounds to the instructress of his children. I, however, was glad to accept this, rather than refuse the situation – which my parents were inclined to think the better plan.

But some weeks more were yet to be devoted to preparation. How long, how tedious those weeks appeared to me! Yet they were happy ones in the main – full of bright hopes and ardent expectations. With what peculiar pleasure I assisted at the making of my new clothes, and, subsequently, the packing of my trunks! But there was a feeling of bitterness mingling with the latter occupation too; and when it was done – when all was ready for my departure on the morrow, and the last night at home approached – a sudden anguish seemed to swell my heart. My dear friends looked so sad, and spoke so very kindly, that I could scarcely keep my eyes from overflowing: but I still affected to be gay. I had taken my last ramble with Mary on the moors, my last walk in the garden, and round the house; I had fed, with her, our pet pigeons for the last time – the pretty creatures that we had tamed to peck their food from our hands: I had given a farewell stroke to all their silky backs as they crowded in my lap. I had tenderly kissed my own peculiar favourites, the pair of snow-white fantails; I had played my last tune on the old familiar piano, and sung my last song to papa: not the last, I hoped, but the last for, what appeared to me, a very long time. And, perhaps, when I did these things again, it would be with different feelings: circumstances might be changed, and this house might never be my settled home again. My dear little friend, the kitten, would certainly be changed: she was already growing a fine cat; and when I returned, even for a hasty visit at Christmas, would, most likely, have forgotten both her playmate and her merry pranks. I had romped with her for the last time; and when I stroked her soft bright fur, while she lay purring herself to sleep in my lap, it was with a feeling of sadness I could not easily disguise. Then, at bed-time, when I retired with Mary to our quiet little chamber, where already my drawers were cleared out and my share of the bookcase was empty – and where, hereafter, she would have to sleep alone, in dreary solitude, as she expressed it – my heart sank more than ever: I felt as if I had been selfish and wrong to persist in leaving her; and when I knelt once more beside our little bed, I prayed for a blessing on her and on my parents more fervently than ever I had done before. To conceal my emotion, I buried my face in my hands, and they were presently bathed in tears. I perceived, on rising, that she had been crying too: but neither of us spoke; and in silence we betook ourselves to our repose, creeping more closely together from the consciousness that we were to part so soon.

But the morning brought a renewal of hope and spirits. I was to depart early; that the conveyance which took me (a gig, hired from Mr Smith, the draper, grocer, and tea-dealer of the village) might return the same day. I rose, washed, dressed, swallowed a hasty breakfast, received the fond embraces of my father, mother, and sister, kissed the cat, to the great scandal of Sally, the maid – shook hands with her, mounted the gig, drew my veil over my face, and then, but not till then, burst into a flood of tears. The gig rolled on; I looked back; my dear mother and sister were still standing at the door, looking after me, and waving their adieux. I returned their salute, and prayed God to bless them from my heart: we descended the hill, and I could see them no more.

'It's a coldish mornin' for you, Miss Agnes,' observed Smith; 'and a darksome un too; but we's, happen, get to yon' spot afore there come much rain to signify.'

'Yes, I hope so,' replied I, as calmly as I could.

'It's comed a good sup last night too.'

'Yes.'

'But this cold wind will, happen, keep it off.'

'Perhaps it will.'

Here ended our colloquy. We crossed the valley, and began to ascend the opposite hill. As we were toiling up, I looked back again: there was the village spire, and the old grey parsonage beyond it, basking in a slanting beam of sunshine – it was but a sickly ray, but the village and surrounding hills were all in sombre shade, and I hailed the wandering beam as a propitious omen to my home. With clasped hands, I fervently implored a blessing on its inhabitants, and hastily turned away; for I saw the sunshine was departing; and I carefully avoided another glance, lest I should see it in gloomy shadow, like the rest of the landscape.

CHAPTER 2

*First Lessons in the Art of Instruction*

As we drove along, my spirits revived again, and I turned, with pleasure, to the contemplation of the new life upon which I was entering. But though it was not far past the middle of September, the heavy clouds and strong north-easterly wind combined to render the day extremely cold and dreary; and the journey seemed a very long one, for, as Smith observed, the roads were 'very heavy'; and certainly his horse was very heavy too: it crawled up the hills, and crept down them, and only condescended to shake its sides in a trot where the road was at a dead level or a very gentle slope, which was rarely the case in those rugged regions; so that it was nearly one o'clock before we reached the place of our destination. Yet, after all, when we entered the lofty iron gateway, when we drove softly up the smooth, well-rolled carriage road, with the green lawn on each side, studded with young trees, and approached the new but stately mansion of Wellwood, rising above its mushroom poplar-groves, my heart failed me, and I wished it were a mile or two farther off. For the first time in my life, I must stand alone: there was no retreating now. I must enter that house, and introduce myself among its strange inhabitants. But how was it to be done? True, I was near nineteen; but, thanks to my retired life and the protecting care of my mother and sister, I well knew that many a girl of fifteen, or under, was gifted with a more womanly address, and greater ease and self-possession, than I was. Yet, if Mrs Bloomfield were a kind, motherly woman, I might do very well, after all; and the children, of course, I should soon be at ease with them – and Mr Bloomfield, I hoped, I should have but little to do with.

'Be calm, be calm, whatever happens,' I said within myself; and truly I kept this resolution so well, and was so fully occupied in steadying my nerves and stilling the rebellious flutter of my heart, that when I was admitted into the hall, and ushered into the presence of Mrs Bloomfield, I almost forgot to answer her polite salutation; and it afterwards struck me that the little I did say was spoken in the tone of one half-dead or half-asleep. The lady, too, was somewhat chilly in her manner, as I discovered when I had time to reflect. She was a tall, spare, stately woman, with thick black hair, cold grey eyes, and extremely sallow complexion.

With due politeness, however, she showed me my bedroom, and left me there to take a little refreshment. I was somewhat dismayed at my appearance on looking in the glass: the cold wind had swelled and reddened my hands, uncurled and entangled my hair, and dyed my face of a pale purple; add to this my collar was horridly crumpled, my frock splashed with mud, my feet clad in stout new boots, and as the trunks were not brought up, there was no remedy; so having smoothed my hair as well as I could, and repeatedly twitched my obdurate collar, I proceeded to clomp down the two flights of stairs, philosophizing as I went; and with some difficulty found my way into the room where Mrs Bloomfield awaited me.

She led me into the dining-room, where the family luncheon had been laid out. Some beefsteaks and half-cold potatoes were set before me; and while I dined upon these, she sat opposite, watching me (as I thought) and endeavouring to sustain something like a conversation − consisting chiefly of a succession of commonplace remarks, expressed with frigid formality: but this might be more my fault than hers, for I really *could* not converse. In fact, my attention was almost wholly absorbed in my dinner: not from ravenous appetite, but from distress at the toughness of the beefsteaks and the numbness of my hands, almost palsied by their five hours' exposure to the bitter wind. I would gladly have eaten the potatoes and let the meat alone, but having got a large piece of the latter on to my plate, I could not be so impolite as to leave it; so, after many awkward and unsuccessful attempts to cut it with the knife, or tear it with the fork, or pull it asunder between them, sensible that the awful lady was spectator to the whole transaction, I at last desperately grasped the knife and fork in my fists, like a child of two years old, and fell to work with all the little strength I possessed. But this needed some apology − with a feeble attempt at a laugh, I said, 'My hands are so benumbed with the cold that I can scarcely handle my knife and fork.'

'I dare say you would find it cold,' replied she, with a cool, immutable gravity that did not serve to reassure me.

When the ceremony was concluded she led me into the sitting-room again, where she rang and sent for the children.

'You will find them not very far advanced in their attainments,' said she, 'for I have had so little time to attend to their education myself, and we have thought them too young for a governess till now; but I think they are clever children, and very apt to learn, especially the little boy: he is, I think, the flower of the flock − a generous, noble-spirited boy, one to be led, but not driven, and remarkable for always speaking the truth. He seems to scorn deception' (this was good news). 'His sister Mary Ann will require watching,' continued she, 'but she is a very good girl upon the whole: though I wish her to be kept out of the nursery as much as possible, as she is now almost six years old, and might acquire bad habits from the nurses. I have ordered her crib to be placed in your room, and if you will be so kind as to overlook her washing and dressing, and take charge of her clothes, she need have nothing further to do with the nursery-maid.'

I replied I was quite willing to do so; and at that moment my young pupils entered the apartment, with their two younger sisters. Master Tom Bloomfield was a well-grown boy of seven, with a somewhat wiry frame, flaxen hair, blue eyes, small turned-up nose, and fair complexion. Mary Ann was a tall girl too, some-what dark like her mother, but with a round full face and a high colour in her cheeks. The second sister was Fanny, a very pretty little girl; Mrs Bloomfield assured me she was a remarkably gentle child, and required encouragement: she had not learned anything yet; but in a few days she would be four years old, and then she might take her first lesson in the alphabet, and be promoted to the schoolroom. The remaining one was Harriet, a little broad, fat, merry, playful thing of scarcely two, that I coveted more than all the rest – but with her I had nothing to do.

I talked to my little pupils as well as I could, and tried to render myself agreeable; but with little success I fear, for their mother's presence kept me under an unpleasant restraint. They, however, were remarkably free from shyness. They seemed bold, lively children, and I hoped I should soon be on friendly terms with them – the little boy especially, of whom I had heard such a favourable character from his mamma. In Mary Ann there was a certain affected simper, and a craving for notice, that I was sorry to observe. But her brother claimed all my attention to himself; he stood bolt upright between me and the fire, with his hands behind his back, talking away like an orator, occasionally interrupting his discourse with a sharp reproof to his sisters when they made too much noise.

'O Tom, what a darling you are!' exclaimed his mother. 'Come and kiss dear mamma; and then won't you show Miss Grey your schoolroom, and your nice new books?'

'I won't kiss *you*, mamma; but I *will* show Miss Grey my schoolroom, and my new books.'

'And *my* schoolroom, and *my* new books, Tom,' said Mary Ann. 'They're mine too.'

'They're *mine*,' replied he decisively. 'Come along, Miss Grey – I'll escort you.'

When the room and books had been shown, with some bickerings between the brother and sister that I did my utmost to appease or mitigate, Mary Ann brought me her doll, and began to be very loquacious on the subject of its fine clothes, its bed, its chest of drawers, and other appurtenances; but Tom told her to hold her clamour, that Miss Grey might see his rocking-horse, which, with a most important bustle, he dragged forth from its corner into the middle of the room, loudly calling on me to attend to it. Then, ordering his sister to hold the reins, he mounted, and made me stand for ten minutes, watching how manfully he used his whip and spurs. Meantime, however, I admired Mary Ann's pretty doll, and all its possessions; and then told Mr Tom he was a capital rider, but I hoped he would not use his whip and spurs so much when he rode a real pony.

'Oh, yes, I will!' said he, laying on with redoubled ardour. 'I'll cut into him like smoke! Eeh! my word! but he shall sweat for it.'

This was very shocking: but I hoped in time to be able to work a reformation.

'Now you must put on your bonnet and shawl,' said the little hero, 'and I'll show you my garden.'

'And *mine*,' said Mary Ann.

Tom lifted his fist with a menacing gesture; she uttered a loud, shrill scream, ran to the other side of me, and made a face at him.

'Surely, Tom, you would not strike your sister! I hope I shall *never* see you do that.'

'You will sometimes: I am obliged to do it now and then to keep her in order.'

'But it is not your business to keep her in order, you know – that is for'——

'Well, now go and put on your bonnet.'

'I don't know – it is so very cloudy and cold, it seems likely to rain; – and you know I have had a long drive.'

'No matter – you *must* come; I shall allow of no excuses,' replied the consequential little gentleman. And as it was the first

day of our acquaintance, I though I might as well indulge him. It
was too cold for Mary Ann to venture, so she stayed with her
mamma; to the great relief of her brother, who liked to have me
all to himself.

The garden was a large one, and tastefully laid out; besides
several splendid dahlias, there were some other fine flowers still
in bloom: but my companion would not give me time to examine
them: I must go with him, across the wet grass, to a remote
sequestered corner, the most important place in the grounds,
because it contained *his* garden. There were two round beds,
stocked with a variety of plants. In one there was a pretty little
rose tree. I paused to admire its lovely blossoms.

'Oh, never mind that!' said he contemptuously. 'That's only
*Mary Ann's* garden, look, THIS is mine.'

After I had observed every flower, and listened to a dis-
quisition on every plant, I was permitted to depart; but first,
with great pomp, he plucked a polyanthus and presented it to
me, as one conferring a prodigious favour. I observed, on the
grass, about his garden, certain apparatus of sticks and cord, and
asked what they were.

'Traps for birds.'

'Why do you catch them?'

'Papa says they do harm.'

'And what do you do with them when you catch them?'

'Different things. Sometimes I give them to the cat; sometimes
I cut them in pieces with my penknife; but the next, I mean to
roast alive.'

'And why do you mean to do such a horrible thing?'

'For two reasons; first, to see how long it will live – and then,
to see what it will taste like.'

'But don't you know it is extremely wicked to do such things.
Remember, the birds can feel as well as you; and think, how
would you like it yourself.'

'Oh, that's nothing! I'm not a bird, and I can't feel what I do
to them.'

'But you will have to feel it some time, Tom: you have heard
where wicked people go to when they die; and if you don't leave
off torturing innocent birds, remember, you will have to go
there, and suffer just what you have made them suffer.'

'Oh, pooh! I shan't. Papa knows how I treat them, and he

never blames me for it: he says it is just what *he* used to do when *he* was a boy. Last summer he gave me a nest full of young sparrows, and he saw me pulling off their legs and wings, and heads, and never said anything; except that they were nasty things, and I must not let them soil my trousers: and Uncle Robson was there too, and he laughed, and said I was a fine boy.'

'But what would your mamma say?'

'Oh, she doesn't care! she says it's a pity to kill the pretty singing birds, but the naughty sparrows, and mice and rats, I may do what I like with. So now, Miss Grey, you see it is *not* wicked.'

'I still think it is, Tom; and perhaps your papa and mamma would think so too, if they thought much about it. – However,' I internally added, 'they may say what they please, but I am determined you shall do nothing of the kind, as long as I have power to prevent it.'

He next took me across the lawn to see his mole-traps, and then into the stack-yard to see his weasel-traps: one of which, to his great joy, contained a dead weasel; and then into the stable to see, not the fine carriage horses, but a little rough colt, which he informed me had been bred on purpose for him, and he was to ride it as soon as it was properly trained. I tried to amuse the little fellow, and listened to all his chatter as complacently as I could; for I thought if he had any affections at all, I would endeavour to win them; and then, in time, I might be able to show him the error of his ways: but I looked in vain for that generous, noble spirit his mother talked of; though I could see he was not without a certain degree of quickness and penetration, when he chose to exert it.

When we re-entered the house it was nearly tea-time. Master Tom told me that, as papa was from home, he and I and Mary Ann were to have tea with mamma, for a treat; for, on such occasions, she always dined at luncheon time with them, instead of at six o'clock. Soon after tea, Mary Ann went to bed, but Tom favoured us with his company and conversation till eight. After he was gone, Mrs Bloomfield further enlightened me on the subject of her children's dispositions and acquirements, and on what they were to learn, and how they were to be managed, and cautioned me to mention their defects to no one but herself. My mother had warned me before to mention them as little as possible to *her*, for people did not like to be told of their children's faults, and so I concluded I was to keep silence on them altogether. About half-past nine, Mrs Bloomfield invited me to partake of a frugal supper of cold meat and bread. I was glad when that was over, and she took her bedroom candlestick and retired to rest; for though I wished to be pleased with her, her company was extremely irksome to me; and I could not help feeling that she was cold, grave, and forbidding – the very opposite of the kind, warm-hearted matron my hopes had depicted her to be.

CHAPTER 3

## A Few More Lessons

I rose next morning with a feeling of hopeful exhilaration, in spite of the disappointments already experienced; but I found the dressing of Mary Ann was no light matter, as her abundant hair was to be smeared with pomade, plaited in three long tails, and tied with bows of ribbon: a task my unaccustomed fingers found great difficulty in performing. She told me her nurse could do it in half the time, and, by keeping up a constant fidget of impatience, contrived to render me still longer. When all was done, we went into the schoolroom, where I met my other pupil, and chatted with the two till it was time to go down to breakfast. That meal being concluded, and a few civil words having been exchanged with Mrs Bloomfield, we repaired to the schoolroom again, and commenced the business of the day. I found my pupils very backward, indeed; but Tom, though averse to every species of mental exertion, was not without abilities. Mary Ann could scarcely read a word, and was so careless and inattentive that I could hardly get on with her at all. However, by dint of great labour and patience, I managed to get something done in the course of the morning, and then accompanied my young charge out into the garden and adjacent grounds, for a little recreation before dinner. There we got on tolerably together, except that I found they had no notion of going with *me*: I must go with *them* wherever they chose to lead me. I must run, walk, or stand, exactly as it suited their fancy. This, I thought, was reversing the order of things; and I found it doubly disagreeable, as on this as well as subsequent occasions they seemed to prefer the dirtiest places and the most dismal occupations. But there was no remedy; either I must follow them, or keep entirely apart from them, and thus appear neglectful of my charge. To-day, they manifested a particular attachment to a well at the bottom of the lawn, where they persisted in dabbling with sticks and pebbles for above half-an-hour. I was in constant fear that their mother would see them from the window, and blame me for allowing them thus to draggle their clothes and wet their feet and hands, instead of taking exercise; but no arguments, commands, or entreaties could draw them away. If *she* did not see them, some one else did – a gentleman on horseback had entered the gate and was proceeding up the road; at the distance of a few paces from us he paused, and calling to the children in a waspish, penetrating tone, bade them 'Keep out of that water.' 'Miss Grey,' said he, '(I suppose it *is* Miss Grey), I am surprised that you should allow them to dirty their clothes in that manner! Don't you see how Miss Bloomfield has soiled her frock? and that Master Bloomfield's socks are quite wet? and both of them without gloves? Dear, dear! Let me *request* that in future you will keep them *decent* at least!' so saying, he turned away, and continued his ride up to the house. This was Mr Bloomfield. I was surprised that he should nominate his children Master and Miss Bloomfield; and still more so that he should speak so uncivilly to me, their governess, and a perfect stranger to himself. Presently the bell rang to summon us in. I dined with the children at one, while he and his lady took their luncheon at the same table. His conduct there did not greatly raise him in my estimation. He was a man of ordinary stature – rather below than above – and rather thin than stout, apparently between thirty and forty years of age: he had a large mouth, pale, dingy complexion, milky blue eyes, and hair the colour of a hempen cord. There was a roast leg of mutton before him: he helped Mrs Bloomfield, the children, and me, desiring me to cut up the children's meat; then, after twisting about the mutton in various directions, and eyeing it from different points, he pronounced it not fit to be eaten, and called for the cold beef.

'What is the matter with the mutton, my dear?' asked his mate.

'It is quite overdone. Don't you taste, Mrs Bloomfield, that all the goodness is roasted out of it? And can't you see that all that nice, red gravy is completely dried away?'

'Well, I think the *beef* will suit you.'

The beef was set before him, and he began to carve, but with the most rueful expressions of discontent.

'What is the matter with the *beef*, Mr Bloomfield? I'm sure I thought it was very nice.'

'And so it *was* very nice. A nicer joint could not be; but it is *quite* spoiled,' replied he dolefully.

'How so?'

'How so? Why, don't you see how it is cut? Dear – dear! it is quite shocking!'

'They must have cut it wrong in the kitchen, then, for I'm sure, I carved it quite properly here yesterday.'

'No *doubt* they cut it wrong in the kitchen – the savages! Dear – dear! Did ever any one see such a fine piece of beef so completely ruined? But remember that, in future, when a decent dish leaves this table, they shall not *touch* it in the kitchen. Remember *that*, Mrs Bloomfield!'

Notwithstanding the ruinous state of the beef, the gentlman managed to cut himself some delicate slices, part of which he ate in silence. When he next spoke, it was, in a less querulous tone, to ask what there was for dinner.

'Turkey and grouse,' was the concise reply.

'And what besides?'

'Fish.'

'What kind of fish?'

'I don't know.'

'*You don't know?*' cried he, looking solemnly up from his plate, and suspended his knife and fork in astonishment.

'No. I told the cook to get some fish – I did not particularize what.'

'Well, that beats everything! A lady professes to keep house, and doesn't even know that fish is for dinner! professes to order fish, and doesn't specify what!'

'Perhaps, Mr Bloomfield, you will order dinner yourself in future.'

Nothing more was said; and I was glad to get out of the room with my pupils; for I never felt so ashamed and uncomfortable in my life for anything that was not my own fault.

In the afternoon we applied to lessons again: then went out again; then had tea in the schoolroom; then I dressed Mary Ann for dessert; and when she and her brother had gone down to the dining-room, I took the opportunity of beginning a letter to my dear friends at home: but the children came up before I had half completed it. At seven I had to put Mary Ann to bed; then I played with Tom till eight, when he, too, went; and I finished my letter and unpacked my clothes, which I had hitherto found no opportunity for doing, and, finally, went to bed myself.

But this is a very favourable specimen of a day's proceedings.

My task of instruction and surveillance, instead of becoming easier as my charges and I got better accustomed to each other, became more arduous as their characters unfolded. The name of governess, I soon found, was a mere mockery as applied to me: my pupils had no more notion of obedience than a wild, un-broken colt. The habitual fear of their father's peevish temper, and the dread of the punishments he was wont to inflict when irritated, kept them generally within bounds in his immediate presence. The girls, too, had some fear of their mother's anger; and the boy might occasionally be bribed to do as she bid him by the hope of a reward: but I had no rewards to offer; and as for punishments, I was given to understand, the parents reserved that privilege to themselves; and yet they expected me to keep my pupils in order. Other children might be guided by the fear of anger, and the desire of approbation; but neither the one nor the other had any effect upon these.

Master Tom, not content with refusing to be ruled, must needs set up as a ruler, and manifested a determination to keep not only his sisters, but his governess, in order, by violent manual and pedal applications; and, as he was a tall, strong boy of his years, this occasioned no trifling inconvenience. A few sound boxes on the ear, on such occasions, might have settled the matter easily enough; but as, in that case, he might make up some story to his mother, which she would be sure to believe, as she had such unshaken faith in his veracity – though I had already discovered it to be by no means unimpeachable – I determined to refrain from striking him, even in self-defence;

and, in his most violent moods, my only resource was to throw him on his back, and hold his hands and feet till the frenzy was somewhat abated. To the difficulty of preventing him from doing what he ought not, was added that of forcing him to do what he ought. Often he would positively refuse to learn, or to repeat his lessons, or even to look at his book. Here, again, a good birch rod might have been serviceable; but, as my powers were so limited, I must make the best use of what I had.

As there were no settled hours for study and play, I resolved to give my pupils a certain task, which, with moderate attention, they could perform in a short time; and till this was done, however weary I was, or however perverse they might be, nothing short of parental interference should induce me to suffer them to leave the schoolroom; even if I should sit with my chair against the door to keep them in. Patience, Firmness, and Perseverance were my only weapons; and these I resolved to use to the utmost. I determined always strictly to fulfil the threats and promises I made; and, to that end, I must be cautious to threaten and promise nothing that I could not perform. Then, I would carefully refrain from all useless irritability and indulgence of my own ill-temper: when they behaved tolerably, I would be as kind and obliging as it was in my power to be, in order to make the widest possible distinction between good and bad conduct; I would reason with them, too, in the simplest and most effective manner. When I reproved them, or refused to gratify their wishes, after a glaring fault, it should be more in sorrow than in anger: their little hymns and prayers I would make plain and clear to their understanding; when they said their prayers at night, and asked pardon for their offences, I would remind them of the sins of the past day, solemnly, but in perfect kindness, to avoid raising a spirit of opposition; penitential hymns should be said by the naughty; cheerful ones by the comparatively good; and every kind of instruction I would convey to them, as much as possible, by entertaining discourse – apparently with no other object than their present amusement in view.

By these means I hoped, in time, both to benefit the children and to gain the approbation of their parents; and also to convince my friends at home that I was not so wanting in skill and prudence as they supposed. I knew the difficulties I had to contend with were great; but I knew (at least I believed) unremitting patience and perseverance could overcome them; and night and morning I implored Divine assistance to this end. But either the children were so incorrigible, the parents so unreasonable, or myself so mistaken in my views, or so unable to carry them out, that my best intentions and strenuous efforts seemed productive of no better result than sport to the children, dissatisfaction to their parents, and torment to myself.

The task of instruction was as arduous for the body as the mind. I had to run after my pupils to catch them, to carry or drag them to the table, and often forcibly to hold them there till the lesson was done. Tom I frequently put into a corner, seating myself before him in a chair, with a book which contained the little task that must be said or read, before he was released, in my hand. He was not strong enough to push both me and the chair away, so he would stand twisting his body and face into the most grotesque and singular contortions – laughable, no doubt, to an unconcerned spectator, but not to me – and uttering loud yells and doleful outcries, intended to represent weeping, but wholly without the accompaniment of tears. I knew this was done solely for the purpose of annoying me; and, therefore, however I might inwardly tremble with impatience and irritation, I manfully strove to suppress all visible signs of molestation and affected to sit with calm indifference, waiting till it should please him to cease this pastime, and prepare for a run in the garden, by casting his eye on the book and reading or repeating the few words he was required to say. Sometimes he was determined to do his writing badly; and I had to hold his hand to prevent him from purposely blotting or disfiguring the paper. Frequently I threatened that, if he did not do better, he should have another line: then he would stubbornly refuse to write this line; and I, to save my word, had finally to resort to the expedient of holding his fingers upon the pen, and forcibly drawing his hand up and down, till, in spite of his resistance, the line was in some sort completed.

Yet Tom was by no means the most unmanageable of my pupils: sometimes, to my great joy, he would have the sense to see that his wisest policy was to finish his tasks, and go out and amuse himself till I and his sisters came to join him; which frequently was not at all, for Mary Ann seldom followed his example in this particular: she apparently preferred rolling on the floor to any other amusement: down she would drop like a leaden weight; and when I, with great difficulty, had succeeded in rooting her thence, I had still to hold her up with one arm, while with the other I held the book from which she was to read or spell her lesson. As the dead weight of the big girl of six became too heavy for one arm to bear, I transferred it to the other; or, if both were weary of the burden, I carried her into a corner, and told her she might come out when she should find the use of her feet, and stand up: but she generally preferred lying there like a log till dinner or tea time, when, as I could not deprive her of her meals, she must be liberated, and would come crawling out with a grin of triumph on her round, red face. Often she would stubbornly refuse to pronouce some particular word in her lesson; and now I regret the lost labour I have had in trying to conquer her obstinacy. If I had passed it over as a matter of no consequence, it would have been better for both parties, than vainly striving to overcome it as I did; but I thought it my absolute duty to crush this vicious tendency in the bud; and so it was, if I could have done it; and, had my powers been less limited, I might have enforced obedience; but, as it was, it was a trial of strength between her and me, in which she generally came off victorious; and every victory served to encourage and strengthen her for a future contest. In vain I argued, coaxed, entreated, threatened, scolded; in vain I kept her in from play, or, if obliged to take her out, refused to play with her, or to speak kindly, or have anything to do with her; in vain I tried to set before her the advantages of doing as she was bid, and being loved, and kindly treated in consequence, and the disadvantages of persisting in her absurd perversity. Sometimes, when she would ask me to do something for her, I would answer –

'Yes, I will, Mary Ann, if you will only say that word. Come! you'd better say it at once, and have no more trouble about it.'

'No.'

'Then, of course, I can do nothing for you.'

With me, at her age, or under, neglect and disgrace were the most dreadful of punishment; but on her they made no impression. Sometimes, exasperated to the utmost pitch, I would shake her violently by the shoulder, or pull her long hair, or put her in the corner; for which she punished me with loud, shrill, piercing screams, that went through my head like a knife. She knew I hated this, and when she had shrieked her utmost, would look into my face with an air of vindictive satisfaction, exclaiming – '*Now*, then! *that's* for you!' And then shriek again and again, till I was forced to stop my ears. Often these dreadful cries would bring Mrs Bloomfield up to inquire what was the matter?

'Mary Ann is a naughty girl, ma'am.'

'But what are these shocking screams?'

'She is screaming in a passion.'

'I never heard such a dreadful noise! You might be killing her. Why is she not out with her brother?'

'I cannot get her to finish her lessons.'

'But Mary Ann must be a *good* girl, and finish her lessons.' This was blandly spoken to the child. 'And I hope I shall *never* hear such terrible cries again!'

And fixing her cold, stony eyes upon me with a look that could not be mistaken, she would shut the door, and walk away. Sometimes I would try to take the little obstinate creature by surprise, and casually ask her the word while she was thinking of something else; frequently she would begin to say it, and then suddenly check herself, with a provoking look that seemed to say, 'Ah! I'm too sharp for you; you shan't trick it out of me, either.'

On another occasion, I pretended to forget the whole affair; and talked and played with her as usual, till night, when I put her to bed; then bending over her, while she lay all smiles and good-humour, just before departing, I said, as cheerfully and kindly as before –

'Now, Mary Ann, just tell me that word before I kiss you good-night: you are a good girl now, and, of course, you will say it.'

'No, I won't.'

'Then I can't kiss you.'

'Well, I don't care.'

In vain I expressed my sorrow; in vain I lingered for some symptom of contrition; she really 'didn't care', and I left her alone, and in darkness, wondering most of all at this last proof of insensate stubbornness. In *my* childhood I could not imagine a more afflictive punishment than for my mother to refuse to kiss me at night: the very idea was terrible. More than the idea I never felt, for, happily, I never committed a fault that was deemed worthy of such a penalty; but once I remember, for some transgression of my sister's, our mother thought proper to inflict it upon her: what *she* felt, I cannot tell; but my sympathetic tears and suffering for her sake, I shall not soon forget.

Another troublesome trait in Mary Ann was her incorrigible propensity to keep running into the nursery, to play with her little sisters and the nurse. This was natural enough, but, as it was against her mother's express desire, I, of course, forbade her to do so, and did my utmost to keep her with me; but that only increased her relish for the nursery, and the more I strove to keep her out of it, the oftener she went, and the longer she stayed: to the great dissatisfaction of Mrs Bloomfield, who, I well knew, would impute all the blame of the matter to me. Another of my trials was the dressing in the morning: at one time she would not be washed; at another she would not be dressed, unless she might wear some particular frock, that I knew her mother would not like her to have; at another she would scream and run away if I attempted to touch her hair. So that, frequently, when, after much trouble and toil, I had, at length, succeeded in bringing her down, the breakfast was nearly half over; and black looks from 'mamma', and testy observations from 'papa', spoken at me, if not to me, were sure to be my meed: for few things irritated the latter so much as want of punctuality at meal times. Then, among the minor annoyances, was my inability to satisfy Mrs Bloomfield with her daughter's dress; and the child's hair 'was never fit to be seen'. Sometimes, as a powerful reproach to me, she would perform the office of tire-woman herself, and then complain bitterly of the trouble it gave her.

When little Fanny came into the schoolroom, I hoped she would be mild and inoffensive, at least; but a few days, if not a few hours, sufficed to destroy the illusion: I found her a mischievous, intractable little creature, given up to falsehood and deception, young as she was, and alarmingly fond of exercising her two favourite weapons of offence and defence; that of spitting in the faces of those who incurred her displeasure, and bellowing like a bull when her unreasonable desires were not gratified. As she, generally, was pretty quiet in her parents' presence, and they were impressed with the notion of her being a remarkably gentle child, her falsehoods were readily believed, and her loud uproars led them to suspect harsh and injudicious treatment on my part; and when, at length, her bad disposition became manifest even to their prejudiced eyes, I felt that the whole was attributed to me.

'What a naughty girl Fanny is getting!' Mrs Bloomfield would say to her spouse. 'Don't you observe, my dear, how she is altered since she entered the schoolroom? She will soon be as bad as the other two; and, I am sorry to say, they have quite deteriorated of late.'

'You may say that,' was the answer. 'I've been thinking that same myself. I thought when we got them a governess they'd improve; but, instead of that, they get worse and worse: I don't know how it is with their learning; but their habits, I know, make no sort of improvement; they get rougher, and dirtier, and more unseemly, every day.'

I knew this was all pointed at me; and these, and all similar innuendoes, affected me far more deeply than any open accusations would have done; for against the latter I should have been roused to speak in my own defence: now I judged it my wisest plan to subdue every resentful impulse, suppress every sensitive shrinking, and go on perseveringly, doing my best; for, irksome as my situation was, I earnestly wished to retain it. I thought, if I could struggle on with unremitting firmness and integrity, the children would in time become more humanized: every month would contribute to make them some little wiser, and, consequently, more manageable; for a child of nine or ten as frantic and ungovernable as these at six and seven would be a maniac.

I flattered myself I was benefiting my parents and sister by my continuance here; for small as the salary was, I still was earning something, and with strict economy I could easily manage to have something to spare for them, if they would favour me by taking it. Then it was by my own will that I had got the place; I had brought all this tribulation on myself, and I was determined to bear it; nay, more than that, I did not even regret the step I had taken. I longed to show my friends that, even now, I was competent to undertake the charge, and able to acquit myself honourably to the end; and if ever I felt it degrading to submit so quietly, or intolerable to toil so constantly, I would turn towards my home, and say within myself –

They may crush, but they shall not subdue me!
'Tis of thee that I think, not of them.

About Christmas I was allowed to visit home; but my holiday was only of a fortnight's duration: 'for,' said Mrs Bloomfield, 'I thought, as you had seen your friends so lately, you would not care for a longer stay.' I left her to think so still: but she little knew how long, how wearisome, those fourteen weeks of absence had been to me; how intensely I had longed for my holidays, how greatly I was disappointed at their curtailment. Yet she was not to blame in this; I had never told her my feelings, and she could not be expected to divine them; I had not been with her a full term, and she was justified in not allowing me a full vacation.

## CHAPTER 4
## *The Grandmamma*

I spare my readers the account of my delight on coming home, my happiness while there – enjoying a brief space of rest and liberty in that dear, familiar place, among the loving and the loved – and my sorrow on being obliged to bid them, once more, a long adieu.

I returned, however, with unabated vigour to my work – a more arduous task than any one can imagine, who has not felt something like the misery of being charged with the care and direction of a set of mischievous turbulent rebels, whom his utmost exertions cannot bind to their duty; while, at the same time, he is responsible for their conduct to a higher power, who exacts from him what cannot be achieved without the aid of the superior's more potent authority: which, either from indolence, or the fear of becoming unpopular with the said rebellious gang, the latter refuses to give. I can conceive few situations more harassing than that wherein, however you may long for success, however you may labour to fulfil your duty, your efforts are baffled and set at naught by those beneath you, and unjustly censured and misjudged by those above.

I have not enumerated half the vexatious propensities of my pupils, or half the troubles resulting from my heavy responsibilities, for fear of trespassing too much upon the reader's patience; as, perhaps, I have already done: but my design, in writing the few last pages, was not to amuse, but to benefit those whom it might concern: he that has no interest in such matters will doubtless have skipped them over with a cursory glance, and, perhaps, a malediction against the prolixity of the writer; but if a parent has, therefrom, gathered any useful hint, or an unfortunate governess received thereby the slightest benefit, I am well rewarded for my pains.

To avoid trouble and confusion, I have taken my pupils one by one, and discussed their various qualities; but this can give no adequate idea of being worried by the whole three together; when, as was often the case, all were determined to 'be naughty, and to tease Miss Grey, and put her in a passion'.

Sometimes, on such occasions, the thought had suddenly occurred to me – 'If *they* could see me now!' meaning, of course, my friends at home; and the idea of how they would pity me has made me pity myself – so greatly that I have had the utmost difficulty to restrain my tears: but I have restrained them, till my little tormentors were gone to dessert, or cleared off to bed (my only prospects of deliverance), and then, in all the bliss of solitude, I have given myself up to the luxury of an unrestricted burst of weeping. But this was a weakness I did not often indulge: my employments were too numerous, my leisure moments too precious, to admit of much time being given to fruitless lamentations.

I particularly remember one wild, snowy afternoon, soon after my return in January; the children had all come up from dinner, loudly declaring that they meant 'to be naughty'; and they had well kept their resolution, though I had talked myself hoarse, and wearied every muscle in my throat, in the vain attempt to reason them out of it. I had got Tom pinned up in a corner, whence, I told him, he should not escape till he had done his appointed task. Meantime, Fanny had possessed herself of my work-bag, and was rifling its contents – and spitting into it besides. I told her to let it alone, but to no purpose, of course. 'Burn it, Fanny!' cried Tom; and *this* command she hastened to obey. I sprang to snatch it from the fire, and Tom darted to the door. 'Mary Ann, throw her desk out of the window!' cried he: and my precious desk, containing my letters and papers, my small amount of cash, and all my valuables, was about to be precipitated from the three-storey window. I flew to rescue it. Meanwhile Tom had left the room, and was rushing down the stairs, followed by Fanny. Having secured my desk, I ran to catch them, and Mary Ann came scampering after. All three escaped me, and ran out of the house into the garden, where they plunged about in the snow, shouting and screaming in exultant glee.

What must I do? If I followed them, I should probably be unable to capture one, and only drive them farther away; if I did not, how was I to get them in? and what would their parents think of me, if they saw or heard the children rioting, hatless, bonnetless, gloveless, and bootless, in the deep, soft snow? While I stood in this perplexity, just without the door, trying, by grim looks and angry words, to awe them into subjection, I heard a voice behind me, in harshly piercing tones exclaiming –

'Miss Grey! Is it possible? What, in the devil's name, can you be thinking about?'

'I can't get them in, sir,' said I, turning round, and beholding Mr Bloomfield, with his hair on end, and his pale blue eyes bolting from their sockets.

'But I INSIST upon their being got in!' cried he, approaching nearer, and looking perfectly ferocious.

'Then, sir, you must call them yourself, if you please, for they won't listen to me,' I replied, stepping back.

'Come in with you, you filthy brats; or I'll horsewhip you every one!' roared he; and the children instantly obeyed. 'There, you see! they come at the first word!'

'Yes, when *you* speak.'

'And it's very strange, that when you've the care of 'em, you've no better control over them than that! – Now, there they are – gone upstairs with their nasty snowy feet! Do go after 'em and see them made decent, for Heaven's sake!'

That gentleman's mother was then staying in the house; and, as I ascended the stairs and passed the drawing-room door, I had the satisfaction of hearing the old lady declaiming aloud to her daughter-in-law to this effect (for I could only distinguish the most emphatic words) –

'Gracious Heavens!——never in all my life——!——get their death as sure as——! Do you think, my dear, she's a *proper person*? Take my word for it'——

I heard no more; but that sufficed.

The senior Mrs Bloomfield had been very attentive and civil to me; and till now I had thought her a nice, kind-hearted, chatty old body. She would often come to me and talk in a confidential strain; nodding and shaking her head, and gesticulating with hands and eyes, as a certain class of old ladies are wont to do: though I never knew one that carried the peculiarity to so great an extent. She would even sympathize with me for the trouble I had with the children, and express at times, by half sentences, interspersed with nods and knowing winks, her sense of the injudicious conduct of their mamma in so restricting my power, and neglecting to support me with her authority. Such a mode of testifying disapprobation was not much to my taste; and I generally refused to take it in, or understand anything more than was openly spoken; at least, I never went farther than an implied acknowledgment that, if matters were otherwise ordered, my task would be a less difficult one, and I should be better able to guide and instruct my charge; but now I must be doubly cautious. Hitherto, though I saw the old lady had her defects (of which one was a proneness to proclaim her perfections), I had always been wishful to excuse them, and to give her credit for all the virtues she professed, and even imagine others yet untold. Kindness, which had been the food of my life through so many years, had lately been so entirely denied me, that I welcomed with grateful joy the slightest semblance of it. No wonder, then, that my heart warmed to the old lady, and always gladdened at her approach and regretted her departure.

But now, the few words luckily or unluckily heard in passing had wholly revolutionized my ideas respecting her: now I looked upon her as hypocritical and insincere, a flatterer, and a spy upon my words and deeds. Doubtless it would have been my interest still to meet her with the same cheerful smile and tone of respectful cordiality as before; but I could not, if I would: my manner altered with my feelings, and became so cold and shy that she could not fail to notice it. She soon did notice it, and *her* manner altered too: the familiar nod was changed to a stiff bow, the gracious smile gave place to a glare of Gorgon ferocity; her vivacious loquacity was entirely transferred from me to 'the darling boys and girls', whom she flattered and indulged more absurdly than ever their mother had done.

I confess I was somewhat troubled at this change: I feared the consequences of her displeasure, and even made some efforts to recover the ground I had lost – and with better apparent success than I could have anticipated. At one time I, merely in common civility, asked after her cough; immediately her long visage relaxed into a smile, and she favoured me with a particular history of that and her other infirmities, followed by an account of her pious resignation, delivered in the usual emphatic, declamatory style, which no writing can portray.

'But there's one remedy for all, my dear, and that's resignation' (a toss of the head), 'resignation to the will of Heaven!' (an uplifting of the hands and eyes). 'It has always supported me through all my trials, and always will do' (a succession of nods). 'But then, it isn't everybody that can say that' (a shake of the head); 'but I'm one of the pious ones, Miss Grey!' (a very significant nod and toss). 'And, thank Heaven, I always was' (another nod), 'and I glory in it!' (an emphatic clasping of the hands and shaking of the head). And with several texts of Scripture, misquoted or misapplied, and religious exclamations so redolent of the ludicrous in the style of delivery and manner of bringing in, if not in the expressions themselves, that I decline repeating them, she withdrew; tossing her large head in high good-humour – with herself at least – and left me hoping that, after all, she was rather weak than wicked.

At her next visit to Wellwood House, I went so far as to say I was glad to see her looking so well. The effect of this was magical: the words, intended as a mark of civility, were received as a flattering compliment; her countenance brightened up, and from that moment she became as gracious and benign as heart could wish – in outward semblance at least. From what I now saw of her, and what I heard from the children, I knew that, in order to gain her cordial friendship, I had but to utter a word of flattery at each convenient opportunity: but this was against my principles; and for lack of this, the capricious old dame soon deprived me of her favour again, and I believe did me much secret injury.

She could not greatly influence her daughter-in-law against

me, because between that lady and herself there was a mutual dislike – chiefly shown by her in secret detractions and calumniations; by the other, in an excess of frigid formality in her demeanour; and no fawning flattery of the elder could thaw away the wall of ice which the younger interposed between them. But with her son, the old lady had better success: he would listen to all she had to say, provided she could soothe his fretful temper, and refrain from irritating him by her own asperities; and I have reason to believe that she considerably strengthened his prejudice against me. She would tell him that I shamefully neglected the children, and even his wife did not attend to them as she ought; and that he must look after them himself, or they would all go to ruin.

Thus urged, he would frequently give himself the trouble of watching them from the windows during their play; at times he would follow them through the grounds, and too often came suddenly upon them while they were dabbling in the forbidden well, talking to the coachman in the stables, or revelling in the filth of the farm-yard – and I, meanwhile, wearily standing by, having previously exhausted my energy in vain attempts to get them away. Often, too, he would unexpectedly pop his head into the schoolroom while the young people were at meals, and find them spilling their milk over the table and themselves, plunging their fingers into their own or each other's mugs, or quarrelling over their victuals like a set of tiger's cubs. If I were quiet at the moment, I was conniving at their disorderly conduct; if (as was frequently the case) I happened to be exalting my voice to enforce order, I was using undue violence, and setting the girls a bad example by such ungentleness of tone and language.

I remember one afternoon in spring when, owing to the rain, they could not go out; but, by some amazing good fortune, they had all finished their lessons, and yet abstained from running down to tease their parents – a trick that annoyed me greatly, but which, on rainy days, I seldom could prevent their doing; because, below, they found novelty and amusement – especially when visitors were in the house; and their mother, though she bid me keep them in the schoolroom, would never chide them for leaving it, or trouble herself to send them back. But this day they appeared satisfied with their present abode, and what is more wonderful still, seemed disposed to play together without depending on me for amusement, and without quarrelling with each other. Their occupation was a somewhat puzzling one: they were all squatted together on the floor by the window, over a heap of broken toys and a quantity of birds' eggs – or rather eggshells, for the contents had luckily been abstracted. These shells they had broken up and were pounding into small fragments, to what end I could not imagine; but so long as they were quiet and not in positive mischief, I did not care; and, with a feeling of unusual repose, I sat by the fire, putting the finishing stitches to a frock for Mary Ann's doll; intending, when that was done, to begin a letter to my mother. Suddenly, the door opened, and the dingy head of Mr Bloomfield looked in.

'All very quiet here! What are you doing ?' said he. 'No harm *to-day*, at least,' thought I. But he was of a different opinion. Advancing to the window, and seeing the children's occupations, he testily exclaimed – 'What in the world are you about?'

'We're grinding egg-shells, papa!' cried Tom.

'How *dare* you make such a mess, you little devils? Don't you see what confounded work you're making of the carpet?' (the carpet was a plain brown drugget). 'Miss Grey, did you know what they were doing?'

'Yes, sir.'

'*You knew* it?'

'Yes.'

'You *knew* it! and you actually sat there and permitted them to go on without a word of reproof!'

'I didn't think they were doing any harm.'

'Any harm! Why, look there! Just look at that carpet, and see – was there ever anything like it in a Christian house before? No wonder your room is not fit for a pigsty – no wonder your pupils are worse than a litter of pigs! – no wonder – Oh! I declare, it puts me quite past my patience!' and he departed, shutting the door after him with a bang, that made the children laugh.

'It puts *me* quite past my patience too!' muttered I, getting up; and, seizing the poker, I dashed it repeatedly into the cinders, and stirred them up with unwonted energy; thus easing my irritation, under pretence of mending the fire.

After this, Mr Bloomfield was continually looking in to see if the schoolroom was in order; and, as the children were continu- ally littering the floor with fragments of toys, sticks, stones, stubble, leaves, and other rubbish, which I could not prevent their bringing, or oblige them to gather up, and which the servants refused to 'clean after them', I had to spend a considerable portion of my valuable leisure moments on my knees upon the floor in painfully reducing things to order. Once I told them that they should not taste their supper till they had picked up everything from the carpet; Fanny might have hers when she had taken up a certain quantity, Mary Ann when she had gathered twice as many, and Tom was to clear away the rest. Wonderful to state, the girls did their part; but Tom was in such a fury that he flew upon the table, scattered the bread and milk about the floor, struck his sisters, kicked the coals out of the coal-pan, attempted to over-throw the table and chairs, and seemed inclined to make a Douglas-larder of the whole contents of the room: but I seized upon him, and, sending Mary Ann to call her mamma, held him, in spite of kicks, blows, yells, and execrations, till Mrs Bloomfield made her appearance.

'What is the matter with my boy?' said she.

And when the matter was explained to her, all she did was to send for the nursery-maid to put the room in order, and bring Master Bloomfield his supper.

'There now,' cried Tom triumphantly, looking up from his viands with his mouth almost too full for speech. 'There now, Miss Grey: you see I have got my supper in spite of you: and I haven't picked up a single thing!'

The only person in the house who had any real sympathy for me was the nurse; for she had suffered like afflictions, though in a smaller degree; as she had not the task of teaching, nor was she so responsible for the conduct of her charge.

'Oh, Miss Grey!' she would say, 'you have some trouble with them childer!'

'I have indeed, Betty; and I dare say you know what it is.'

'Ay, I do so! But I don't vex myself o'er 'em as you do. And then, you see, I hit 'em a slap sometimes: and them little uns – I give 'em a good whipping now and then: there's nothing else will do for 'em, as what they say. Howsoever, I've lost my place for it.'

'Have you, Betty? I heard you were going to leave.'

'Eh, bless you, yes! Missis gave me warning a three-wik sin'. She told me afore Christmas how it mud be, if I hit 'em again; but I couldn't hold my hand off 'em at nothing. I know not how *you* do, for Miss Mary Ann's worse by the half nor her sisters!'

36

CHAPTER 5
*The Uncle*

Besides the old lady, there was another relative of the family whose visits were a great annoyance to me – this was 'Uncle Robson', Mrs Bloomfield's brother; a tall, self-sufficient fellow, with dark hair and sallow complexion like his sister, a nose that seemed to disdain the earth, and little grey eyes, frequently half closed, with a mixture of real stupidity and affected contempt of all surrounding objects. He was a thick-set, strongly-built man, but he had found some means of compressing his waist into a remarkably small compass; and that, together with the un-natural stiffness of his form, showed that the lofty-minded, manly Mr Robson, the scorner of the female sex, was not above the foppery of stays. He seldom deigned to notice me; and, when he did, it was with a certain supercilious insolence of tone and manner that convinced me he was no gentleman: though it was intended to have a contrary effect. But it was not for that I disliked his coming, so much as for the harm he did the children – encouraging all their evil propensities, and undoing, in a few minutes, the little good it had taken me months of labour to achieve.

Fanny and little Harriet he seldom condescended to notice; but Mary Ann was something of a favourite. He was continually encouraging her tendency to affectation (which I had done my utmost to crush), talking about her pretty face, and filling her head with all manner of conceited notions concerning her personal appearance (which I had instructed her to regard as dust in the balance compared with the cultivation of her mind and manners); and I never saw a child so susceptible of flattery as she was. Whatever was wrong, in either her or her brother, he would encourage by laughing at, if not by actually praising: people little know the injury they do to children by laughing at their faults, and making a pleasant jest of what their true friends have endeavoured to teach them to hold in grave abhorrence.

Though not a positive drunkard, Mr Robson habitually swallowed great quantities of wine, and took with relish an occasional glass of brandy and water. He taught his nephew to imitate him in this to the utmost of his ability, and to believe that the more wine and spirits he could take, and the better he liked them, the more he manifested his bold and manly spirit, and rose superior to his sisters. Mr Bloomfield had not much to say against it, for his favourite beverage was gin and water; of which he took a considerable portion every day, by dint of constant sipping – and to that I chiefly attributed his dingy complexion and waspish temper.

Mr Robson likewise encouraged Tom's propensity to persecute the lower creation, both by precept and example. As he frequently came to course or shoot over his brother-in-law's grounds, he would bring his favourite dogs with him; and he treated them so brutally that, poor as I was, I would have given a sovereign any day to see one of them bite him, provided the animal could have done it with impunity. Sometimes, when in a very complacent mood, he would go a-bird-nesting with the children: a thing that irritated and annoyed me exceedingly; as, by frequent and persevering attempts, I flattered myself I had partly shown them the evil of this pastime, and hoped, in time, to bring them to some general sense of justice and humanity; but ten minutes' bird-nesting with Uncle Robson, or even a laugh from him at some relation of their former barbarities, was sufficient at once to destroy the effect of my whole elaborate course of reasoning and persuasion. Happily, however, during that spring, they never, but once, got anything but empty nests, or eggs – being too impatient to leave them till the birds were hatched; that once, Tom, who had been with his uncle into the neighbouring plantation, came running in high glee into the garden, with a brood of little callow nestlings in his hands. Mary Ann and Fanny, whom I was just bringing out, ran to admire his spoils, and to beg each a bird for themselves. 'No, not one!' cried Tom. 'They're all mine: Uncle Robson gave them to me – one, two, three, four, five – you shan't touch one of them! no, not one, for your lives!' continued he exultingly; laying the nest on the ground, and standing over it with his legs wide apart, his hands thrust into his breeches-pockets, his body bent forward, and his face twisted into all manner of contortions in the ecstasy of his delight.

'But you shall see me fettle 'em off. My word, but I *will* wallop 'em! See if I don't now. By gum! but there's rare sport for me in that nest.'

'But, Tom,' said I, 'I shall not allow you to torture those birds. They must either be killed at once or carried back to the place you took them from, that the old birds may continue to feed them.'

'But you don't know where that is, madam: it's only me and Uncle Robson that knows that.'

'But if you don't tell me, I shall kill them myself – much as I hate it.'

'You daren't. You daren't touch them for your life! because you know papa and mamma and Uncle Robson would be angry. Ha, ha! I've caught you there, miss!'

'I shall do what I think is right in a case of this sort without consulting any one. If your papa and mamma don't happen to approve of it, I shall be sorry to offend them; but your Uncle Robson's opinions, of course, are nothing to me.'

So saying – urged by a sense of duty – at the risk of both making myself sick and incurring the wrath of my employers – I got a large stone that had been reared up for a mouse-trap by the gardener, then, having once more vainly endeavoured to persuade the little tyrant to let the birds be carried back, I asked what he intended to do with them. With fiendish glee he commenced a list of torments; and while he was busied in the relation, I dropped the stone upon his intended victims and crushed them flat beneath it. Loud were the outcries, terrible the execrations, consequent upon this daring outrage; Uncle Robson had been coming up the walk with his gun, and was just then pausing to kick his dog. Tom flew towards him, vowing he would make him kick me instead of Juno. Mr Robson leant upon his gun, and laughed excessively at the violence of his nephew's passions, and the bitter maledictions and opprobrious epithets he heaped upon me. 'Well, you *are* a good 'un!' exclaimed he, at length, taking up his weapon and proceeding towards the house. 'Damme, but the lad has some spunk in him, too. Curse me, if ever I saw a nobler little scoundrel than that. He's beyond petticoat government already: by God! he defies mother, granny, governess, and all! Ha, ha, ha! Never mind, Tom, I'll get you another brood to-morrow.'

'If you do, Mr Robson, I shall kill them too,' said I.

'Humph!' replied he, and having honoured me with a broad stare – which, contrary to his expectations, I sustained without flinching – he turned away with an air of supreme contempt, and stalked into the house. Tom next went to tell his mamma. It was not her way to say much on any subject; but, when she next saw me, her aspect and demeanour were doubly dark and chill. After some casual remark about the weather, she observed –

'I am sorry, Miss Grey, you should think it necessary to interfere with Master Bloomfield's amusements; he was *very* much distressed about your destroying the birds.'

'When Master Bloomfield's amusements consist in injuring sentient creatures,' I answered, 'I think it my duty to interfere.'

'You seem to have forgotten,' she said calmly, 'that the creatures were all created for our convenience.'

I thought that doctrine admitted some doubt, but merely replied –

'If they were, we have no right to torment them for our amusement.'

'I think,' said she, 'a child's amusement is scarcely to be weighed against the welfare of a soulless brute.'

'But, for the child's own sake, it ought not to be encouraged to have such amusements,' answered I, as meekly as I could, to make up for such unusual pertinacity. 'Blessed are the merciful, for they shall obtain mercy.'

'Oh! of course; but that refers to our conduct towards each other.'

'The merciful man shows mercy to his beast,' I ventured to add.

'I think *you* have not shown much mercy,' replied she, with a short, bitter laugh; 'killing the poor birds by wholesale in that shocking manner, and putting the dear boy to such misery for a mere whim.'

I judged it prudent to say no more. This was the nearest approach to a quarrel I ever had with Mrs Bloomfield; as well as the greatest number of words I ever exchanged with her at one time, since the day of my first arrival.

But Mr Robson and old Mrs Bloomfield were not the only guests whose coming to Wellwood House annoyed me; every visitor disturbed me more or less; not so much because they neglected me (though I did feel their conduct strange and disagreeable in that respect) as because I found it impossible to keep my pupils away from them, as I was repeatedly desired to do:

Tom must talk to them, and Mary Ann must be noticed by them. Neither the one nor the other knew what it was to feel any degree of shamefacedness, or even common modesty. They would indecently and clamorously interrupt the conversation of their elders, tease them with the most impertinent questions, roughly collar the gentlemen, climb their knees uninvited, hang about their shoulders or rifle their pockets, pull the ladies' gowns, disorder their hair, tumble their collars, and importunately beg for their trinkets.

Mrs Bloomfield had the sense to be shocked and annoyed at all this, but she had not sense to prevent it: she expected me to prevent it. But how could I – when the guests, with their fine clothes and new faces, continually flattered and indulged them, out of complaisance to their parents – how could *I*, with my homely garments, everyday face, and honest words, draw them away? I strained every nerve to do so: by striving to amuse them I endeavoured to attract them to my side; by the exertion of such authority as I possessed, and by such severity as I dared to use, I tried to deter them from tormenting the guests; and by reproaching their unmannerly conduct, to make them ashamed to repeat it. But they knew no shame; they scorned authority which had no terrors to back it; and as for kindness and affection, either they had no hearts, or such as they had were so strongly guarded, and so well concealed, that I, with all my efforts, had not yet discovered how to reach them.

But soon my trials in this quarter came to a close – sooner than I either expected or desired; for one sweet evening towards the close of May, as I was rejoicing in the near approach of the holidays, and congratulating myself upon having made some progress with my pupils (as far as their learning went at least, for I *had* instilled *something* into their heads, and I had at length brought them to be a little – a very little – more rational about getting their lessons done in time to leave some space for recreation, instead of tormenting themselves and me all day long to no purpose), Mrs Bloomfield sent for me, and calmly told me that after Midsummer my services would be no longer required. She assured me that my character and general conduct were unexceptionable; but the children had made so little improvement since my arrival, that Mr Bloomfield and she felt it their duty to seek some other mode of instruction. Though superior to most children of their years in abilities, they were decidedly behind them in attainments: their manners were uncultivated, and their tempers unruly. And this she attributed to a want of sufficient firmness, and diligent, persevering care on my part.

Unshaken firmness, devoted diligence, unwearied perseverance, unceasing care, were the very qualifications on which I had secretly prided myself; and by which I had hoped in time to overcome all difficulties, and obtain success at last. I wished to say something in my own justification: but in attempting to speak, I felt my voice falter; and rather than testify any emotion, or suffer the tears to overflow that were already gathering in my eyes, I chose to keep silence, and bear all like a self-convicted culprit.

Thus was I dismissed, and thus I sought my home. Alas! what would they think of me? unable, after all my boasting, to keep my place, even for a single year, as governess to three small children, whose mother was asserted by my own aunt to be a 'very nice woman'. Having been thus weighed in the balance and found wanting, I need not hope they would be willing to try me again. And this was an unwelcome thought; for vexed, harassed, disappointed as I had been, and greatly as I had learned to love and value my home, I was not yet weary of adventure, nor willing to relax my efforts. I knew that all parents were not like Mr and Mrs Bloomfield, and I was certain all children were not like theirs. The next family must be different, and any change must be for the better. I had been seasoned by adversity, and tutored by experience, and I longed to redeem my lost honour in the eyes of those whose opinion was more than that of all the world to me.

CHAPTER 6

## The Parsonage Again

For a few months I remained peaceably at home, in the quiet enjoyment of liberty and rest, and genuine friendship, from all of which I had fasted so long; and in the earnest prosecution of my studies, to recover what I had lost during my stay at Wellwood

House, and to lay in new stores for future use. My father's health was still very infirm, but not materially worse than when I last saw him; and I was glad I had it in my power to cheer him by my return, and to amuse him with singing his favourite songs.

No one triumphed over my failure, or said I had better have taken his or her advice, and quietly stayed at home. All were glad to have me back again, and lavished more kindness than ever upon me, to make up for the sufferings I had undergone; but not one would touch a shilling of what I had so cheerfully earned and so carefully saved, in the hope of sharing it with them. By dint of pinching here, and scraping there, our debts were already nearly paid. Mary had had good success with her drawings; but our father had insisted upon *her* likewise keeping all the produce of her industry to herself. All we could spare from the supply of our humble wardrobe and our little casual expenses he directed us to put into the savings' bank; saying we knew not how soon we might be dependent on that alone for support; for he felt he had not long to be with us, and what would become of our mother and us when he was gone, God only knew!

Dear papa! if he had troubled himself less about the afflictions that threatened us in case of his death, I am convinced that dreaded event would not have taken place so soon. My mother would never suffer him to ponder on the subject if she could help it.

'Oh, Richard!' exclaimed she, on one occasion, 'if you would but dismiss such gloomy subjects from your mind, you would live as long as any of us; at least you would live to see the girls married, and yourself a happy grandfather, with a canty old dame for your companion.'

My mother laughed, and so did my father; but his laugh soon perished in a dreary sigh.

'*They* married – poor penniless things!' said he, 'who will take them, I wonder!'

'Why, nobody shall that isn't thankful for them. Wasn't I penniless when you took me? and you *pretended*, at least, to be vastly pleased with your acquisition. But it's no matter whether they get married or not: we can devise a thousand honest ways of making a livelihood. And I wonder, Richard, you can think of bothering your head about our *poverty* in case of your death; as if *that* would be anything compared with the calamity of losing you – an affliction that you well know would swallow up all others, and which you ought to do your utmost to preserve us from: and there is nothing like a cheerful mind for keeping the body in health.'

'I know, Alice, it's wrong to keep repining as I do, but I cannot help it: you must bear with me.'

'I *won't* bear with you, if I can alter you,' replied my mother: but the harshness of her words was undone by the earnest affection of her tone and pleasant smile, that made my father smile again, less sadly and less transiently than was his wont.

'Mamma,' said I, as soon as I could find an opportunity of speaking with her alone, 'my money is but little, and cannot last long; if I could increase it, it would lessen papa's anxiety on one subject at least. I cannot draw like Mary, and so the best thing I could do would be to look out for another situation.'

'And so you would actually try again, Agnes?'

'Decidedly, I would.'

'Why, my dear, I should have thought you had had enough of it.'

'I know,' said I, 'everybody is not like Mr and Mrs Bloomfield'——

'Some are worse,' interrupted my mother.

'But not many, I think,' replied I, 'and I'm sure all children are not like theirs; for I and Mary were not: we always did as you bid us, didn't we?'

'Generally: but then, I did not spoil you; and you were not perfect angels after all: Mary had a fund of quiet obstinacy, and you were somewhat faulty in regard to temper; but you were very good children on the whole.'

'I know I was sulky sometimes, and I should have been glad to see these children sulky sometimes too; for then I could have understood them: but they never were, for they *could* not be offended, nor hurt, nor ashamed: they could not be unhappy in any way, except when they were in a passion.'

'Well, if they *could* not, it was not their fault: you cannot expect stone to be as pliable as clay.'

'No, but still it is very unpleasant to live with such unimpressible, incomprehensible creatures. You cannot love them; and if you could, your love would be utterly thrown away; they could neither return it, nor value, nor understand it. But, however, even if I should stumble on such a family again, which is quite unlikely, I have all this experience to begin with, and I should manage better another time; and the end and aim of this preamble is, let me try again.'

'Well, my girl, you are not easily discouraged, I see: I am glad of that. But, let me tell you, you are a good deal paler and thinner than when you first left home; and we cannot have you undermining your health to hoard up money, either for yourself or others.'

'Mary tells me I am changed too; and I don't much wonder at it, for I was in a constant state of agitation and anxiety all day long: but next time I am determined to take things coolly.'

After some further discussion, my mother promised once more to assist me, provided I would wait and be patient; and I left her to broach the matter to my father, when and how she deemed it most advisable: never doubting her ability to obtain his consent. Meantime, I searched, with great interest, the advertising columns of the newspapers, and wrote answers to every 'Wanted a Governess' that appeared at all eligible; but all my letters, as well as the replies, when I got any, were dutifully shown to my mother; and she, to my chagrin, made me reject the situations one after another: these were low people, these were too exacting in their demands, and these too niggardly in their remuneration.

'Your talents are not such as every poor clergyman's daughter possesses, Agnes,' she would say, 'and you must not throw them away. Remember, you promised to be patient: there is no need of hurry: you have plenty of time before you, and may have plenty of chances yet.'

At length, she advised me to put an advertisement, myself, in the paper, stating my qualifications, etc.

'Music, singing, drawing, French, Latin, and German,' said she, 'are no mean assemblage: many will be glad to have so much in one instructor; and this time you shall try your fortune in a somewhat higher family – in that of some genuine thorough-bred gentleman; for such are far more likely to treat you with proper respect and consideration than those purse-proud tradespeople and arrogant upstarts. I have known several among the higher ranks who treated their governesses quite as one of the family; though some, I allow, are as insolent and exacting as any one else can be: for there are good and bad in all classes.'

The advertisement was quickly written and despatched. Of the two parties who answered it, but one would consent to give me fifty pounds, the sum my mother bade me name as the salary I should require; and here I hesitated about engaging myself, as I feared the children would be too old, and their parents would require some one more showy, or more experienced, if not more accomplished than I. But my mother dissuaded me from declining it on that account: I should do vastly well, she said, if I would only throw aside my diffidence, and acquire a little more confidence in myself. I was just to give a plain, true statement of my acquirements and qualifications, and name what stipulations I chose to make, and then await the result. The only stipulation I ventured to propose, was that I might be allowed two months' holidays during the year to visit my friends, at Midsummer and Christmas. The unknown lady, in her reply, made no objection to this, and stated that, as to my acquirements, she had no doubt I should be able to give satisfaction; but in the engagement of governesses, she considered those things as but subordinate points; as, being situated in the neighbourhood of O——, she could get masters to supply any deficiencies in that respect: but, in her opinion, next to unimpeachable morality, a mild and cheerful temper and obliging disposition were the most essential requisites.

My mother did not relish this at all, and now made many objections to my accepting the situation; in which my sister warmly supported her: but, unwilling to be baulked again, I overruled them all; and, having first obtained the consent of my father (who had, a short time previously, been apprised of these transactions), I wrote a most obliging epistle to my unknown correspondent, and, finally, the bargain was concluded.

It was decreed that on the last day of January I was to enter upon my new office as governess in the family of Mr Murray, of Horton Lodge, near O——, about seventy miles from our village: a formidable distance to me, as I had never been above twenty miles from home in all the course of my twenty years' sojourn on earth; and as, moreover, every individual in that family and in the neighbourhood was utterly unknown to myself and all my acquaintances. But this rendered it only the more piquant to me. I had now, in some measure, got rid of the *mauvaise honte* that had formerly oppressed me so much; there was a pleasing excitement in the idea of entering these unknown regions, and making my way alone among its strange inhabitants. I now flattered myself I was going to see something of the world: Mr Murray's residence was near a large town, and not in a manufacturing district, where the people had nothing to do but make money; his rank, from what I could gather, appeared to be higher than that of Mr Bloomfield; and, doubtless, he was one of those genuine thorough-bred gentry my mother spoke of, who would treat his governess with due consideration as a respectable well-educated lady, the instructor and guide of his children, and not a mere upper servant. Then my pupils being older, would be more rational, more teachable, and less troublesome than the last: they would be less confined to the schoolroom, and not require that constant labour and incessant watching; and, finally, bright visions mingled with my hopes, with which the care of children and the mere duties of a governess had little or nothing to do. Thus, the reader will see that I had no claim to be regarded as a martyr to filial piety, going forth to sacrifice peace and liberty for the sole purpose of laying up stores for the comfort and support of my parents; though certainly the comfort of my father, and the future support of my mother, had a large share in my calculations; and fifty pounds appeared to me no ordinary sum. I must have decent clothes becoming my station; I must, it seemed, put out my washing, and also pay for my four annual journeys between Horton Lodge and home; but with strict attention to economy, surely twenty pounds, or little more, would cover those expenses, and then there would be thirty for the bank, or little less: what a valuable addition to our stock! Oh, I *must* struggle to keep this situation, whatever it might be! both for my own honour among my friends and for the solid services I might render them by my continuance there.

# Horton Lodge

The 31st of January was a wild, tempestuous day: there was a strong north wind, with a continual storm of snow drifting on the ground and whirling through the air. My friends would have had me delay my departure, but fearful of prejudicing my employers against me by such want of punctuality at the commencement of my undertaking, I persisted in keeping the appointment.

I will not inflict upon my readers an account of my leaving home on that dark winter morning: the fond farewells, the long, long journey to O——, the solitary waitings in inns for coaches or trains – for there were some railways then – and, finally, the meeting at O—— with Mr Murray's servant, who had been sent with the phaeton to drive me from thence to Horton Lodge. I will just state that the heavy snow had thrown such impediments in the way of both horses and steam-engines, that it was dark some hours before I reached my journey's end, and that a most bewildering storm came on at last, which made the few miles' space between O—— and Horton Lodge a long and formidable passage. I sat resigned, with the cold, sharp snow drifting through my veil and filling my lap, seeing nothing, and wondering how the unfortunate horse and driver could make their way even as well as they did: and indeed it was but a toilsome, creeping style of progression, to say the best of it. At length we paused; and, at the call of the driver, some one unlatched and rolled back upon their creaking hinges what appeared to be the park gates. Then we proceeded along a smoother road, whence, occasionally, I perceived some huge hoary mass gleaming through the darkness, which I took to be a portion of a snow-clad tree. After a considerable time we paused again, before the stately portico of a large house with long windows descending to the ground.

I rose with some difficulty from under the superincumbent snow-drift, and alighted from the carriage, expecting that a kind and hospitable reception would indemnify me for the toils and hardships of the day. A gentlemanly person in black opened the door, and admitted me into a spacious hall, lighted by an amber-coloured lamp suspended from the ceiling; he led me through this, along a passage, and, opening the door of a back room, told me that was the schoolroom. I entered, and found two young ladies and two young gentlemen – my future pupils, I supposed. After a formal greeting, the elder girl, who was trifling over a piece of canvas and a basket of German wools, asked if I should like to go upstairs. I replied in the affirmative, of course.

'Matilda, take a candle, and show her her room,' said she.

Miss Matilda, a strapping hoyden of about fourteen, with a short frock and trousers, shrugged her shoulders and made a slight grimace, but took a candle and proceeded before me, up the back stairs (a long, steep, double flight), and through a long, narrow passage, to a small but tolerably comfortable room. She them asked me if I would take some tea or coffee. I was about to answer No; but remembering that I had taken nothing since seven o'clock that morning, and feeling faint in consequence, I said I would take a cup of tea. Saying she would tell 'Brown', the young lady departed; and by the time I had divested myself of my heavy, wet cloak, shawl, bonnet, etc., a mincing damsel came to say the young ladies desired to know whether I would take my tea up there or in the schoolroom. Under the plea of fatigue, I chose to take it there. She withdrew; and, after a while, returned again with a small tea-tray, and placed it on the chest of drawers which served as a dressing-table. Having civilly thanked her, I asked at what time I should be expected to rise in the morning.

'The young ladies and gentlemen breakfast at half-past eight, ma'am,' said she; 'they rise early; but, as they seldom do any lessons before breakfast, I should think it will do if you rise soon after seven.'

I desired her to be so kind as to call me at seven, and, promising to do so, she withdrew. Then, having broken my long fast on a cup of tea and a little thin bread and butter, I sat down beside the small, smouldering fire, and amused myself with a hearty fit of crying; after which, I said my prayers, and then, feeling considerably relieved, began to prepare for bed. Finding that none of my luggage was brought up, I instituted a search for the bell; and failing to discover any signs of such a convenience in any corner of the room, I took my candle and ventured through the long passage, and down the steep stairs, on a voyage of discovery. Meeting a well dressed female on the way, I told her what I wanted; but not without considerable hesitation, as I was not quite sure whether it was one of the upper servants, or Mrs Murray herself: it happened, however, to be the lady's-maid. With the air of one conferring an unusual favour, she vouchsafed to undertake the sending up of my things; and when I had re-entered my room, and waited and wondered a long time (greatly fearing that she had forgotten or neglected to perform her promise, and doubting whether to keep waiting or go to bed, or go down again), my hopes, at length, were revived by the sound of voices and laughter, accompanied by the tramp of feet along the passage; and presently the luggage was brought in by a rough-looking maid and a man, neither of them very respectful in their demeanour to me. Having shut the door upon their retiring footsteps, and unpacked a few of my things, I betook myself to rest; gladly enough, for I was weary in body and mind.

It was with a strange feeling of desolation, mingled with a strong sense of the novelty of my situation, and a joyless kind of curiosity concerning what was yet unknown, that I awoke the next morning; feeling like one whirled away by enchantment, and suddenly dropped from the clouds into a remote and un-known land, widely and completely isolated from all he had ever seen or known before; or like a thistle-seed borne on the wind to some strange nook of uncongenial soil, where it must lie long enough before it can take root and germinate, extracting nourishment from what appears so alien to its nature: if, indeed, it ever can. But this gives no proper idea of my feelings at all; and no one that has not lived such a retired, stationary life as mine can possibly imagine what they were: hardly even if he has known what it is to awake some morning and find himself in Port Nelson, in New Zealand, with a world of waters between himself and all that knew him.

I shall not soon forget the peculiar feeling with which I raised my blind and looked out upon the unknown world: a wide, white wilderness was all that met my gaze; a waste of

> Deserts tossed in snow,
> And heavy-laden groves.

I descended to the schoolroom with no remarkable eagerness to join my pupils, though not without some feeling of curiosity respecting what a further acquaintance would reveal. One thing, among others of more obvious importance, I determined with myself – I must begin with calling them Miss and Master. It seemed to me a chilling and unnatural piece of punctilio between the children of a family and their instructor and daily companion; especially where the former were in their early childhood, as at Wellwood House; but even there my calling the little Bloomfields by their simple names had been regarded as an offensive liberty: as their parents had taken care to show me, by carefully designating them *Master* and *Miss* Bloomfield, etc., in speaking to me. I had been very slow to take the hint, because the whole affair struck me as so very absurd; but now I determined to be wiser, and begin at once with as much form and ceremony as any member of the family would be likely to require: and indeed, the children being so much older, there would be less difficulty; though the little words Miss and Master seemed to have a surprising effect in repressing all familiar, open-hearted kindness, and extinguishing every gleam of cordiality that might arise between us.

As I cannot, like Dogberry, find it in my heart to bestow *all* my tediousness upon the reader, I will not go on to bore him with a minute detail of all the discoveries and proceedings of this and the following day. No doubt he will be amply satisfied with a slight sketch of the different members of the family, and a general view of the first year or two of my sojourn among them.

To begin with the head: Mr Murray was, by all accounts, a blustering, roystering country squire; a devoted fox-hunter, a skilful horse-jockey and farrier, an active, practical farmer, and a hearty *bon-vivant*. By all accounts, I say; for, except on Sundays, when he went to church, I never saw him from month to month: unless, in crossing the hall or walking in the grounds, the figure of a tall, stout gentleman, with scarlet cheeks and crimson nose, happened to come across me; on which occasions, if he passed near enough to speak, an unceremonious nod, accompanied by a 'Morning, Miss Grey', or some such brief salutation, was usually vouchsafed. Frequently, indeed, his loud laugh reached me from afar; and oftener still I heard him swearing and blaspheming against the footmen, groom, coachman, or some other hapless dependent.

Mrs Murray was a handsome, dashing lady of forty, who certainly required neither rouge nor padding to add to her charms; and whose chief enjoyments were, or seemed to be, in giving or frequenting parties, and in dressing at the very top of the fashion. I did not see her till eleven o'clock on the morning of my arrival; when she honoured me with a visit, just as my mother might step into the kitchen to see a new servant-girl: yet not so, either, for my mother would have seen her immediately after her arrival, and not waited till next day; and, moreover, she would have addressed her in a more kind and friendly manner, and given her some words of comfort as well as a plain exposition of her duties; but Mrs Murray did neither the one nor the other. She just stepped into the schoolroom on her return from ordering dinner in the housekeeper's room, bade me good-morning, stood for two minutes by the fire, said a few words about the weather and the 'rather rough' journey I must have had yesterday; petted her youngest child – a boy of ten – who had just been wiping his mouth and hands on her gown, after indulging in some savoury morsel from the housekeeper's stores; told me what a sweet, good boy he was; and then sailed out, with a self-complacent smile upon her face: thinking, no doubt, that she had done quite enough for the present, and had been delightfully condescending into the bargain. Her children evidently held the same opinion, and I alone thought otherwise.

After this she looked in upon me once or twice, during the absence of my pupils, to enlighten me concerning my duties towards them. For the girls she seemed anxious only to render them as superficially attractive and showily accomplished as they could possibly be made, without present trouble or discomfort to themselves; and I was to act accordingly – to study and strive to amuse and oblige, instruct, refine, and polish, with the least possible exertion on their part, and no exercise of authority on mine. With regard to the two boys, it was much the same; only instead of accomplishments, I was to get the greatest possible quantity of Latin grammar and Valpy's *Delectus* into their heads, in order to fit them for school – the greatest possible quantity, at least, *without* trouble to themselves. John might be a 'little high-spirited', and Charles might be a 'little nervous and tedious'——

'But at all events, Miss Grey,' said she, 'I hope *you* will keep your temper, and be mild and patient throughout; especially with the dear little Charles: he is so extremely nervous and susceptible, and so utterly unaccustomed to anything but the tenderest treatment. You will excuse my naming these things to you; for the fact is, I have hitherto found all the governesses, even the very best of them, faulty in this particular. They wanted that meek and quiet spirit, which St Matthew, or some of them, says is better than the putting on of apparel – you will know the passage to which I allude, for you are a clergyman's daughter. But I have no doubt you will give satisfaction in this respect as well as the rest. And remember, on all occasions, when any of the young people do anything improper, if persuasion and gentle remonstrance will not do, let one of the others come and tell me; for I can speak to them more plainly than it would be proper for you to do. And make them as happy as you can, Miss Grey, and I dare say you will do very well.'

I observed that while Mrs Murray was so extremely solicitous for the comfort and happiness of her children, and continually talking about it, she never once mentioned mine; though they were at home surrounded by friends, and I an alien among strangers; and I did not yet know enough of the world not to be considerably surprised at this anomaly.

Miss Murray, otherwise Rosalie, was about sixteen when I came, and decidedly a very pretty girl; and in two years longer, as time more completely developed her form and added grace to her carriage and deportment, she became positively beautiful; and that in no common degree. She was tall and slender, yet not thin; perfectly formed, exquisitely fair, though not without a brilliant, healthy bloom; her hair, which she wore in a profusion of long ringlets, was of a very light brown inclining to yellow; her eyes were pale blue, but so clear and bright that few would wish them darker; the rest of her features were small, not quite regular, and not remarkably otherwise: but altogether you could not hesitate to pronounce her a very lovely girl. I wish I could say as much for mind and disposition as I can for her form and face.

Yet think not I have any dreadful disclosures to make: she was lively, light-hearted, and could be very agreeable with those who did not cross her will. Towards me, when I first came, she was cold and haughty, then insolent and overbearing; but on a further acquaintance, she gradually laid aside her airs, and in time became as deeply attached to me as it was possible for *her* to be to one of my character and position: for she seldom lost sight, for above half-an-hour at a time, of the fact of my being a hireling and a poor curate's daughter. And yet, upon the whole, I believe she respected me more than she herself was aware of; because I was the only person in the house who steadily professed good principles, habitually spoke the truth, and generally endeavoured to make inclination bow to duty: and this I say, not, of course, in commendation of myself, but to show the unfortunate state of the family to which my services, were, for the present, devoted. There was no member of it in whom I regretted this sad want of principle so much as Miss Murray herself; not only because she had taken a fancy to me, but because there was so much of what was pleasant and prepossessing in herself, that, in spite of her failings, I really liked her – when she did not rouse my indignation, or ruffle my temper by *too* great a display of her faults. These, however, I would fain persuade myself, were rather the effect of her education than her disposition: she had never been perfectly taught the distinction between right and wrong; she had, like her brothers and sisters, been suffered, from infancy, to tyrannize over nurses, governesses, and servants; she had not been taught to moderate her desires, to control her temper or bridle her will, or to sacrifice her own pleasure for the good of others. Her temper being naturally good, she was never violent or morose, but from constant indulgence and habitual scorn of reason, she was often testy and capricious; her mind had never been cultivated: her intellect, at best, was somewhat shallow; she possessed considerable vivacity, some quickness of perception, and some talent for music and the acquisition of languages, but till fifteen she had troubled herself to acquire nothing; – then the love of display had roused her faculties, and induced her to apply herself, but only to the more showy accomplishments. And when I came it was the same: every thing was neglected but French, German, music, singing, dancing, fancy-work, and a little drawing – such drawing as might produce the greatest show with the smallest labour, and the principal parts of which were generally done by me. For music and singing, besides my occasional instructions, she had the attendance of the best master the country afforded; and in these accomplishments, as well as in dancing, she certainly attained great proficiency. To music, indeed, she devoted too much of her time: as, governess though I was, I frequently told her; but her mother thought that if *she* liked it, she *could* not give too much time to the acquisition of so attractive an art. Of fancy-work I knew nothing but what I gathered from my pupil and my own observation; but no sooner was I initiated, than she made me useful in twenty different ways: all the tedious parts of her work were shifted on to my shoulders; such as stretching the frames, stitching in the canvas, sorting the wools and silks, putting in the grounds, counting the stitches, rectifying mistakes, and finishing the pieces she was tired of.

At sixteen, Miss Murray was something of a romp, yet not more so than is natural and allowable for a girl of that age; but at seventeen, that propensity, like all other things, began to give way to the ruling passion, and soon was swallowed up in the all-absorbing ambition to attract and dazzle the other sex. But enough of her: now let us turn to her sister.

Miss Matilda Murray was a veritable hoyden, of whom little need be said. She was about two years and a half younger than her sister; her features were larger, her complexion much darker. She might possibly make a handsome woman; but she was far too big-boned and awkward ever to be called a pretty girl, and at present she cared little about it. Rosalie knew all her charms, and thought them even greater than they were, and valued them more highly than she ought to have done, had they been three times as great; Matilda thought she was well enough, but cared little about the matter; still less did she care about the cultivation of her mind, and the acquisition of ornamental accomplishments. The manner in which she learnt her lessons and practised her music was calculated to drive any governess to despair. Short and easy as her tasks were, if done at all, they were slurred over, at any time and in any way; but generally at the least convenient times, and in the way least beneficial to herself, and least satisfactory to me: the short half-hour of practising was horribly strummed through; she, meantime, unsparingly abusing me, either for interrupting her with corrections, or for not rectifying her mistakes before they were made, or something equally unreasonable. Once or twice I ventured to remonstrate with her seriously for such irrational conduct; but on each of those occasions I received such reprehensive expostulations from her mother as convinced me that, if I wished to keep the situation, I must even let Miss Matilda go on in her own way.

When her lessons were over, however, her ill-humour was generally over too: while riding her spirited pony, or romping with the dogs or her brothers and sister, but especially with her dear brother John, she was as happy as a lark. As an animal, Matilda was all right, full of life, vigour, and activity; as an intelligent being, she was barbarously ignorant, indocile, careless, and irrational; and consequently, very distressing to one who had the task of cultivating her understanding, reforming her manners, and aiding her to acquire those ornamental attainments which, unlike her sister, she despised as much as the rest. Her mother was partly aware of her deficiencies, and gave me many a lecture as to how I should try to form her tastes, and endeavour to rouse and cherish her dormant vanity; and, by insinuating, skilful flattery, to win her attention to the desired objects – which I would not do; and how I should prepare and smooth the path of learning till she could glide along it without the least exertion to herself: which I could not, for nothing can be taught to any purpose without some little exertion on the part of the learner.

As a moral agent, Matilda was reckless, headstrong, violent, and unamenable to reason. One proof of the deplorable state of her mind was, that from her father's example she had learned to swear like a trooper. Her mother was greatly shocked at the 'unladylike trick', and wondered 'how she had picked it up'. 'But you can soon break her of it, Miss Grey,' said she: 'it is only a habit, and if you will just gently remind her every time she does so, I am sure she will soon lay it aside.' I not only 'gently reminded' her, I tried to impress upon her how wrong it was, and how distressing to the ears of decent people; but all in vain: I was only answered by a careless laugh, and, 'Oh, Miss Grey, how shocked you are! I'm so glad!' Or, 'Well! I can't help it; papa shouldn't have taught me: I learned it all from him; and maybe a bit from the coachman.'

Her brother John, *alias* Master Murray, was about eleven when I came: a fine, stout, healthy boy, frank and good-natured in the main, and might have been a decent lad had he been properly educated; but now he was as rough as a young bear, boisterous, unruly, unprincipled, untaught, unteachable – at least, for a governess under his mother's eye. His masters at school might be able to manage him better – for to school he was sent, greatly to my relief, in the course of a year; in a state, it is true, of scandalous ignorance as to Latin, as well as the more useful though more neglected things: and this, doubtless, would all be laid to the account of his education having been entrusted to an ignorant female teacher, who had presumed to take in hand what she was wholly incompetent to perform. I was not delivered from his brother till full twelve months after, when he also was despatched in the same state of disgraceful ignorance as the former.

Master Charles was his mother's peculiar darling. He was little more than a year younger than John, but much smaller, paler, and less active and robust; a pettish, cowardly, capricious, selfish little fellow, only active in doing mischief, and only clever in inventing falsehoods: not simply to hide his faults, but, in mere malicious wantonness, to bring odium upon others. In fact, Master Charles was a very great nuisance to me: it was a trial of patience to live with him peaceably; to watch over him was worse; and to teach him, or pretend to teach him, was inconceivable. At ten years old he could not read correctly the easiest line in the simplest book; and as, according to his mother's principle, he was to be told every word before he had time to hesitate or examine its orthography, and never even to be informed, as a stimulant to exertion, that other boys were more forward than he, it is not surprising that he made but little progress during the two years I had charge of his education. His minute portions of Latin grammar, etc., were to be repeated over to him till he chose to say he knew them, and then he was to be helped to say them; if he made mistakes in his little easy sums in arithmetic, they were to be shown him at once, and the sum done for him, instead of his being left to exercise his faculties in finding them out himself; so that, of course, he took no pains to avoid mistakes, but frequently set down his figures at random, without any calculation at all.

I did not invariably confine myself to these rules: it was against my conscience to do so; but I seldom could venture to deviate from them in the slightest degree without incurring the wrath of my little pupil, and subsequently of his mamma; to whom he would relate my transgressions, maliciously exaggerated, or adorned with embellishments of his own; and often, in consequence, was I on the point of losing or resigning my situation. But, for their sakes at home, I smothered my pride and suppressed my indignation, and managed to struggle on till my little tormentor was despatched to school; his father declaring that home education was 'no go for him, it was plain; his mother spoiled him outrageously, and his governess could make no hand of him at all'.

A few more observations about Horton Lodge and its ongoings, and I have done with dry description for the present. The house was a very respectable one; superior to Mr Bloomfield's, both in age, size, and magnificence; the garden was not so tastefully laid out; but instead of the smooth-shaven lawn, the young trees guarded by palings, the grove of upstart poplars, and the plantation of firs, there was a wide park, stocked with deer, and beautified by fine old trees. The surrounding country itself was pleasant, as far as fertile fields, flourishing trees, quiet green lanes, and smiling hedges with wild flowers scattered along their banks, could make it; but it was depressingly flat to one born and nurtured among the rugged hills of ——.

We were situated nearly two miles from the village church, and, consequently, the family carriage was put in requisition every Sunday morning, and sometimes oftener. Mr and Mrs Murray generally thought it sufficient to show themselves at church once in the course of the day; but frequently the children preferred going a second time to wandering about the grounds all the day with nothing to do. If some of my pupils chose to walk and take me with them, it was well for me; for otherwise my position in the carriage was, to be crushed into the corner farthest from the open window, and with my back to the horses: a position which invariably made me sick; and, if I were not actually obliged to leave the church in the middle of the service, my devotions were disturbed with a feeling of langour and sickliness, and the tormenting fear of its becoming worse; and a depressing headache was generally my companion throughout the day, which would otherwise have been one of welcome rest, and holy, calm enjoyment.

'It's very odd, Miss Grey, that the carriage should always make you sick: it never makes *me*,' remarked Miss Matilda.

'Nor me either,' said her sister, 'but I daresay it would, if I sat where she does – such a nasty, horrid place, Miss Grey; I wonder how you can bear it!'

'I am obliged to bear it, since no choice is left me,' I might have answered; but in tenderness for their feelings I only replied – 'Oh! it is but a short way, and if I am not sick in church, I don't mind it.'

If I were called upon to give a description of the usual divisions and arrangements of the day, I should find it a very difficult matter. I had all my meals in the schoolroom with my pupils, at such times as suited their fancy: sometimes they would ring for dinner before it was half-cooked; sometimes they would keep it waiting on the table for above an hour, and then be out of humour because the potatoes were cold, and the gravy covered with cakes of solid fat; sometimes they would have tea at four; frequently, they would storm at the servants because it was not in precisely at five; and when these orders were obeyed, by way of encouragement to punctuality, they would keep it on the table till seven or eight.

Their hours of study were managed in much the same way; my judgment or convenience was never once consulted. Sometimes Matilda and John would determine 'to get all the plaguy business over before breakfast', and send the maid to call me up at half-past five, without any scruple or apology; sometimes, I was told to be ready precisely at six, and, having dressed in a hurry, came down to an empty room, and after waiting a long time in suspense, discovered that they had changed their minds, and were still in bed; or perhaps, if it were a fine summer morning, Brown would come to tell me that the young ladies and gentlemen had taken a holiday, and were gone out; and then I was kept waiting for breakfast till I was almost ready to faint: they having fortified themselves with something before they went.

Often they would do their lessons in the open air; which I had nothing to say against: except that I frequently caught cold by sitting on the damp grass, or from exposure to the evening dew, or some insidious draught, which seemed to have no injurious effect on them. It was quite right that they should be hardy; yet, surely, they might have been taught some consideration for others who were less so. But I must not blame them for what was, perhaps, my own fault; for I never made any particular objections to sitting where they pleased; foolishly choosing to risk the consequences, rather than trouble them for my convenience. Their indecorous manner of doing their lessons was quite as remarkable as the caprice displayed in their choice of time and place. While receiving my instructions, or repeating what they had learned, they would lounge upon the sofa, lie on the rug, stretch, yawn, talk to each other, or look out of the window; whereas, I could not so much as stir the fire, or pick up the handkerchief I had dropped, without being rebuked for inattention by one of my pupils, or told that 'mamma would not like me to be so careless'.

The servants, seeing in what little estimation the governess was held by both parents and children, regulated their behaviour by the same standard. I have frequently stood up for them, at the risk of some injury to myself, against the tyranny and injustice of their young masters and mistresses; and I always endeavoured to give them as little trouble as possible: but they entirely neglected my comfort, despised my requests, and slighted my directions. All servants, I am convinced, would not have done so; but domestics in general, being ignorant and little accustomed to reason and reflection, are too easily corrupted by the careless-ness and bad example of those above them; and these, I think, were not of the best order to begin with.

I sometimes felt myself degraded by the life I led, and ashamed of submitting to so many indignities; and sometimes I thought myself a fool for caring so much about them, and feared I must be sadly wanting in Christian humility, or that charity which 'suffereth long and is kind, seeketh not her own, is not easily provoked, beareth all things, endureth all things'. But, with time and patience, matters began to be slightly ameliorated: slowly, it is true, and almost imperceptibly; but I got rid of my male pupils (that was no trifling advantage), and the girls, as I intimated before concerning one of them, became a little less insolent, and began to show some symptoms of esteem. 'Miss Grey was a queer creature: she never flattered, and did not praise them half enough; but whenever she did speak favourably of them, or anything belonging to them, they could be quite sure her approbation was sincere. She was very obliging, quiet, and peaceable in the main, but there were some things that put her out of temper: they did not much care for that, to be sure, but still it was better to keep her in tune; as when she was in a good humour she would talk to them, and be very agreeable and amusing sometimes, in her way; which was quite different to mamma's, but still very well for a change. She had her own opinions on every subject, and kept steadily to them – very tiresome opinions they often were; as she was always thinking of what was right and what was wrong, and had a strange reverence for matters connected with religion, and an unaccountable liking for good people.'

CHAPTER 8

*The 'Coming-Out'*

At eighteen, Miss Murray was to emerge from the quiet obscurity of the schoolroom into the full blaze of the fashionable world – as much of it, at least, as could be had out of London; for her papa could not be persuaded to leave his rural pleasures and pursuits even for a few weeks' residence in town. She was to make her *début* on the 3rd of January, at a magnificent ball which her mamma proposed to give to all nobility and choice gentry of O—— and its neighbourhood for twenty miles round. Of course, she looked forward to it with the wildest impatience, and the most extravagant anticipations of delight.

'Miss Grey,' said she, one evening, a month before the all-important day, as I was perusing a long and extremely interesting letter of my sister's – which I had just glanced at in the morning to see that it contained no very bad news, and kept till now, unable before to find a quiet moment for reading it – 'Miss Grey, do put away that dull, stupid letter, and listen to me! I'm sure my talk must be far more amusing than that.'

She seated herself on the low stool at my feet; and I, suppressing a sigh of vexation, began to fold up the epistle.

'You should tell the good people at home not to bore you with such long letters,' said she; 'and above all, do bid them write on proper note-paper, and not on those great vulgar sheets. You should see the charming little ladylike notes mamma writes to her friends.'

'The good people at home,' replied I, 'know very well that the longer their letters are, the better I like them. I should be very sorry to receive a charming little ladylike note from any of them; and I thought you were too much of a lady yourself, Miss Murray, to talk about the "vulgarity" of writing on a large sheet of paper.'

'Well, I only said it to tease you. But now I want to talk about the ball; and to tell you that you positively must put off your holidays till it is over.'

'Why so? – I shall not be present at the ball.'

'No, but you will see the rooms decked out before it begins, and hear the music, and, above all, see me in my splendid new dress. I shall be so charmng, you'll be ready to worship me – you really must stay.'

'I should like to see you very much; but I shall have many opportunities of seeing you equally charming on the occasion of some of the numberless balls and parties that are to be, and I cannot disappoint my friends by postponing my return so long.'

'Oh, never mind your friends! Tell them we won't let you go.'

'But, to say the truth, it would be a disappointment to myself: I long to see them as much as they to see me – perhaps more.'

'Well, but it is such a short time.'

'Nearly a fortnight by my computation; and, besides, I cannot bear the thoughts of a Christmas spent from home: and, moreover, my sister is going to be married.'

'Is she – when?'

'Not till next month: but I want to be there to assist her in making preparations, and to make the best of her company while we have her.'

'Why didn't you tell me before?'

'I've only got the news in this letter, which you stigmatize as dull and stupid, and won't let me read.'

'To whom is she to be married?'

'To Mr Richardson, the vicar of a neighbouring parish.'

'Is he rich?'

'No; only comfortable.'

'Is he handsome?'

'No; only decent.'

'Young?'

'No; only middling.'

'O mercy! what a wretch! What sort of a house is it?'

A quiet little vicarage, with an ivy-clad porch, an old-fashioned garden, and'——

'O stop! – you'll make me sick. How *can* she bear it?'

'I expect she'll not only be able to bear it, but to be very happy. You did not ask me if Mr Richardson were a good, wise, or amiable man; I could have answered Yes, to all these questions – at least so Mary thinks, and I hope she will not find herself mistaken.'

'But – miserable creature! how can she think of spending her life there, cooped up with that nasty old man; and *no* hope of change?'

'He is not old: he's only six or seven and thirty; and she herself is twenty-eight, and as sober as if she were fifty.'

'Oh! that's better then – they're well matched: but do they call him the "worthy vicar"?'

'I don't know; but if they do, I believe he merits the epithet.'

'Mercy, how shocking! and will she wear a white apron, and make pies and puddings?'

'I don't know about the white apron, but I dare say she will make pies and puddings now and then; but that will be no great hardship, as she had done it before.'

'And will she go about in a plain shawl, and a large straw bonnet, carrying tracts and bone soup to her husband's poor parishioners?'

'I'm not clear about that; but I dare say she will do her best to make them comfortable in body and mind, in accordance with our mother's example.'

CHAPTER 9

*The Ball*

'Now, Miss Grey,' exclaimed Miss Murray, immediately I entered the schoolroom, after having taken off my outdoor garments, upon returning from my four weeks' recreation, 'Now – shut the door, and sit down, and I'll tell you all about the ball.'

'No, – damn it, no!' shouted Miss Matilda. 'Hold your tongue, can't ye? and let me tell her about my new mare – *such* a splendour, Miss Grey! a fine blood mare'——

'Do be quiet, Matilda; and let me tell my news first.'

'No, no, Rosalie; you'll be such a damned long time over it – she shall hear me first – I'll be hanged if she doesn't!'

'I'm sorry to hear, Miss Matilda, that you've not got rid of that shocking habit yet.'

'Well, I can't help it: but I'll never say a wicked word again, if you'll only listen to me, and tell Rosalie to hold her confounded tongue.'

Rosalie remonstrated, and I thought I should have been torn in pieces between them; but Miss Matilda having the loudest voice, her sister at length gave in, and suffered her to tell her story first: so I was doomed to hear a long account of her splendid mare, its breeding and pedigree, its paces, its action, its spirit, etc., and of her own amazing skill and courage in riding it; concluding with an assertion that she could clear a five-barred gate 'like winking', that papa said she might hunt the next time the hounds met, and mamma had ordered a bright scarlet hunting-habit for her.

'Oh, Matilda! what stories you are telling!' exclaimed her sister.

'Well,' answered she, no whit abashed, 'I know I *could* clear a five-barred gate if I tried, and papa *will* say I may hunt, and mamma *will* order the habit when I ask it.'

'Well, now get along,' replied Miss Murray; 'and do, dear Matilda, try to be a little more ladylike. Miss Grey, I wish you *would* tell her not to use such shocking words; she *will* call her horse a mare: it is so *inconceivably* shocking! and then she uses such dreadful expressions in describing it: she *must* have learned it from the grooms. It nearly puts me into fits when she begins.'

'I learned it from papa, you ass! and his jolly friends,' said the young lady, vigorously cracking a hunting-whip, which she habitually carried in her hand. 'I'm as good a judge of horse-flesh as the best of 'm.'

'Well, now get along, you shocking girl! I really shall take a fit if you go on in such a way. And now, Miss Grey, attend to me; I'm going to tell you about the ball. You must be dying to hear about it, I know. Oh, *such* a ball! You never saw or heard, or read, or dreamt of anything like it in all your life! The

decorations, the entertainment, the supper, the music were indescribable! and then the guests! There were two noblemen,
three baronets, and five titled ladies, and other ladies and
gentlemen innumerable. The ladies, of course, were of no consequence to me, except to put me in a good humour with myself,
by showing how ugly and awkward most of them were; and the
best, mamma told me, – the most transcendent beauties among
them, were nothing to me. As for *me* Miss Grey – I'm so *sorry*
you didn't see me! I was *charming* – wasn't I, Matilda?'

'Middling.'

'No, but I really *was* – at least so mamma said – and Brown
and Williamson. Brown said she was sure no gentleman could
set eyes on me without falling in love that minute; and so I may
be allowed to be a little vain. I know you think me a shocking,
conceited, frivolous girl; but then, you know, I don't atttribute it
*all* to my personal attractions: I give some praise to the
hairdresser, and some to my exquisitely lovely dress – you must
see it to-morrow – white gauze over pink satin – and so *sweetly*
made! and a necklace and bracelet of beautiful, large pearls!'

'I've no doubt you looked very charming: but should that
delight you so very much?'

'Oh, no! – not that alone! but then, I was so much admired;
and I made so *many* conquests in that one night – you'd be
astonished to hear'——

'But what good will they do you?'

'What good! Think of any woman asking that!'

'Well, I should think one conquest would be enough; and too
much, unless the subjugation were mutual.'

'Oh, but you know I never agree with you on those points.
Now, wait a bit, and I'll tell you my principal admirers – those
who made themselves very conspicuous that night and after: for
I've been to two parties since. Unfortunately the two noblemen,
Lord G—— and Lord F——, were married, or I might have
condescended to be particularly gracious to *them*; as it was, I did
not: though Lord F——, who hates his wife, was evidently much
struck with me. He asked me to dance with him twice – he is a
charming dancer, by-the-bye, and so am I, you can't think how
well I did – I was astonished at myself. My lord was very
complimentary too – rather too much so in fact – and I thought
proper to be a little haughty and repellant; but I had the pleasure

of seeing his nasty, cross wife ready to perish with spite and vexation'——

'Oh, Miss Murray, you don't mean to say that such a thing could really give you pleasure! However cross or'——

'Well, I know it's very wrong; but never mind! I mean to be good sometime – only don't preach now, there's a good creature. I haven't told you half yet. Let me see. Oh! I was going to tell you how many unmistakable admirers I had: Sir Thomas Ashby was one, – Sir Hugh Meltham and Sir Broadley Wilson are old codgers, only fit companions for papa and mamma. Sir Thomas is young, rich, and gay; but an ugly beast, nevertheless: however, mamma says I should not mind that after a few months' acquaintance. Then there was Henry Meltham, Sir Hugh's younger son: rather good-looking, and a pleasant fellow to flirt with: but *being* a younger son, that is all he is good for; then there was young Mr Green, rich enough, but of no family, and a great stupid fellow, a mere country booby; and then, our good rector, Mr Hatfield: an *humble* admirer he ought to consider himself; but I fear he has forgotten to number humility among his stock of Christian virtues.'

'Was Mr Hatfield at the ball?'

'Yes, to be sure. Did you think he was too good to go?'

'I thought he might consider it unclerical.'

'By *no* means. He did not profane his cloth by dancing! but it was with difficulty he could refrain, poor man: he looked as if he were dying to ask my hand just for *one* set; and – oh! by-the-bye – he's got a new curate: that seedy old fellow Mr Bligh has got his long-wished-for living at last, and is gone.'

'And what is the new one like?'

'Oh, *such* a beast! Weston his name is. I can give you his description in three words – an insensate, ugly, stupid blockhead. That's four, but no matter – enough of *him* now.'

Then she returned to the ball and gave me a further account of her deportment there, and at the several parties she had since attended; and further particulars respecting Sir Thomas Ashby and Messrs Meltham, Green, and Hatfield, and the ineffaceable impression she had wrought upon each of them.

'Well, which of the four do you like best?' said I, suppressing my third or fourth yawn.

'I detest them all!' replied she, shaking her bright ringlets in vivacious scorn.

'That means, I suppose, I like them all – but which most?'

'No, I really detest them all; but Harry Meltham is the handsomest and most amusing, and Mr Hatfield the cleverest, Sir Thomas the wickedest, and Mr Green the most stupid. But the one I'm to have, I suppose, if I'm doomed to have any of them, is Sir Thomas Ashby.'

'Surely not, if he's so wicked, and if you dislike him?'

'Oh, I don't mind his being wicked: he's all the better for that; and as for disliking him – I shouldn't greatly object to being Lady Ashby of Ashby Park, if I must marry. But if I could be always young, I would be always single. I should like to enjoy myself thoroughly, and coquet with all the world, till I am on the verge of being called an old maid; and then to escape the infamy of that, after having made ten thousand conquests, to break all their hearts save one, by marrying some high-born, rich, indulgent husband, whom, on the other hand, fifty ladies were dying to have.'

'Well, as long as you entertain these views, keep single by all means, and never marry at all: not even to escape the infamy of old-maidenhood.'

## CHAPTER 10
## *The Church*

'Well, Miss Grey, what do you think of the new curate?' asked Miss Murray, on our return from church the Sunday after the recommencement of our duties.

'I can scarcely tell,' was my reply: 'I have not even heard him preach.'

'Well, but you saw him, didn't you?'

'Yes, but I cannot pretend to judge of a man's character by a single cursory glance at his face.'

'But isn't he ugly?'

'He did not strike me as being particularly so; I don't dislike that cast of countenance: but the only thing I particularly noticed about him was his style of reading; which appeared to me good – infinitely better, at least, than Mr Hatfield's. He read the Lessons as if he were bent on giving full effect to every passage: it seemed as if the most careless person could not have helped attending, nor the most ignorant have failed to understand; and the prayers he read as if he were not reading at all, but praying earnestly and sincerely from his own heart.'

'Oh, yes, that's all he is good for: he can plod through the service well enough; but he has not a single idea beyond it.'

'How do you know?'

'Oh! I know perfectly well; I am an excellent judge in such matters. Did you see how he went out of church? stumping along – as if there were nobody there but himself – never looking to the right hand or the left, and evidently thinking of nothing but just getting out of the church, and, perhaps, home to his dinner: his great stupid head could contain no other idea.'

'I suppose you would have had him cast a glance into the squire's pew,' said I, laughing at the vehemence of her hostility.

'Indeed! I should have been highly indignant if he had dared to do such a thing!' replied she, haughtily tossing her head; then, after a moment's reflection, she added – 'Well, well! I suppose he's good enough for his place: but I'm glad I'm not dependent on *him* for amusement – that's all. Did you see how Mr Hatfield hurried out to get a bow from me, and be in time to put us into the carriage?'

'Yes,' answered I; internally adding, 'and I thought it somewhat derogatory to his dignity as a clergyman to come flying from the pulpit in such eager haste to shake hands with the squire, and hand his wife and daughters into their carriage: and, moreover, I owe him a grudge for nearly shutting me out of it'; for, in fact, though I was standing before his face, close beside the carriage steps, waiting to get in, he would persist in putting them up and closing the door, till one of the family stopped him by calling out that the governess was not in yet; then, without a word of apology, he departed, wishing them good-morning, and leaving the footman to finish the business.

*Nota bene.* – Mr Hatfield never spoke to me, neither did Sir Hugh or Lady Meltham, nor Mr Harry or Miss Meltham, nor Mr Green or his sisters, nor any other lady or gentleman who frequented that church: nor, in fact, any one that visited at Horton Lodge.

Miss Murray ordered the carriage again, in the afternoon, for herself and her sister: she said it was too cold for them to enjoy themselves in the garden: and besides, she believed Harry Meltham would be at church. 'For,' said she, smiling slily at her own fair image in the glass, 'he has been a most exemplary attendant at church these last few Sundays: you would think he was quite a good Christian. And you may go with us, Miss Grey: I want you to see him; he is so greatly improved since he returned from abroad – you can't think! And besides, then you will have an opportunity of seeing the beautiful Mr Weston again, and of hearing him preach.'

I did hear him preach, and was decidedly pleased with the evangelical truth of his doctrine, as well as the earnest simplicity of his manner, and the clearness and force of his style. It was truly refreshing to hear such a sermon, after being so long accustomed to the dry, prosy discourses of the former curate, and the still less edifying harangues of the rector. Mr Hatfield would come sailing up the aisle, or rather sweeping along like a whirlwind, with his rich silk gown flying behind him and rustling against the pew doors, mount the pulpit like a con-queror ascending his triumphal car; then, sinking on the velvet cushion in an attitude of studied grace, remain in silent pros-tration for a certain time; then mutter over a Collect, and gabble through the Lord's Prayer, rise, draw off one bright lavender glove, to give the congregation the benefit of his sparkling rings, lightly pass his fingers through his well-curled hair, flourish a cambric handkerchief, recite a very short passage, or, perhaps, a mere phrase of Scripture, as a headpiece to his discourse, and, finally, deliver a composition which, as a composition, might be considered good, though far too studied and too artificial to be pleasing to me: the propositions were well laid down, the arguments logically conducted; and yet it was sometimes hard to listen quietly throughout without some slight demonstrations of disapproval or impatience.

His favourite subjects were Church discipline, rites and cere-monies, apostolical succession, the duty of reverence and obedience to the clergy, the atrocious criminality of dissent, the absolute necessity of observing all the forms of godliness, the reprehensible presumption of individuals who attempted to think for themselves in matters connected with religion, or to be guided by their own interpretations of Scripture, and occasionally (to please his wealthy parishioners) the necessity of deferential obedience from the poor to the rich – supporting his maxims and exhortations throughout with quotations from the Fathers: with whom he appeared to be far better acquainted than with the Apostles and Evangelists, and whose importance he seemed to consider at least equal to theirs. But now and then he gave us a sermon of a different order – what some would call a very good one; but sunless and severe: representing the Deity as a terrible task-master, rather than a benevolent father. Yet, as I listened, I felt inclined to think the man was sincere in all he said: he must have changed his views, and become decidedly religious; gloomy and austere, yet still devout. But such illusions were usually dissipated, on coming out of church, by hearing his voice in jocund colloquy with some of the Melthams or Greens, or, perhaps, the Murrays themselves; probably laughing at his own sermon, and hoping that he had given the rascally people something to think about; perchance, exulting in the thought that old Betty Holmes would now lay aside the sinful indulgence of her pipe, which had been her daily solace for upwards of thirty years; that George Higgins would be frightened out of his Sabbath evening walks, and Thomas Jackson would be sorely troubled in his conscience, and shaken in his sure and certain hope of a joyful resurrection at the last day.

Thus, I could not but conclude that Mr Hatfield was one of those who 'bind heavy burdens, and grievous to be borne, and lay them upon men's shoulders, while they themselves will not move them with one of their fingers', and who 'make the word of God of none effect by their traditions, teaching for doctrines the commandments of men'. I was well pleased to observe that the new curate resembled him, as far as I could see, in none of these particulars.

'Well, Miss Grey, what do you think of him now?' said Miss Murray, as we took our places in the carriage after service.

'No harm still,' replied I.

'No harm!' repeated she, in amazement. 'What do you mean?'

'I mean, I think no worse than I did before.'

'No worse! I should think not indeed – quite the contrary! Is he not greatly improved?'

'Oh, yes; very much indeed,' replied I; for I had now discovered it was Harry Meltham she meant, not Mr Weston. That gentleman had eagerly come forward to speak to the young ladies: a thing he would hardly have ventured to do had their mother been present; he had likewise politely handed them into the carriage. He had not attempted to shut me out, like Mr Hatfield; neither, of course, had he offered me his assistance (I should not have accepted it if he had), but as long as the door remained open he had stood smirking and chatting with them, and then lifted his hat and departed to his own abode: but I had scarcely noticed him all the time. My companions, however, had been more observant; and, as we rolled along, they discussed between them not only his looks, words, and actions, but every feature of his face, and every article of his apparel.

'You shan't have him all to yourself, Rosalie,' said Miss Matilda at the close of this discussion; 'I like him: I know he'd make a nice, jolly companion for me.'

'Well, you're quite welcome to him, Matilda,' replied her sister, in a tone of affected indifference.

'And I'm sure,' continued the other, 'he admires me quite as much as he does you; doesn't he, Miss Grey?'

'I don't know; I'm not acquainted with his sentiments.'

'Well, but he *does* though.'

'My *dear* Matilda! nobody will ever admire you till you get rid of your rough, awkward manners.'

'Oh, stuff! Harry Meltham likes such manners; and so do papa's friends.'

'Well, you *may* captivate old men and younger sons; but nobody else, I am sure, will ever take a fancy to you.'

'I don't care: I'm not always grubbing after money, like you and mamma. If my husband is able to keep a few good horses and dogs, I shall be quite satisfied; and all the rest may go to the devil!'

'Well, if you use such shocking expressions, I'm sure no real gentleman will ever venture to come near you. Really, Miss Grey, you should not let her do so.'

'I can't possibly prevent it, Miss Murray.'

'And you're quite mistaken, Matilda, in supposing that Harry Meltham admires you: I assure you he does nothing of the kind.'

Matilda was beginning an angry reply; but, happily, our journey was now at an end; and the contention was cut short by the footman opening the carriage door, and letting down the steps for our descent.

## Chapter 11

# *The Cottagers*

As I had now only one regular pupil – though she contrived to give me as much trouble as three or four ordinary ones, and though her sister still took lessons in German and drawing – I had considerably more time at my own disposal than I had ever been blessed with before since I had taken upon me the governess's yoke; which time I devoted partly to correspondence with my friends, partly to reading, study, and the practice of music, singing, etc., partly to wandering in the grounds or adjacent fields, with my pupils if they wanted me, alone if they did not.

Often, when they had no more agreeable occupation at hand, the Misses Murray would amuse themselves with visiting the poor cottagers on their father's estate, to receive their flattering homage, or to hear the old stories or gossiping news of the garrulous old women; or, perhaps, to enjoy the purer pleasure of making the poor people happy with their cheering presence and their occasional gifts, so easily bestowed, so thankfully received. Sometimes I was called upon to accompany one or both of the sisters in these visits; and sometimes I was desired to go alone, to fulfil some promise which they had been more ready to make than to perform; to carry some small donation, or read to one who was sick or seriously disposed: and thus I made a few acquaintances among the cottagers; and, occasionally, I went to see them on my own account.

I generally had more satisfaction in going alone than with either of the young ladies; for they, chiefly owing to their defective education, comported themselves towards their inferiors in a manner that was highly disagreeable for me to witness. They never, in thought, exchanged places with them; and, consequently, had no consideration for their feelings, regarding them as an order of beings entirely different from themselves. They would watch the poor creatures at their meals, making uncivil remarks about their food, and their manner of eating; they would laugh at their simple notions and provincial expressions, till some of them scarcely durst venture to speak; they would call the grave elderly men and women old fools and silly old blockheads to their faces; and all this without meaning to offend. I could see that the people were often hurt and annoyed by such conduct, though their fear of the 'grand ladies' prevented them from testifying any resentment; but *they* never perceived it. They thought that, as these cottagers were poor and untaught, they must be stupid and brutish; and as long as they, their superiors, condescended to talk to them, and to give them shillings and half-crowns, or articles of clothing, they had a right to amuse themselves, even at their expense; and the people must adore them as angels of light, condescending to minister to their necessities, and enlighten their humble dwellings.

I made many and various attempts to deliver my pupils from these delusive notions without alarming their pride – which was easily offended, and not soon appeased – but with little apparent result; and I know not which was the more reprehensible of the two: Matilda was more rude and boisterous; but from Rosalie's womanly age and ladylike exterior better things were expected: yet she was as provokingly careless and inconsiderate as a giddy child of twelve.

One bright day in the last week of February, I was walking in the park, enjoying the threefold luxury of solitude, a book, and pleasant weather; for Miss Matilda had set out on her daily ride, and Miss Murray was gone in the carriage with her mamma to pay some morning calls. But it struck me that I ought to leave these selfish pleasures, and the park with its glorious canopy of bright blue sky, the west wind sounding through its yet leafless branches, the snow-wreaths still lingering in its hollows, but melting fast beneath the sun, and the graceful deer browsing on its moist herbage, already assuming the freshness and verdure of spring – and go to the cottage of one Nancy Brown, a widow, whose son was at work all day in the fields, and who was afflicted with an inflammation in the eyes, which had for some time incapacitated her from reading: to her own great grief, for she was a woman of a serious, thoughtful turn of mind. I accordingly went, and found her alone, as usual, in her little, close, dark cottage, redolent of smoke and confined air, but as tidy and clean as she could make it. She was seated beside her little fire (consisting of a few red cinders and a bit of stick), busily knitting, with a small sackcloth cushion at her feet, placed for the accommodation of her gentle friend the cat: who was seated thereon, with her long tail half encircling her velvet paws, and her half-closed eyes dreamily gazing on the low, crooked fender.

'Well, Nancy, how are you to-day?'

'Why, middling, miss, i' myseln – my eyes is no better, but I'm a deal easier i' my mind nor I have been,' replied she, rising to welcome me with a contented smile: which I was glad to see, for Nancy had been somewhat afflicted with religious melancholy. I congratulated her upon the change. She agreed that it was a great blessing, and expressed herself 'right down thankful for it'; adding, 'If it please God to spare my sight, and make me so as I can read my Bible again, I think I shall be as happy as a queen.'

'I hope He will, Nancy,' replied I; 'and, meantime, I'll come and read to you now and then, when I have a little time to spare.'

With expressions of grateful pleasure, the poor woman moved to get me a chair; but, as I saved her the trouble, she busied herself with stirring the fire, and adding a few more sticks to the decaying embers; and then, taking her well-used Bible from the shelf, dusted it carefully, and gave it me. On my asking if there was any particular part she should like me to read, she answered –

'Well, Miss Grey, if it's all the same to you I should like to hear that chapter in the first Epistle of St John, that says, "God is love, and he that dwelleth in love dwelleth in God, and God in him."'

With a little searching, I found these words in the fourth chapter. When I came to the seventh verse she interrupted me, and, with needless apologies for such a liberty, desired me to read it very slowly, that she might take it all in, and dwell on every word; hoping I would excuse her, as she was but a 'simple body'.

'The wisest person,' I replied, 'might think over each of these verses for an hour, and be all the better for it; and I would rather read them slowly than not.'

Accordingly, I finished the chapter as slowly as need be, and at the same time as impressively as I could; my auditor listened most attentively all the while, and sincerely thanked me when I had done. I sat still about half a minute to give her time to reflect upon it; when, somewhat to my surprise, she broke the pause by asking me how I liked Mr Weston?

'I don't know,' I replied, a little startled by the suddenness of the question; 'I think he preaches very well.'

'Ay, he does so; and talks well too.'

'Does he?'

'He does. Maybe, you haven't seen him — not to talk to him much, yet?'

'No, I never see any one to talk to — except the young ladies of the Hall.'

'Ah; they're nice, kind young ladies; but they can't talk as he does.'

'Then he comes to see you, Nancy?'

'He does, miss; and I'se thankful for it. He comes to see all us poor bodies a deal ofter nor Maister Bligh, or th' Rector ever did; an' it's well he does, for he's always welcome: we can't say as much for th' Rector — there is 'at says they're fair feared on him. When he comes into a house, they say he's sure to find summut wrong, and begin a calling 'em as soon as he crosses th' doorstuns: but maybe he thinks it his duty-like to tell 'em what's wrong. And very oft he comes o' purpose to reprove folk for not coming to church, or not kneeling an' standing when other folk does, or going to the Methody chapel, or summut o' that sort: but I can't say 'at he ever fund much fault wi' me. He came to see me once or twice, afore Maister Weston come, when I was so ill troubled in my mind; and as I had only very poor health besides, I made bold to send for him — and he came right enough. I was sore distressed, Miss Grey — thank God, it's owered now — but when I took my Bible, I could get no comfort of it at all. That very chapter 'at you've just been reading troubled me as much as aught — "He that loveth not, knoweth not God." It seemed fearsome to me; for I felt that I loved neither God nor man as I should do, and could not, if I tried ever so. And th' chapter afore, where it says — "He that is born of God cannot commit sin." And another place where it says — "Love is the fulfilling of the Law." And many, many others, miss: I should fair weary you out, if I was to tell them all. But all seemed to condemn me, and to show me 'at I was not in the right way; and as I knew not how to get into it, I sent our Bill to beg Maister Hatfield to be as kind as look in on me some day; and when he came, I told him all my troubles.'

'And what did he say, Nancy?'

'Why, miss, he seemed to scorn me. I might be mista'en – but he like gave a sort of a whistle, and I saw a bit of a smile on his face; and he said, "Oh, it's all stuff! You've been among the Methodists, my good woman." But I tell'd him I'd never been near the Methodies. And then he said –

'"Well," says he, "you must come to church, where you'll hear the Scriptures properly explained, instead of sitting poring over your Bible at home."

'But I told him I always used coming to church when I had my health; but this very cold winter weather I hardly durst venture so far – and me so bad wi' th' rheumatiz and all.

'But he says, "It'll do your rheumatiz good to hobble to church: there's nothing like exercise for the rheumatiz. You can walk about the house well enough; why can't you walk to church? The fact is," says he, "you're getting too fond of your ease. It's always easy to find excuses for shirking one's duty."

'But then, you know, Miss Grey, it wasn't so. However, I told him I'd try. "But please, sir," says I, "If I do go to church, what the better shall I be? I want to have my sins blotted out, and to feel that they are remembered no more against me, and that the love of God is shed abroad in my heart; and if I can get no good by reading my Bible an' saying my prayers at home, what good shall I get by going to church?"

'"The church," says he, "is the place appointed by God for His worship. It's your duty to go there as often as you can. If you want comfort, you must seek it in the path of duty" – an' a deal more he said, but I cannot remember all his fine words. However, it all came to this, that I was to come to church as oft as ever I could, and bring my Prayer-book with me, an' read up all the sponsers after the clerk, an' stand, an' kneel, an' sit, an' do all as I should, and take the Lord's Supper at every opportunity, an' hearken his sermons, and Maister Bligh's, an' it 'ud be all right: if I went on doing my duty, I should get a blessing at last.

'"But if you get no comfort that way," says he, "it's all up."

'"Then, sir," says I, "should you think I'm a reprobate?"

'"Why," says he – he says, "if you do your best to get to heaven and can't manage it, you must be one of those that seek to enter in at the strait gate and shall not be able."

'An' then he asked me if I'd seen any of the ladies o' th' Hall about that mornin': so I told him where I had seen the young missis go on th' Moss-lane; – an' he kicked my poor cat right across th' floor, an' went after 'em as gay as a lark: but I was very sad. That last word o' his fair sunk into my heart, an' lay there like a lump o' lead, till I was weary to bear it.

'Howsoever, I follered his advice: I thought he meant it all for th' best, though he *had* a queer way with him. But you know, miss, he's rich an' young, and such-like cannot right understand the thoughts of a poor old woman such as me. But howsoever, I did my best to do all as he bade me – but maybe I'm plaguing you, miss, wi' my chatter.'

'Oh no, Nancy! Go on and tell me all.'

'Well, my rheumatiz got better – I know not whether wi' going to church or not, but one frosty Sunday I got this cold i' my eyes. Th' inflammation didn't come on all at once like, but bit by bit – but I wasn't going to tell you about my eyes, I was talking about my trouble o' mind; – and to tell the truth, Miss Grey, I don't think it was anyways eased by coming to church – nought to speak on, at least: I like got my health better, but that didn't mend my soul. I hearkened and hearkened the ministers, and read an' read at my Prayer-book; but it was all like sounding brass and a tinkling cymbal: the sermons I couldn't understand, an' th' Prayer-book only served to show me how wicked I was, that I could read such good words an' never be no better for it, and oftens feel it a sore labour an' a heavy task beside, instead of a blessing and a privilege as all good Christians does. It seemed like as all were barren an' dark to me. And then, them dreadful words, "Many shall seek to enter in, and shall not be able." They like as they fair dried up my sperrit.

'But one Sunday, when Maister Hatfield gave out about the sacrament, I noticed where he said, "If there be any of you that cannot quiet his own conscience, but requireth further comfort or counsel, let him come to me, or some other discreet and learned minister of God's word, and open his grief!" So, next Sunday morning, afore service, I just looked into the vestry, an' began a talking to th' Rector again. I hardly could fashion to take such a liberty, but I thought when my soul was at stake I shouldn't stick at a trifle. But he said he hadn't time to attend to me then.

'"And, indeed," says he, "I've nothing to say to you but what I've said before. Take the sacrament, of course, and go on doing your duty; and if that won't serve you, nothing will. So don't bother me any more."

'So then, I went away. But I heard Maister Weston – Maister Weston was there, miss – this was his first Sunday at Horton, you know, an' he was i' th' vestry in his surplice, helping th' Rector on with his gown.'

'Yes, Nancy.'

'And I heard him ask Maister Hatfield who I was; an' he says, "Oh, she's a canting old fool."'

'And I was very ill grieved, Miss Grey; but I went to my seat, and I tried to do my duty as aforetime: but I like got no peace. An' I even took the sacrament; but I felt as though I were eating and drinking to my own damnation all th' time. So I went home, sorely troubled.

'But next day, afore I'd gotten fettled up – for indeed, miss, I'd no heart to sweeping an' fettling, an' washing pots; so I sat me down i' th' muck – who should come in but Maister Weston! I started siding stuff then, an' sweeping an' doing; and I expected he'd begin a calling me for my idle ways, as Maister Hatfield would a' done; but I was mista'en: he only bid me good mornin' like, in a quiet dacent way. So I dusted him a chair, an' fettled up th' fireplace abit; but I hadn't forgotten th' Rector's words, so says I, "I wonder, sir, you should give yourself that trouble, to come so far to see a 'canting old fool', such as me."

'He seemed taken aback at that; but he would fain persuade me 'at the Rector was only in jest; and when that wouldn't do, he says, "Well, Nancy, you shouldn't think so much about it: Mr Hatfield was a little out of humour just then: you know we're none of us perfect – even Moses spoke unadvisedly with his lips. But now sit down a minute, if you can spare the time, and tell me all your doubts and fears; and I'll try to remove them."

'So I sat me down anent him. He was quite a stranger, you know, Miss Grey, and even *younger* nor Maister Hatfield, I believe; an' I had thought him not so pleasant-looking as him, and rather a bit crossish, at first to look at; but he spake so civil like – and when th' cat, poor thing, jumped on to his knee, he only stroked her, and gave a bit of a smile: so I thought that was a good sign; for once, when she did so to th' Rector, he knocked her off, like as it might be in scorn and anger, poor thing. But you can't expect a cat to know manners like a Christian, you know, Miss Grey.'

'No; of course not, Nancy. But what did Mr Weston say then?'

'He said naught; but he listened to me as steady an' patient as could be, an' never a bit o' scorn about him; so I went on, an' told him all, just as I've telled you – an' more too.

'"Well," says he, "Mr Hatfield was quite right in telling you to persevere in doing your duty; but in advising you to go to church and attend to the service, and so on, he didn't mean that was the whole of a Christian's duty: he only thought you might there learn what more was to be done, and be led to take delight in those exercises, instead of finding them a task and a burden. And if you had asked him to explain those words that trouble you so much, I think he would have told you, that if many shall seek to enter in at the strait gate and shall not be able, it is their own sins that hinder them; just as a man with a large sack on his back might wish to pass through a narrow doorway, and find it impossible to do so unless he would leave his sack behind him. But you, Nancy, I dare say, have no sins that you would not gladly throw side if you knew how?"

'"Indeed, sir, you speak truth," said I.

'"Well," says he, "you know the first and greatest commandment – and the second, which is like unto it – on which two commandments hang all the law and the prophets? You say you cannot love God; but it strikes me that if you rightly consider who and what He is, you cannot help it. He is your father, your best friend: every blessing, everything good, pleasant, or useful, comes from Him; and everything evil, everything you have reason to hate, to shun, or to fear, comes from Satan – *His* enemy as well as ours. And for *this* cause was God manifest in the flesh, that He might destroy the works of the devil: in one word, God is LOVE; and the more of love we have within us, the nearer we are to Him, and the more of His spirit we possess."

'"Well, sir," I said, "if I can always think on these things, I think I might well love God: but how can I love my neighbours, when they vex me, and be so contrairy and sinful as some on 'em is?"

'"It may seem a hard matter," says he, "to love our neighbours, who have so much of what is evil about them, and whose faults so often awaken the evil that lingers within ourselves; but remember that *He* made them, and *He* loves them; and whosoever loveth him that begat, loveth him that is begotten also. And if God so loveth us that He gave His only begotten Son to die for us, we ought also to love one another. But if you cannot feel positive affection for those who do not care for you, you can at least try to do to them as you would they should do unto you: you can endeavour to pity their failings and excuse their offences, and to do all the good you can to those about you. And if you accustom yourself to this, Nancy, the very effort itself will make you love them in some degree – to say nothing of the goodwill your kindness would beget in them, though they might have little else that is good about them. If we love God and wish to serve Him, let us try to be like Him, to do His work, to labour for His glory – which is the good of man – to hasten the coming of His kingdom, which is the peace and happiness of all the world: however powerless we may seem to be, in doing all the good we can through life, the humblest of us may do much towards it; and let us dwell in love, that He may dwell in us and we in Him. The more happiness we bestow, the more we shall receive, even here; and the greater will be our reward in heaven when we rest from our labours." I believe, miss, them is his very words, for I've thought 'em ower many a time. An' then he took that Bible, an' read bits here and there, an' explained 'em as clear as the day: and it seemed like as a new light broke in on my soul; an' I felt a fair glow about my heart, an' only wished poor Bill an' all the world could ha' been there, an' heard it all, an' rejoiced wi' me.

'After he was gone, Hannah Rogers, one o' th' neighbours, came in and wanted me to help her to wash. I telled her I couldn't just then, for I hadn't set on th' potaties for th' dinner, nor washed up th' breakfast stuff yet. So then she began a-calling me for my nasty idle ways. I was a little bit vexed at first, but I never said nothing wrong to her; I only telled her, like all in a quiet way, 'at I'd had th' new parson to see me; but I'd get done as quick as ever I could, an' then come an' help her. So then she softened down; and my heart like as it warmed towards her, an' in a bit we was very good friends. An' so it is, Miss Grey, "a soft answer turneth away wrath; but grievous words stir up anger". It isn't only in them you speak to, but in yourself.'

'Very true, Nancy, if we could always remember it.'

'Ay, if we could!'

'And did Mr Weston ever come to see you again?'

'Yes, many a time; and since my eyes has been so bad, he's sat an' read to me by the half-hour together: but you know, miss, he has other folks to see, and other things to do – God bless him! An' that next Sunday he preached *such* a sermon! His text was, "Come unto me all ye that labour and are heavy laden, and I will give you rest," and them two blessed verses that follows. You wasn't there, miss, you was with your friends then – but it made me *so* happy! And I *am* happy now, thank God! an' I take a pleasure, now, in doing little bits o' jobs for my neighbours – such as a poor old body 'at's half blind can do; and they take it kindly of me, just as he said. You see, miss, I'm knitting a pair o' stockings now; – they're for Thomas Jackson; he's a queerish old body, an' we've had many a bout at threaping, one anent t' other; an' at times we've differed sorely. So I thought I couldn't do better nor knit him a pair o' warm stockings: an' I've felt to like him a deal better, poor old man, sin' I began. It's turned out just as Maister Weston said.'

'Well, I'm very glad to see you so happy, Nancy, and so wise: but I must go now; I shall be wanted at the Hall,' said I; and bidding her good-bye, I departed, promising to come again when I had time, and feeling nearly as happy as herself.

At another time, I went to read to a poor labourer who was in the last stage of consumption. The young ladies had been to see him, and somehow a promise of reading had been extracted from them; but it was too much trouble, so they begged *me* to do it instead. I went, willingly enough; and there too I was gratified with the praises of Mr Weston, both from the sick man and his wife. The former told me that he derived great comfort and benefit from the visits of the new parson, who frequently came to see him, and was 'another guess sort of man' to Mr Hatfield; who before the other's arrival at Horton had now and then paid him a visit; on which occasions he would always insist upon having the cottage door kept open, to admit the fresh air for his own convenience, without considering how it might injure the sufferer: and having opened his Prayer-book and hastily read over a part of the Service for the Sick, would hurry away again: if he did not stay to administer some harsh rebuke to the afflicted wife, or to make some thoughtless, not to say heartless, observation, rather calculated to increase than diminish the troubles of the suffering pair.

'Whereas,' said the man, 'Maister Weston 'ull pray with me quite in a different fashion, an' talk to me as kind as owt; an' oft read to me too, an' sit beside me just like a brother.'

'Just for all the world!' exclaimed his wife; 'an' about a three wik sin', when he seed how poor Jem shivered wi' cold, an' what pitiful fires we kept, he axed if wer stock of coals was nearly done. I told him it was, an' we was ill set to get more: but you know, mum, I didn't think o' him helping us; but howsoever, he sent us a sack o' coals next day; an' we've had good fires ever sin: an' a great blessing it is, this winter time. But that's his way, Miss Grey: when he comes into a poor body's house a-seein' sick folk, he like notices what they most stand i' need on; an' if he thinks they can't readily get it therseln, he never says nowt about it, but just gets it for 'em. An' it isn't everybody 'at 'ud do that, 'at has as little as he has: for you know, mum, he's nowt at all to live on but what he gets fra' th' rector, an' that's little enough, they say.'

I remembered then, with a species of exultation, that he had frequently been styled a vulgar brute by the amiable Miss Murray, because he wore a silver watch, and clothes not quite so bright and fresh as Mr Hatfield's.

In returning to the lodge I felt very happy, and thanked God that I had now something to think about: something to dwell on as a relief from the weary monotony, the lonely drudgery, of my present life: for I *was* lonely. Never, from month to month, from year to year, except during my brief intervals of rest at home, did I see one creature to whom I could open my heart, or freely speak my thoughts with any hope of sympathy, or even comprehension: never one, unless it were poor Nancy Brown, with whom I could enjoy a single moment of real social intercourse, or whose conversation was calculated to render me better, wiser, or happier than before; or who, as far as I could see, could be greatly benefited by mine. My only companions had been unamiable children, and ignorant, wrong-headed girls; from whose fatiguing folly unbroken solitude was often a relief most earnestly desire and dearly prized. But to be restricted to such associates was a serious evil, both in its immediate effects and the consequences that were likely to ensue. Never a new idea or stirring thought came to me from without: and such as rose within me were, for the most part, miserably crushed at once, or doomed to sicken and fade away, because they could not see the light.

Habitual associates are known to exercise a great influence over each other's minds and manners. Those whose actions are for ever before our eyes, whose words are ever in our ears, will naturally lead us, albeit against our will, slowly, gradually, imperceptibly, perhaps, to act and speak as they do. I will not presume to say how far this irresistible power of assimilation extends; but if one civilized man were doomed to pass a dozen years amid a race of intractable savages, unless he had power to improve them, I greatly question whether, at the close of that period, he would not have become, at least, a barbarian himself. And I, as I could not make my young companions better, feared exceedingly that they would make me worse – would gradually bring my feelings, habits, capacities, to the level of their own; without, however, imparting to me their lightheartedness and cheerful vivacity.

Already I seemed to feel my intellect deteriorating, my heart petrifying, my soul contracting; and I trembled lest my very moral perceptions should become deadened, my distinctions of right and wrong confounded, and all my better faculties be sunk, at last, beneath the baneful influence of such a mode of life. The gross vapours of earth were gathering around me, and closing in upon my inward heaven; and thus it was that Mr Weston rose at length upon me, appearing like the morning-star in my horizon, to save me from the fear of utter darkness; and I rejoiced that I had now a subject for contemplation that was above me, not beneath. I was glad to see that all the world was not made up of Bloomfields, Murrays, Hatfields, Ashbys, etc.; and that human excellence was not a mere dream of the imagination. When we hear a little good and no harm of a person, it is easy and pleasant to imagine more: in short, it is needless to analyse all my thoughts; but Sunday was now become a day of peculiar delight to me (I was now almost broken in to the back corner in the carriage), for I liked to hear him – and I liked to see him, too; though I knew he was not handsome, or even what is called agreeable, in outward aspect: but, certainly, he was not ugly.

In stature he was a little, a very little, above the middle size; the outline of his face would be pronounced too square for beauty, but to me it announced decision of character; his dark brown hair was not carefully curled like Mr Hatfield's, but simply brushed aside over a broad white forehead; the eyebrows, I suppose, were too projecting, but from under those dark brows there gleamed an eye of singular power, brown in colour, not large, and somewhat deep-set, but strikingly brilliant, and full of expression; there was character, too, in the mouth, something that bespoke a man of firm purpose and a habitual thinker; and when he smiled – but I will not speak of that yet, for, at the time I mention, I had never seen him smile: and, indeed, his general appearance did not impress me with the idea of a man given to such a relaxation, nor of such an individual as the cottagers described him. I had early formed my opinion of him; and, in spite of Miss Murray's objurgations, was fully convinced that he was a man of strong sense, firm faith, and ardent piety, but thoughtful and stern: and when I found that to his other good qualities was added that of true benevolence and gentle, considerate kindness, the discovery, perhaps, delighted me the more, as I had not been prepared to expect it.

CHAPTER 12
## The Shower

The next visit I paid to Nancy Brown was in the second week in March: for, though I had many spare minutes during the day, I seldom could look upon an hour as entirely my own; since, where everything was left to the caprices of Miss Matilda and her sister, there could be no order or regularity. Whatever occupation I chose, when not actually busied about them or their concerns, I had, as it were, to keep my loins girded, my shoes on my feet, and my staff in my hand; for not to be immediately forthcoming when called for was regarded as a grave and inexcusable offence: not only by my pupils and their mother, but by the very servant, who came in breathless haste to call me, exclaiming, 'You're to go to the schoolroom *directly*, mum – the young ladies is WAITING!!' Climax of horror! actually waiting for their governess!!!

But this time I was pretty sure of an hour or two to myself; for Matilda was preparing for a long ride, and Rosalie was dressing for a dinner party at Lady Ashby's: so I took the opportunity of repairing to the widow's cottage, where I found her in some anxiety about her cat, which had been absent all day. I comforted her with as many anecdotes of that animal's roving propensities as I could recollect. 'I'm feared o' th' gamekeepers,' said she, 'that's all 'at I think on. If th' young gentlemen had been at home, I should a' thought they'd been setting their dogs at her, an' worried her, poor thing, as they did *many* a poor thing's cat; but I haven't that to be feared on now.' Nancy's eyes were better, but still far from well: she had been trying to make a Sunday shirt for her son, but told me she could only bear to do a little bit at it now and then, so that it progressed but slowly, though the poor lad wanted it sadly. So I proposed to help her a little, after I had read to her, for I had plenty of time that evening, and need not return till dusk. She thankfully accepted the offer.

'An' you'll be a bit o' company for me too, miss,' said she; 'I like as I feel lonesome without my cat.' But when I had finished reading, and done the half of a seam, with Nancy's capacious brass thimble fitted on to my finger by means of a roll of paper, I was disturbed by the entrance of Mr Weston, with the identical cat in his arms. I now saw that he could smile, and very pleasantly too.

'I've done you a piece of good service, Nancy,' he began: then seeing me, he acknowledged my presence by a slight bow. I should have been invisible to Hatfield, or any other gentleman of those parts. 'I've delivered your cat,' he continued, 'from the hands, or rather the gun, of Mr Murray's gamekeeper.'

'God bless you, sir!' cried the grateful old woman, ready to weep for joy as she received her favourite from his arms.

'Take care of it,' said he, 'and don't let it go near the rabbit warren, for the gamekeeper swears he'll shoot it if he sees it there again: he would have done so to-day, if I had not been in time to stop him. – I believe it is raining, Miss Grey,' added he, more quietly, observing that I had put aside my work, and was preparing to depart. 'Don't let me disturb you – I shan't stay two minutes.'

'You'll *both* stay while this shower gets owered,' said Nancy, as she stirred the fire, and placed another chair beside it; 'what! there's room for all.'

'I can see better here, thank you, Nancy,' replied I, taking my work to the window, where she had the goodness to suffer me to remain unmolested, while she got a brush to remove the cat's hairs from Mr Weston's coat, carefully wiped the rain from his hat, and gave the cat its supper, busily talking all the time: now thanking her clerical friend for what he had done; now wondering how the cat had found out the warren; and now lamenting the probable consequences of such a discovery. He listened with a quiet, good-natured smile, and at length took a seat in compliance with her pressing invitations, but repeated that he did not mean to stay.

'I have another place to go to,' said he, 'and I see' (glancing at the book on the table) 'some one else has been reading to you.'

'Yes, sir; Miss Grey has been as kind as read me a chapter; an' now she's helping me with a shirt for our Bill – but I'm feared she'll be cold there. Won't you come to th' fire, miss?'

'No, thank you, Nancy, I'm quite warm. I must go as soon as this shower is over.'

'Oh, miss! You said you could stop while dusk!' cried the provoking old woman, and Mr Weston seized his hat.

'Nay, sir,' exclaimed she, 'pray don't go now, while it rains so fast.'

'But it strikes me I'm keeping your visitor away from the fire.'

'No, you're not, Mr Weston,' replied I, hoping there was no harm in a falsehood of that description.

'No, sure!' cried Nancy. 'What, there's lots o' room!'

'Miss Grey,' said he, half-jestingly, as if he felt it necessary to change the present subject, whether he had anything particular to say or not, 'I wish you would make my peace with the squire when you see him. He was by when I rescued Nancy's cat, and did not quite approve of the deed. I told him I thought he might better spare all his rabbits than she her cat, for which audacious assertion he treated me to some rather ungentlemanly language; and I fear I retorted a trifle too warmly.'

'Oh, lawful sir! I hope you didn't fall out wi' th' maister for sake o' my cat! he cannot bide answering again – can th' maister.'

'Oh! it's no matter, Nancy: I don't care about it, really; I said nothing *very* uncivil; and I suppose Mr Murray is accustomed to use rather strong language when he's heated.'

'Ay, sir; it's a pity!'

'And now, I really must go. I have to visit a place a mile beyond this; and you would not have me return in the dark: besides, it has nearly done raining now – so good evening, Nancy. Good evening, Miss Grey.'

'Good evening, Mr Weston; but don't depend upon me for making your peace with Mr Murray, for I never see him – to speak to.'

'Don't you? it can't be helped then,' replied he in dolorous resignation: then with a peculiar half-smile, he added, 'But never mind; I imagine the squire has more to apologize for than I.' And left the cottage.

I went on with my sewing as long as I could see, and then bade Nancy good-evening; checking her too lively gratitude by the undeniable assurance that I had only done for her what she would have done for me, if she had been in my place and I in hers. I hastened back to Horton Lodge, where, having entered the schoolroom, I found the tea-table all in confusion, the tray flooded with slops, and Miss Matilda in a most ferocious humour.

'Miss Grey, whatever have you been about? I've had tea half-an-hour ago, and had to make it myself, and drink it all alone! I wish you *would* come in sooner!'

'I've been to see Nancy Brown. I thought you would not be back from your ride.'

'How could I ride in the rain, I should like to know? That damned pelting shower was vexatious enough – coming on when I was just in full swing: and then to come and find nobody in to tea! – and you know I can't make the tea as I like it.'

'I didn't think of the shower,' replied I (and indeed the thought of its driving her home had never entered my head).

'No, of course; you were under shelter yourself, and you never thought of other people.'

I bore her coarse reproaches with astonishing equanimity, even with cheerfulness; for I was sensible that I had done more good to Nancy Brown than harm to her: and perhaps some other thoughts assisted to keep up my spirits, and impart a relish to the cup of cold, overdrawn tea, and a charm to the otherwise unsightly table; and – I had almost said – to Miss Matilda's unamiable face. But she soon betook herself to the stables, and left me to the quiet enjoyment of my solitary meal.

CHAPTER 13

*The Primroses*

Miss Murray now always went twice to church, for she so loved admiration that she could not bear to lose a single opportunity of obtaining it: and she was so sure of it wherever she showed herself, that whether Harry Meltham and Mr Green were there or not, there was certain to be somebody present who would not be insensible to her charms: besides the Rector, whose official capacity generally obliged him to attend. Usually, also if the weather permitted, both she and her sister would walk home; Matilda, because she hated the confinement of the carriage; she, because she disliked the privacy of it, and enjoyed the company that generally enlivened the first mile of the journey in walking from the church to Mr Green's park-gates: near which commenced the private road to Horton Lodge, which lay in the opposite direction; while the highway conducted in a straight-forward course to the still more distant mansion of Sir Hugh Meltham. Thus there was always a chance of being accompanied, so far, either by Harry Meltham, with or without Miss Meltham, or Mr Green, with perhaps one or both of his sisters, and any gentlemen visitors they might have.

Whether I walked with the young ladies or rode with their parents, depended upon their own capricious will: if they chose to 'take' me, I went; if, for reasons best known to themselves, they chose to go alone, I took my seat in the carriage. I liked walking better, but a sense of reluctance to obtrude my presence on any one who did not desire it always kept me passive on these and similar occasions; and I never inquired into the causes of their varying whims. Indeed, this was the best policy – for to submit and oblige was the governess's part, to consult their own pleasure was that of the pupils. But when I did walk, the first half of the journey was generally a great nuisance to me. As none of the before-mentioned ladies and gentlemen ever noticed me, it was disagreeable to walk beside them, as if listening to what they said, or wishing to be thought one of them, while they talked over me, or across; and if their eyes, in speaking, chanced to fall on me, it seemed as if they looked on vacancy – as if they either did not see me, or were very desirous to make it appear so.

It was disagreeable, too, to walk behind, and thus appear to acknowledge my own inferiority; for, in truth, I considered myself pretty nearly as good as the best of them, and wished them to know that I did so, and not to imagine that I looked upon myself as a mere domestic, who knew her own place too well to walk beside such fine ladies and gentlemen as they were – though her young ladies might choose to have her with them, and even condescend to converse with her when no better company were at hand. Thus – I am almost ashamed to confess it – but indeed I gave myself no little trouble in my endeavours (if I did keep up with them) to appear perfectly unconscious or regardless of their presence, as if I were wholly absorbed in my own reflections, or the contemplation of surrounding objects; or, if I lingered behind, it was some bird or insect, some tree or flower, that attracted my attention, and having duly examined that, I would pursue my walk alone, at a leisurely pace, until my pupils had bidden adieu to their companions, and turned off into the quiet, private road.

One such occasion I particularly well remember: it was a lovely afternoon about the close of March; Mr Green and his sisters had sent their carriage back empty, in order to enjoy the bright sunshine and balmy air in a sociable walk home along with their visitors, Captain Somebody and Lieutenant Somebody-else (a couple of military fops), and the Misses Murray, who, of course, contrived to join them. Such a party was highly agreeable to Rosalie; but not finding it equally suitable to my taste, I presently fell back, and began to botanize and entomologize along the green banks and budding hedges, till the company was considerably in advance of me, and I could hear the sweet song of the happy lark; then my spirit of misanthropy began to melt away beneath the soft, pure air and genial sunshine: but sad thoughts of early childhood, and yearnings for departed joys, or for a brighter future lot, arose instead. As my eyes wandered over the steep banks covered with young grass and green-leaved plants, and surmounted by budding hedges, I longed intensely for some familiar flower that might recall the woody dales or green hill-sides of home: the brown moorlands, of course, were out of the question. Such a discovery would make my eyes gush out with water, no doubt; but that was one of my greatest enjoyments now. At length I descried, high up between the twisted roots of an oak, three lovely primroses, peeping so sweetly from their hiding-place that the tears already started at the sight; but they grew so high above me that I tried in vain to gather one or two, to dream over and to carry with me: I could not reach them unless I climbed the bank, which I was deterred from doing by hearing a footstep at that moment behind me, and was, therefore, about to turn away, when I was startled by the words, 'Allow me to gather them for you, Miss Grey,' spoken in the grave, low tones of a well-known voice. Immediately the flowers were gathered, and in my hand. It was Mr Weston, of course – who else would trouble himself to do so much for *me*?

I thanked him: whether warmly or coldly I cannot tell: but certain I am that I did not express half the gratitude I felt. It was foolish, perhaps, to feel any gratitude at all; but it seemed to me, at that moment, as if this were a remarkable instance of his good-nature: an act of kindness which I could not repay, but never should forget: so utterly unaccustomed was I to receive such civilities, so little prepared to expect them from anyone within fifty miles of Horton Lodge. Yet this did not prevent me from feeling a little uncomfortable in his presence; and I proceeded to follow my pupils at a much quicker pace than before; though perhaps, if Mr Weston had taken the hint and let me pass without another word, I might have repented it an hour after: but he did not. A somewhat rapid walk for me was but an ordinary pace for him.

'Your young ladies have left you alone,' said he.

'Yes, they are occupied with more agreeable company.'

'Then don't trouble yourself to overtake them.'

I slackened my pace; but next moment regretted having done so: my companion did not speak; and I had nothing in the world to say, and feared he might be in the same predicament. At length, however, he broke the pause by asking, with a certain quiet abruptness peculiar to himself, if I liked flowers.

'Yes; very much,' I answered: 'wild flowers especially.'

'*I* like wild flowers,' said he; 'others I don't care about, because I have no particular associations connected with them – except one or two. What are your favourite flowers?'

'Primroses, bluebells, and heath-blossoms.'

'Not violets?'

'No; because, as you say, I have no particular associations connected with them; for there are no sweet violets among the hills and valleys round my home.'

'It must be a great consolation to you to have a home, Miss Grey,' observed my companion after a short pause: 'however remote, or however seldom visited, still it is something to look to.'

'It is so much that I think I could not live without it,' replied I, with an enthusiasm of which I immediately repented; for I thought it must have sounded essentially silly.

'Oh yes, you could,' said he, with a thoughtful smile. 'The ties that bind us to life are tougher than you imagine, or than any one can who has not felt how roughly they may be pulled without breaking. You might be miserable without a home, but even *you* could live; and not *so* miserably as you suppose. The human heart is like india-rubber: a little swells it, but a great deal will not burst it. If "a little more than nothing will disturb it, little less than all things will suffice" to break it. As in the outer members of our frame, there is a vital power inherent in itself, that strengthens it against external violence. Every blow that shakes it will serve to harden it against a future stroke; as constant labour thickens the skin of the hand, and strengthens its muscles instead of wasting them away: so that a day of arduous toil that might excoriate a lady's palm would make no sensible impression on that of a hardy ploughman.

'I speak from experience – partly my own. There was a time when I thought as you do – at least, I was fully persuaded that home and its affections were the only things that made life tolerable: that, if deprived of these, existence would become a burden hard to be endured; but now I have no home – unless you would dignify my two hired rooms at Horton by such a name; – and not twelve months ago I lost the last and dearest of my early friends; and yet, not only I live, but I am not wholly destitute of hope and comfort, even for this life: though I must acknowledge that I can seldom enter even an humble cottage at the close of day, and see its inhabitants gathered peaceably around their cheerful hearth, without a feeling *almost* of envy at their domestic enjoyment.'

'You don't know what happiness lies before you yet,' said I: 'you are now only in the commencement of your journey.'

'The best of happiness,' replied he, 'is mine already – the power and the will to be useful.'

We now approached a stile communicating with a footpath that conducted to a farm-house, where, I suppose, Mr Weston purposed to make himself 'useful'; for he presently took leave of me, crossed the stile, and traversed the path with his usual firm, elastic tread, leaving me to ponder his words as I continued my course alone. I had heard before that he had lost his mother not many months before he came. She then was the last and dearest of his early friends; and he had *no home*. I pitied him from my heart: I almost wept for sympathy. And this, I thought, accounted for the shade of premature thoughtfulness that so frequently clouded his brow, and obtained for him the reputation of a morose and sullen disposition with the charitable Miss Murray and all her kin. 'But,' thought I, 'he is not so miserable as I should be under such a deprivation: he leads an active life; and a wide field for useful exertion lies before him. He can *make* friends; and he can make a home too, if he pleases; and, doubtless, he will please some time. God grant the partner of that home may be worthy of his choice, and make it a happy one – such a home as he deserves to have! And how delightful it would be to'—— But no matter what I thought.

I began this book with the intention of concealing nothing; that those who liked might have the benefit of perusing a fellow-creature's heart: but we have *some* thoughts that all the angels in heaven are welcome to behold, but not our brother-men – not even the best and kindest amongst them.

By this time the Greens had taken themselves to their own abode, and the Murrays had turned down the private road, whither I hastened to follow them. I found the two girls warm in an animated discussion on the respective merits of the two young officers; but on seeing me Rosalie broke off in the middle of a sentence to exclaim, with malicious glee –

'Oh, ho, Miss Grey! you're come at last, are you? No *wonder* you lingered so long behind; and no *wonder* you always stand up so vigorously for Mr Weston when I abuse him. Ah, ha! I see it all now!'

'Now, come, Miss Murray, don't be foolish,' said I, attempting a good-natured laugh; 'you know such nonsense can make no impression on me.'

But she still went on talking such intolerable stuff – her sister helping her with appropriate fiction coined for the occasion – that I thought it necessary to say something in my own justification.

'What folly all this is!' I exclaimed. 'If Mr Weston's road happened to be the same as mine for a few yards, and if he chose to exchange a word or two in passing, what is there so remarkable in that? I assure you, I never spoke to him before: except once.'

'Where? where? and when?' cried they eagerly.

'In Nancy's cottage.'

'Ah, ha! you've met him there, have you?' exclaimed Rosalie, with exultant laughter. 'Ah! now, Matilda, I've found out why she's so fond of going to Nancy Brown's! she goes there to flirt with Mr Weston.'

'Really, that is not worth contradicting! – I only saw him there once, I tell you – and how could I know he was coming?'

Irritated as I was at their foolish mirth and vexatious imputations, the uneasiness did not continue long; when they had had their laugh out, they returned again to the captain and lieutenant; and, while they disputed and commented upon them, my indignation rapidly cooled; the cause of it was quickly forgotten, and I turned my thoughts into a pleasanter channel. Thus we proceeded up the park, and entered the hall; and as I ascended the stairs to my own chamber, I had but one thought within me: my heart was filled to overflowing with one single earnest wish. Having entered the room, and shut the door, I fell upon my knees and offered up a fervent but not impetuous prayer: 'Thy will be done,' I strove to say throughout; but, 'Father, all things are possible with Thee, and may it be Thy will,' was sure to follow. That wish – that prayer – both men and women would have scorned me for – 'But Father, *Thou* wilt *not* despise!' I said, and felt that it was true. It seemed to me that another's welfare was at least as ardently implored for as my own; nay, even *that* was the principal object of my heart's desire. I might have been deceiving myself; but that idea gave me confidence to ask, and power to hope I did not ask in vain. As for the primroses, I kept two of them in a glass in my room until they were completely withered, and the housemaid threw them out; and the petals of the other I pressed between the leaves of my Bible – I have them still, and mean to keep them always.

CHAPTER 14

*The Rector*

The following day was as fine as the preceding one. Soon after breakfast Miss Matilda, having galloped and blundered through a few unprofitable lessons, and vengeably thumped the piano for an hour, in a terrible humour with both me and it because her mamma would not give her a holiday, had betaken herself to her favourite places of resort, the yards, the stables, and the dog-kennels; and Miss Murray was gone forth to enjoy a quiet ramble with a new fashionable novel for her companion, leaving me in the schoolroom hard at work upon a water-colour drawing which I had promised to do for her, and which she insisted upon my finishing that day.

At my feet lay a little rough terrier. It was the property of Miss Matilda; but she hated the animal, and intended to sell it, alleging that it was quite spoiled. It was really an excellent dog of its kind; but she affirmed it was fit for nothing, and had not even the sense to know its own mistress.

The fact was, she had purchased it when but a small puppy, insisting at first that no one should touch it but herself; but, soon becoming tired of so helpless and troublesome a nursling, she had gladly yielded to my entreaties to be allowed to take charge of it; and I, by carefully nursing the little creature from infancy to adolescence, of course, had obtained its affections: a reward I should have greatly valued, and looked upon as far outweighing all the trouble I had had with it, had not poor Snap's grateful feelings exposed him to many a harsh word and many a spiteful kick and pinch from his owner, and were he not now in danger of being 'put away', in consequence, or transferred to some rough, stony-hearted master. But how could I help it? I could not make the dog hate me, by cruel treatment; and she would not propitiate him by kindness.

However, while I thus sat, working away with my pencil, Mrs Murray came half-sailing, half-bustling into the room.

'Miss Grey,' she began, – 'dear! how can you sit at your drawing such a day as this?' (She thought I was doing it for my own pleasure.) 'I *wonder* you don't put on your bonnet and go out with the young ladies.'

'I think, ma'am, Miss Murray is reading; and Miss Matilda is amusing herself with her dogs.'

'If you would try to amuse Miss Matilda yourself a little more, I think she would not be *driven* to seek amusement in the companionship of dogs and horses, and grooms, so much as she is; and if you would be a little more cheerful and conversable with Miss Murray, she would not so often go wandering in the fields with a book in her hand. However, I don't want to vex you,' added she, seeing, I suppose, that my cheeks burned and my hand trembled with some unamiable emotion. 'Do, pray, try not to be so touchy, – there's no speaking to you else. And tell me if you know where Rosalie is gone: and why she likes to be so much alone?'

'She says she likes to be alone when she has a new book to read.'

'But why can't she read it in the park or the garden? – why should she go into the fields and lanes? And how is it that that Mr Hatfield so often finds her out? She told me last week he'd walked his horse by her side all up Moss Lane; and now I'm sure it was he I saw from my dressing-room window, walking so briskly past the park-gates, and on towards the field where she so frequently goes. I wish you would go and see if she is there; and just gently remind her that it is not proper for a young lady of her rank and prospects to be wandering about by herself in that manner, exposed to the attentions of any one that presumes to address her; like some poor neglected girl that has no park to walk in, and no friends to take care of her: and tell her that her papa would be extremely angry if he knew of her treating Mr Hatfield in the familiar manner that I fear she does; and – oh! if you – if *any* governess had but half a mother's watchfulness – half a mother's anxious care, I should be saved this trouble; and you would see at once the necessity of keeping your eye upon her, and making your company agreeable to – Well, go – go; there's no time to be lost,' cried she, seeing that I had put away my drawing materials, and was waiting in the doorway for the conclusion of her address.

According to her prognostications, I found Miss Murray in her favourite field just without the park; and, unfortunately, not alone; for the tall, stately figure of Mr Hatfield was slowly sauntering by her side.

Here was a poser for me. It was my duty to interrupt the *tête-à-tête*: but how was it to be done? Mr Hatfield could not be driven away by so insignificant a person as I; and to go and place myself on the other side of Miss Murray, and intrude my un-welcome presence upon her without noticing her companion, was a piece of rudeness I could not be guilty of; neither had I the courage to cry aloud from the top of the field that she was wanted elsewhere. So I took the intermediate course of walking slowly but steadily towards them; resolving, if my approach failed to scare away the beau, to pass by and tell Miss Murray her mamma wanted her.

She certainly looked very charming as she strolled lingering along under the budding horse-chestnut trees that stretched their long arms over the park-palings, with her closed book in one hand, and in the other a graceful sprig of myrtle, which served her as a very pretty plaything; her bright ringlets escaping pro-fusely from her little bonnet, and gently stirred by the breeze, her fair cheek flushed with gratified vanity, her smiling blue eyes, now shyly glancing towards her admirer, now gazing downward at her myrtle sprig. But Snap, running before me, interrupted her in the middle of some half-pert, half-playful repartee, by catching hold of her dress and vehemently tugging thereat; till Mr Hatfield, with his cane, administered a resounding thwack upon the animal's skull, and sent it yelping back to me, with a clamorous outcry that afforded the reverend gentleman great amusement: but seeing me so near, he thought, I suppose, he might as well be taking his departure; and as I stooped to caress the dog, with ostentatious pity to show my disapproval of his severity, I heard him say –

'When shall I see you again, Miss Murray?'

'At church, I suppose,' replied she, 'unless your business chance to bring you here again at the precise moment when I happen to be walking by.'

'I could always manage to have business here, if I knew precisely when and where to find you.'

'But if I would, I could not inform you, for I am so im-methodical, I never can tell to-day what I shall do to-morrow.'

'Then give me that, meantime, to comfort me,' said he, half jestingly and half in earnest, extending his hand for the sprig of myrtle.

'No, indeed, I shan't.'

'Do! *pray* do! I shall be the most miserable of men if you don't. You cannot be so cruel as to deny me a favour so easily granted, and yet so highly prized!' pleaded he, as ardently as if his life depended on it.

By this time I stood within a very few yards of them, impatiently waiting his departure.

'There then! take it and go,' said Rosalie.

He joyfully received the gift, murmured something that made her blush and toss her head, but with a little laugh that showed her displeasure was entirely affected; and then with a courteous salutation withdrew.

'Did you ever see such a man, Miss Grey?' said she, turning to me; 'I'm so *glad* you came! I thought I never *should* get rid of him; and I was so terribly afraid of papa seeing him.'

'Has he been with you long?'

'No, not long, but he's so extremely impertinent: and he's always hanging about, pretending his business or his clerical duties require his attendance in these parts, and really watching for poor me, and pouncing upon me wherever he sees me.'

'Well, your mamma thinks you ought not to go beyond the park or garden without some discreet, matronly person like me to accompany you, and keep off all intruders. She descried Mr Hatfield hurrying past the park-gates, and forthwith despatched me with instructions to seek you up and to take care of you, and likewise to warn'——

'Oh, mamma's so tiresome! As if I couldn't take care of myself. She bothered me before about Mr Hatfield; and I told her she might trust me: I never should forget my rank and station for the most delightful man that ever breathed. I wish he would go down on his knees to-morrow, and implore me to be his wife, that I might just show her how mistaken she is in supposing that I could ever—— Oh, it provokes me so! To think that I could be such a fool as to fall in *love*! It is quite beneath the dignity of a woman to do such a thing. Love! I detest the word! as applied to one of our sex, I think it a perfect insult. A preference I *might* acknowledge; but never for one like poor Mr Hatfield, who has not seven hundred a year to bless himself with. I like to talk to him, because he's so clever and amusing – I wish Sir Thomas Ashby were half as nice; besides, I must have *somebody* to flirt

with, and no one else has the sense to come here; and when we
go out, mamma won't let me flirt with anybody but Sir Thomas
– if he's there; and if he's *not* there, I'm bound hand and foot, for
fear somebody should go and make up some exaggerated story,
and put it into his head that I'm engaged, or likely to be engaged,
to somebody else; or, what is more probable, for fear his nasty
old mother should see or hear of my ongoings, and conclude that
I'm not a fit wife for her excellent son: as if the said son were not
the greatest scamp in Christendom; and as if any woman of
common decency were not a world too good for him.'

'Is it really so, Miss Murray? and does your mamma know it,
and yet wish you to marry him?'

'To be sure she does! She knows more against him than I do, I
believe: she keeps it from me lest I should be discouraged; not
knowing how little I care about such things. For it's no great
matter, really: he'll be all right when he's married, as mamma
says; and reformed rakes make the best husbands, *everybody*
knows. I only wish he were not so ugly – *that's* all *I* think about:
but then there's no choice here in the country; and papa *will not*
let us go to London'——

'But I should think Mr Hatfield would be far better.'

'And so he would, if he were lord of Ashby Park – there's not a
doubt of it: but the fact is, I *must* have Ashby Park, whoever
shares it with me.'

'But Mr Hatfield thinks you like him all this time; you don't
consider how bitterly he will be disappointed when he finds
himself mistaken.'

'*No*, indeed! It will be a proper punishment for his presumption – for ever *daring* to think I could like him. I should
enjoy nothing so much as lifting the veil from his eyes.'

'The sooner you do it the better, then.'

'No; I tell you, I like to amuse myself with him. Besides, he
doesn't really think I like him. I take good care of that: you don't
know how cleverly I manage. He may presume to think he can
*induce* me to like him; for which I shall punish him as he
deserves.'

'Well, mind you don't give too much reason for such presumption – that's all,' replied I.

But all my exhortations were in vain: they only made her
somewhat more solicitous to disguise her wishes and her

thoughts from me. She talked no more to me about the Rector; but I could see that her mind, if not her heart, was fixed upon him still, and that she was intent upon obtaining another interview: for though, in compliance with her mother's request, I was now constituted the companion of her rambles for a time, she still persisted in wandering in the fields and lanes that lay in the nearest proximity to the road; and, whether she talked to me or read the book she carried in her hand, she kept continually pausing to look round her, or gaze up the road to see if any one was coming; and if a horseman trotted by, I could tell by her unqualified abuse of the poor equestrian, whoever he might be, that she hated him *because* he was not Mr Hatfield.

'Surely,' thought I, 'she is not so indifferent to him as she believes herself to be, or would have others to believe her; and her mother's anxiety is not so wholly causeless as she affirms.'

Three days passed away, and he did not make his appearance. On the afternoon of the fourth, as we were walking beside the park-palings in the memorable field, each furnished with a book (for I always took care to provide myself with something to be doing when she did not require me to talk), she suddenly interrupted my studies by exclaiming –

'Oh, Miss Grey! do be so kind as to go and see Mark Wood, and take his wife half-a-crown from me – I should have given or sent it a week ago, but quite forgot. There!' said she, throwing me her purse, and speaking very fast – 'Never mind getting it out now, but take the purse and give them what you like; I would go with you, but I want to finish this volume. I'll come and meet you when I've done it. Be quick, will you – and – oh, wait; hadn't you better read to him a bit? Run to the house and get some sort of a good book. Anything will do.'

I did as I was desired; but, suspecting something from her hurried manner and the suddenness of the request, I just glanced glanced back before I quitted the field, and there was Mr Hatfield about to enter at the gate below. By sending me to the house for a book, she had just prevented my meeting him on the road.

'Never mind!' thought I, 'there'll be no great harm done. Poor Mark will be glad of the half-crown, and perhaps of the good book too; and if the Rector does steal Miss Rosalie's heart, it will only humble her pride a little; and if they do get married at last, it will only save her from a worse fate; and she will be quite a good enough partner for him, and he for her.'

Mark Wood was the consumptive labourer whom I mentioned before. He was now rapidly wearing away. Miss Murray, by her liberality, obtained literally the blessing of him that was ready to perish; for though the half-crown could be of very little service to him, he was glad of it for the sake of his wife and children, so soon to be widowed and fatherless. After I had sat a few minutes, and read a little for the comfort and edification of himself and his afflicted wife, I left them; but I had not proceeded fifty yards before I encountered Mr Weston, apparently on his way to the same abode. He greeted me in his usual quiet, unaffected way, stopped to inquire about the condition of the sick man and his family, and with a sort of unconscious, brotherly disregard to ceremony, took from my hand the book out of which I had been reading, turned over its pages, made a few brief but very sensible remarks, and restored it; then told me about some poor sufferer he had just been visiting, talked a little about Nancy Brown, made a few observations upon my little rough friend the terrier, that was frisking at his feet, and finally upon the beauty of the weather, and departed.

I have omitted to give a detail of his words, from a notion that they would not interest the reader as they did me, and not because I have forgotten them. No; I remember them well; for I thought them over and over again in the course of that day and many succeeding ones, I know not how often; and recalled every intonation of his deep, clear voice, every flash of his quick, brown eye, and every gleam of his pleasant but too transient smile. Such a confession will look very absurd, I fear; but no matter: I have written it: and they that read it will not know the writer.

While I was walking along, happy within, and pleased with all around, Miss Murray came hastening to meet me; her buoyant step, flushed cheek, and radiant smiles showing that she, too, was happy, in her own way. Running up to me, she put her arm through mine, and without waiting to recover breath, began –

'Now, Miss Grey, think yourself highly honoured, for I'm come to tell you my news before I've breathed a word of it to any one else.'

'Well, what is it?'

'Oh, *such* news! In the first place, you must know that Mr
Hatfield came upon me just after you were gone. I was in *such*
a way for fear papa or mamma should see him; but, you know,
I couldn't call you back again, and so I – oh, dear! I can't tell
you all about it now, for there's Matilda, I see, in the park, and
I must go and open my budget to her. But, however, Hatfield
was most uncommonly audacious, unspeakably complimentary, and unprecedentedly tender – tried to be so, at least
– he didn't succeed very well in *that*, because it's not his vein.
I'll tell you all he said another time.'

'But what did *you* say – I'm more interested in that?'

'I'll tell you that, too, at some future period. I happened to be
in a very good humour just then; but, though I was com-
plaisant and gracious enough, I took care not to compromise
myself in any possible way. But, however, the conceited wretch
chose to interpret my amiability of temper his own way, and at
length presumed upon my indulgence so far – what do you
think? – he actually – made me an offer!'

'And you'——

'I proudly drew myself up, and with the greatest coolness
expressed my astonishment at such an occurrence, and hoped
he had seen nothing in my conduct to justify his expectations.
You should have *seen* how his countenance fell! He went
perfectly white in the face. I assured him that I esteemed him
and all that, but could not possibly accede to his proposals; and
if I did, papa and mamma could never be brought to give their
consent.

'"But if they could," said he, "would yours be wanting?"

'"Certainly, Mr Hatfield," I replied, with a cool decision
which quelled all hope at once. Oh, if you had seen how
dreadfully mortified he was – how crushed to the earth by his
disappointment! really, I almost pitied him myself.

'One more desperate attempt, however, he made. After a
silence of considerable duration, during which he struggled to
be calm, and I to be grave – for I felt a strong propensity to
laugh – which would have ruined all – he said, with the ghost
of a smile –

'"But tell me plainly, Miss Murray, if I had the wealth of Sir
Hugh Meltham, or the prospects of his eldest son, would you
still refuse me? answer me truly, upon your honour."

'"Certainly," said I. "That would make no difference what-ever."

'It was a great lie, but he looked so confident in his own attractions still, that I determined not to leave him one stone upon another. He looked me full in the face; but I kept my countenance so well that he could not imagine I was saying anything more than the actual truth.

'"Then it's all over, I suppose," he said, looking as if he could have died on the spot with vexation and the intensity of his despair. But he was angry as well as disappointed. There was he, suffering so unspeakably, and there was I, the pitiless cause of it all, so utterly impenetrable to all the artillery of his looks and words, so calmly cold and proud, he could not but feel some resentment; and with singular bitterness he began –

'"I certainly did not expect this, Miss Murray. I might say something about your past conduct, and the hopes you have led me to foster, but I forbear, on condition'——

'"No conditions, Mr Hatfield!" said I, now truly indignant at his insolence.

'"Then let me beg it as a favour," he replied, lowering his voice at once, and taking a humbler tone: "let me entreat that you will not mention this affair to any one whatever. If you will keep silence about it, there need be no unpleasantness on either side – nothing, I mean beyond what is quite unavoidable: for my own feelings I will endeavour to keep to myself, if I cannot annihilate them – I will try to forgive, if I cannot forget, the cause of my sufferings. I will not suppose, Miss Murray, that you know how deeply you have injured me. I would not have you aware of it; but if, in addition to the injury you have already done me – pardon me, but whether innocently or not, you *have* done it – and if you add to it by giving publicity to this unfortunate affair, or naming it *at all*, you will find that I too can speak, and though you scorned my love, you will hardly scorn my"——

'He stopped, but he bit his bloodless lip, and looked so terribly fierce that I was quite frightened. However, my pride upheld me still, and I answered disdainfully–

'"I do not know what motive you suppose I could have for naming it to any one, Mr Hatfield; but if I were disposed to do so, you would not deter me by threats; and it is scarcely the part of a gentleman to attempt it."

"'Pardon me, Miss Murray," said he, "I have loved you so intensely – I do still adore you so deeply, that I would not willingly offend you; but though I never have loved, and never *can* love any woman as I have loved you, it is equally certain that I never was so ill-treated by any. On the contrary, I have always found your sex the kindest and most tender and obliging of God's creation, till now." (Think of the conceited fellow saying that!) "And the novelty and harshness of the lesson you have taught me to-day, and the bitterness of being disappointed in the only quarter on which the happiness of my life depended, must excuse any appearance of asperity. If my presence is disagreeable to you, Miss Murray," he said (for I was looking about me to show how little I cared for him, so he thought I was tired of him, I suppose), – "if my presence is disagreeable to you, Miss Murray, you have only to promise me the favour I named, and I will relieve you at once. There are many ladies – some even in this parish – who would be delighted to accept what you have so scornfully trampled under your feet. They would be naturally inclined to hate one whose surpassing loveliness has so completely estranged my heart from them and blinded me to their attractions; and a single hint of the truth from me to one of these, would be sufficient to raise such a talk against you as would seriously injure your prospects and diminish your chance of success with any other gentleman you or your mamma might design to entangle."

"'What do you mean, sir?" said I, ready to stamp with passion.

"'I mean that this affair from beginning to end appears to me like a case of arrant flirtation, to say the least of it – such a case as you would find it rather inconvenient to have blazoned through the world: especially with the additions and exaggerations of your female rivals, who would be too glad to publish the matter, if I only gave them a handle to it. But I promise you, on the faith of a gentleman, that no word or syllable that could tend to your prejudice shall ever escape my lips, provided you will"——

"'Well, well, I won't mention it," said I. "You may rely upon my silence, if that can afford you any consolation."

"'You promise it?"

"'Yes," I answered, for I wanted to get rid of him now.

'"Farewell, then!" said he, in a most doleful heart-sick tone; and with a look where pride vainly struggled against despair, he turned and went away: longing, no doubt, to get home, that he might shut himself up in his study and cry – if he doesn't burst into tears before he gets there.'

'But you have broken your promise already,' said I, truly horrified at her perfidy.

'Oh! it's only to you; I know you won't repeat it.'

'Certainly, I shall not: but you say you were going to tell your sister; and she will tell your brothers when they come home, and Brown immediately, if you do not tell her yourself; and Brown will blazon it, or be the means of blazoning it, throughout the country.'

'No, indeed, she won't. We shall not tell her at all, unless it be under the promise of the strictest secrecy.'

'But how can you expect her to keep her promises better than her more enlightened mistress?'

'Well, well, she shan't hear it then,' said Miss Murray, somewhat snappishly.

'But you will tell your mamma, of course,' pursued I; 'and she will tell your papa.'

'Of course, I shall tell mamma, that is the very thing that pleases me so much. I shall now be able to convince her how mistaken she was in her fears about me.'

'Oh, *that's* it, is it? I was wondering what it was that delighted you so much.'

'Yes; and another thing is that I've humbled Mr Hatfield so charmingly; and another – why, you must allow me some share of female vanity: I don't pretend to be without that most essential attribute of our sex – and if you had seen poor Hatfield's intense eagerness of making his ardent declaration, and his flattering proposal, and his agony of mind, that no effort of pride could conceal, on being refused, you would have allowed I had some cause to be gratified.'

'The greater his agony, I should think, the less your cause for gratification.'

'Oh, nonsense!' cried the young lady, shaking herself with vexation. 'You either can't understand me or you won't. If I had not confidence in your magnanimity, I should think you envied me. But you will, perhaps, comprehend this cause of pleasure –

which is as great as any – namely, that I am delighted with myself for my prudence, my self-command, my heartlessness, if you please. I was not a bit taken by surprise, not a bit confused, or awkward, or foolish; I just acted and spoke as I ought to have done, and was completely my own mistress throughout. And here was a man, decidedly good-looking – Jane and Susan Green call him bewitchingly handsome – I suppose they're two of the ladies he pretends would be so glad to have him; but, however, he was certainly a very clever, witty, agreeable companion – not what *you* call clever, but just enough to make him entertaining; and a man one needn't be ashamed of anywhere, and would not soon grow tired of; and to confess the truth, I rather liked him – better even, of late, than Harry Meltham – and he evidently idolized me; and yet, though he came upon me all alone and unprepared, I had the wisdom and the pride, and the strength to refuse him – and so scornfully and coolly as I did: I have good reason to be proud of that!'

'And are you equally proud of having told him that his having the wealth of Sir Hugh Meltham would make no difference to you when that was not the case; and of having promised to tell no one of his misadventure, apparently without the slightest intention of keeping your promise?'

'Of course! what else could I do? You would not have had me – but I see, Miss Grey, you're not in a good temper. Here's Matilda; I'll see what she and mamma have to say about it.'

She left me, offended at my want of sympathy, and thinking, no doubt, that I envied her. I did not – at least, I firmly believed I did not. I was sorry for her; I was amazed, disgusted at her heartless vanity; I wondered why so much beauty should be given to those who made so bad a use of it, and denied to some who would make it a benefit to both themselves and others.

But God knows best, I concluded. There are, I suppose, some men as vain, as selfish, and as heartless as she is, and, perhaps, such women may be useful to punish them.

CHAPTER 15
# *The Walk*

'O dear! I wish Hatfield had not been so precipitate!' said Rosalie next day at four p.m., as, with a portentous yawn, she laid down her worsted-work and looked listlessly towards the window. 'There's no inducement to go out now; and nothing to look forward to. The days will be so long and dull when there are no parties to enliven them; and there are none this week, or next either, that I know of.'

'Pity you were so cross to him,' observed Matilda, to whom this lamentation was addressed. 'He'll never come again: and I suspect you liked him after all. I hoped you would have taken him for your beau, and left dear Harry to me.'

'Humph! my beau must be an Adonis, indeed, Matilda, the admired of all beholders, if I am to be contented with him alone. I'm sorry to lose Hatfield, I confess; but the first decent man, or number of men, that come to supply his place will be more than welcome. It's Sunday to-morrow – I do wonder how he'll look, and whether he'll be able to go through the service. Most likely he'll pretend he's got a cold and make Mr Weston do it all.'

'Not he!' exclaimed Matilda, somewhat contemptuously. 'Fool as he is, he's not so soft as that comes to.'

Her sister was slightly offended; but the event proved Matilda was right: the disappointed lover performed his pastoral duties as usual. Rosalie, indeed, affirmed he looked very pale and dejected; he might be a little paler, but the difference, if any, was scarcely perceptible. As for his dejection, I certainly did not hear his laugh ringing from the vestry as usual, nor his voice loud in hilarious discourse; though I did hear it uplifted in rating the sexton in a manner that made the congregation stare; and in his transits to and from the pulpit and the communion-table there was more of solemn pomp and less of that irreverent, self-confident, or rather self-delighted imperiousness with which he usually swept along – that air that seemed to say, 'You all reverence and adore me, I know; but if any one does not, I defy him to the teeth!' But the most remarkable change was, that he never once suffered his eyes to wander in the direction of Mr Murray's pew, and did not leave the church till we were gone.

Mr Hatfield had doubtless received a very severe blow; but his pride impelled him to use every effort to conceal the effects of it. He had been disappointed in his certain hope of obtaining not only a beautiful, and, to him, highly attractive wife, but one whose rank and fortune might give brilliance to far inferior charms: he was likewise, no doubt, intensely mortified by his repulse, and deeply offended at the conduct of Miss Murray throughout. It would have given him no little consolation to have known how disappointed she was to find him apparently so little moved, and to see that he was able to refrain from casting a single glance at her throughout both services; though, she declared, it showed he was thinking of her all the time, or his eyes would have fallen upon her, if it were only by chance: but if they had so chanced to fall, she would have affirmed it was because they could not resist the attraction. It might have pleased him too, in some degree, to have seen how dull and dissatisfied she was throughout that week (the greater part of it, at least), for lack of her usual source of excitement; and how often she regetted having 'used him up so soon', like a child that, having devoured its plum-cake too hastily, sits sucking its fingers and vainly lamenting its greediness.

At length I was called upon, one fine morning, to accompany her in a walk to the village. Ostensibly she went to get some shades of Berlin wool at a tolerably respectable shop that was chiefly supported by the ladies of the vicinity: really – I trust there is no breach of charity in supposing that she went with the idea of meeting either with the Rector himself, or some other admirer by the way; for as we went along, she kept wondering 'what Hatfield would do or say, if we met him', &c., &c.; as we passed Mr Green's park-gates, she 'wondered whether he was at home – great stupid blockhead'; as Lady Meltham's carriage passed us, she 'wondered what Mr Harry was doing this fine day'; and then began to abuse his elder brother for being 'such a fool as to get married and go and live in London'.

'Why,' said I, 'I thought you wanted to live in London yourself.'

'Yes, because it's so dull here: but then he makes it still duller by taking himself off; and if he were not married I might have him instead of that odious Sir Thomas.'

Then, observing the prints of a horse's feet on the somewhat miry road, she 'wondered whether it was a gentleman's horse', and finally concluded it was, for the impressions were too small to have been made by a 'great, clumsy cart-horse'; and then she 'wondered who the rider could be', and whether we should meet him coming back, for she was sure he had only passed that morning; and lastly, when we entered the village and saw only a few of its humble inhabitants moving about, she 'wondered why the stupid people couldn't keep in their houses; she was sure she didn't want to see their ugly faces, and dirty, vulgar clothes – it wasn't for that she came to Horton!'

Amid all this, I confess, I wondered, too, in secret, whether we should meet or catch a glimpse of somebody else; and as we passed his lodgings, I even went so far as to wonder whether he was at the window. On entering the shop, Miss Murray desired me to stand in the doorway while she transacted her business, and tell her if anyone passed. But alas! there was no one visible besides the villagers, except Jane and Susan Green coming down the single street, apparently returning from a walk.

'Stupid things!' muttered she, as she came out after having concluded her bargain. 'Why couldn't they have their dolt of a brother with them? even *he* would be better than nothing.'

She greeted them, however, with a cheerful smile, and pro-testations of pleasure at the happy meeting equal to their own. They placed themselves one on each side of her, and all three walked away chatting and laughing as young ladies do when they get together, if they be but on tolerably intimate terms. But I, feeling myself to be one too many, left them to their merriment and lagged behind, as usual on such occasions: I had no relish for walking beside Miss Green or Miss Susan like one deaf and dumb, who could neither speak nor be spoken to.

But this time I was not long alone. It struck me, at first, as very odd, that just as I was thinking about Mr Weston he should come up and accost me; but afterwards, on due reflection, I thought there was nothing odd about it, unless it were the fact of his speaking to me; for on such a morning and so near his own abode, it was natural enough that he should be about; and as for my thinking of him, I had been doing that, with little intermis-sion, ever since we set out on our journey; so there was nothing remarkable in that.

'You are alone again, Miss Grey!' said he.

'Yes.'

'What kind of people are those ladies – the Misses Green?'

'I really don't know.'

'That's strange – when you live so near and see them so often!'

'Well, I suppose they are lively, good-tempered girls; but I imagine you must know them better than I do myself, for I never exchanged a word with either of them.'

'Indeed! They don't strike me as being particularly reserved.'

'Very likely they are not so to people of their own class; but they consider themselves as moving in quite a different sphere from me!'

He made no reply to this; but after a short pause, he said –

'I suppose it's these things, Miss Grey, that make you think you cannot live without a home?'

'Not exactly. The fact is I am too socially disposed to be able to live contentedly without a friend; and as the only friends I have, or am likely to have, are at home, if it – or rather, if they were gone – I will not say I could not live – but I would rather not live in such a desolate world.'

'But why do you say the only friends you are likely to have? Are you so unsociable that you cannot make friends?'

'No, but I never made one yet; and in my present position there is no possibility of doing so, or even of forming a common acquaintance. The fault may be partly in myself, but I hope not altogether.'

'The fault is partly in society, and partly, I should think, in your immediate neighbours: and partly, too, in yourself; for many ladies, in your position, would make themselves be noticed and accounted of. But your pupils should be companions for you in some degree; they cannot be many years younger than yourself.'

'Oh, yes, they are good company sometimes; but I cannot call them friends, nor would they think of bestowing such a name on me – they have other companions better suited to their tastes.'

'Perhaps you are too wise for them. How do you amuse yourself when alone – do you read much?'

'Reading is my favourite occupation, when I have leisure for it and books to read.'

From speaking of books in general, he passed to different books in particular, and proceeded by rapid transitions from topic to topic, till several matters, both of taste and opinion, had been discussed considerably within the space of half-an-hour, but without the embellishment of many observations from himself; he being evidently less bent upon communicating his own thoughts and predilections than on discovering mine. He had not the tact, or the art, to effect such a purpose by skilfully drawing out my sentiments or ideas through the real or apparent statement of his own, or leading the conversation by imperceptible gradations to such topics as he wished to advert to: but such gentle abruptness, and such single-minded straightforwardness could not possibly offend me.

'And why should he interest himself at all in my moral and intellectual capacities: what is it to him what I think or feel?' I asked myself. And my heart throbbed in answer to the question.

But Jane and Susan Green soon reached their home. As they stood parleying at the park-gates, attempting to persuade Miss Murray to come in, I wished Mr Weston would go, that she might not see him with me when she turned round; but, unfortunately, his business, which was to pay one more visit to poor Mark Wood, led him to pursue the same path as we did, till nearly the close of our journey. When, however, he saw that Rosalie had taken leave of her friends and I was about to join her, he would have left me and passed on at a quicker pace; but, as he civilly lifted his hat in passing her, to my surprise, instead of returning the salute with a stiff, ungracious bow, she accosted him with one of her sweetest smiles, and, walking by his side, began to talk to him with all imaginable cheerfulness and affability; and so we proceeded all three together.

After a short pause in the conversation, Mr Weston made some remark addressed particularly to me, as referring to something we had been talking of before; but, before I could answer, Miss Murray replied to the observation and enlarged upon it: he rejoined; and, from thence to the close of the interview, she engrossed him entirely to herself. It might be partly owing to my own stupidity, my want of tact and assurance: but I felt myself wronged: I trembled with apprehension; and I listened with envy to her easy, rapid flow of utterance, and saw with anxiety the bright smile with which she looked into his face from time to time: for she was walking a little in advance, for the purpose (as I judged) of being seen as well as heard. If her conversation was light and trivial, it was amusing, and she was never at a loss for something to say, or for suitable words to express it in. There was nothing pert or flippant in her manner now, as when she walked with Mr Hatfield; there was only a gentle, playful kind of vivacity, which I thought must be peculiarly pleasing to a man of Mr Weston's disposition and temperament.

When he was gone she began to laugh, and muttered to herself – 'I thought I could do it!'

'Do what?' I asked.

'Fix that man.'

'What in the world do you mean?'

'I mean that he will go home and dream of me. I have shot him through the heart!'

'How do you know?'

'By many infallible proofs: more especially the look he gave me when he went away. It was not an impudent look – I exonerate him from that – it was a look of reverential, tender adoration. Ha, ha! he's not quite such a stupid blockhead as I thought him!'

I made no answer, for my heart was in my throat, or something like it, and I could not trust myself to speak. 'O God, avert it!' I cried internally – 'for his sake, not for mine!'

Miss Murray made several trivial observations as we passed up the park, to which (in spite of my reluctance to let one glimpse of my feelings appear) I could only answer by monosyllables. Whether she intended to torment me, or merely to amuse herself, I could not tell – and did not much care; but I thought of the poor man and his one lamb, and the rich man with his thousand flocks; and I dreaded I knew not what for Mr Weston, independently of my own blighted hopes.

Right glad was I to get into the house, and find myself alone once more in my own room. My first impulse was to sink into the chair beside the bed; and laying my head on the pillow, to seek relief in a passionate burst of tears: there was an imperative craving for such an indulgence; but alas! I must restrain and swallow back my feelings still: there was the bell – the odious bell for the schoolroom dinner; and I must go down with a calm face, and smile, and laugh, and talk nonsense – yes, and eat, too, if possible, as if all was right, and I was just returned from a pleasant walk.

## CHAPTER 16
### *The Substitution*

Next Sunday was one of the gloomiest of April days – a day of thick, dark clouds and heavy showers. None of the Murrays were disposed to attend church in the afternoon, excepting Rosalie: she was bent upon going as usual; so she ordered the carriage, and I went with her: nothing loth, of course, for at church I might look without fear of scorn or censure upon a form and face more pleasing to me than the most beautiful of God's creations; I might listen without disturbance to a voice more charming than the sweetest music to my ears; I might seem to hold communion with that soul in which I felt so deeply interested, and imbibe its purest thoughts and holiest aspirations, with no alloy to such felicity except the secret reproaches of my conscience, which would too often whisper that I was deceiving my own self, and mocking God with the service of a heart more bent upon the creature than the Creator.

Sometimes such thoughts would give me trouble enough; but sometimes I could quiet them with thinking – it is not the man, it is his goodness that I love. 'Whatsoever things are pure, whatsoever things are lovely, whatsoever things are honest and of good report, think on these things.' We do well to worship God in His works; and I know none of them in which so many of His attributes – so much of His own spirit shines, as in this His faithful servant; whom to know and not to appreciate, were obtuse insensibility in me, who have so little else to occupy my heart.

Almost immediately after the conclusion of the service, Miss Murray left the church. We had to stand in the porch, for it was raining, and the carriage was not yet to come. I wondered at her coming forth so hastily, for neither young Meltham nor Squire Green was there; but I soon found it was to secure an interview with Mr Weston as he came out, which he presently did. Having saluted us both, he would have passed on, but she detained him; first with observations upon the disagreeable weather, and then with asking if he would be so kind as to come some time to-morrow to see the granddaughter of the old woman who kept the porter's lodge, for the girl was ill of a fever, and wished to see him. He promised to do so.

'And at what time will you be most likely to come, Mr
Weston? The old woman will like to know when to expect you –
you know such people think more about having their cottages in
order when decent people come to see them than we are apt to
suppose.'

Here was a wonderful instance of consideration from the
thoughtless Miss Murray. Mr Weston named an hour in the
morning at which he would endeavour to be there. By this time
the carriage was ready, and the footman was waiting, with an
open umbrella, to escort Miss Murray through the churchyard. I
was about to follow; but Mr Weston had an umbrella too, and
offered me the benefit of its shelter, for it was raining heavily.

'No, thank you, I don't mind the rain,' I said. I always lacked
common sense when taken by surprise.

'But you don't *like* it, I suppose? – an umbrella will do you no
harm at any rate,' he replied, with a smile that showed he was
not offended; as a man of worse temper or less penetration
would have been at such a refusal of his aid. I could not deny the
truth of his assertion, and so went with him to the carriage; he
even offered me his hand on getting in: an unnecessary piece of
civility, but I accepted that too, for fear of giving offence. One
glance he gave, one little smile at parting – it was but for a
moment; but therein I read, or thought I read, a meaning that
kindled in my heart a brighter flame of hope than had ever yet
arisen.

'I would have sent the footman back for you, Miss Grey, if
you'd waited a moment – you needn't have taken Mr Weston's
umbrella,' observed Rosalie, with a very unamiable cloud upon
her pretty face.

'I would have come without an umbrella, but Mr Weston
offered me the benefit of his, and I could not have refused it
more than I did without offending him,' replied I, smiling
placidly; for my inward happiness made that amusing which
would have wounded me at another time.

The carriage was now in motion. Miss Murray bent forwards,
and looked out of the window as we were passing Mr Weston.
He was pacing homewards along the causeway, and did not turn
his head.

'Stupid ass!' cried she, throwing herself back again in the seat.
'You don't know *what* you've lost by not looking this way!'

'What has he lost?'

'A bow from me, that would have raised him to the seventh heaven!'

I made no answer. I saw she was out of humour, and I derived a secret gratification from the fact, not that she was vexed, but that she thought she had reason to be so. It made me think my hopes were not entirely the offspring of my wishes and imaginations.

'I mean to take up Mr Weston instead of Mr Hatfield,' said my companion after a short pause, resuming something of her usual cheerfulness. 'The ball at Ashby Park takes place on Tuesday, you know; and mamma thinks it very likely that Sir Thomas will propose to me then: such things are often done in the privacy of the ball-room, when gentlemen are most easily ensnared, and ladies most enchanting. But if I am to be married so soon, I must make the best of the present time: I am determined Hatfield shall not be the only man who shall lay his heart at my feet, and implore me to accept the worthless gift in vain.'

'If you mean Mr Weston to be one of your victims,' said I, with affected indifference, 'you will have to make such overtures yourself that you will find it difficult to draw back when he asks you to fulfil the expectations you have raised.'

'I don't suppose he will ask me to *marry* him – nor should I desire it: that would be *rather* too much presumption! but I intend him to feel my power. He has felt it already, indeed: but he shall *acknowledge* it too; and what visionary hopes he may have, he must keep to himself, and only amuse me with the result of them – for a time.'

'Oh! that some kind spirit would whisper those words in his ear!' I inwardly exclaimed. I was far too indignant to hazard a reply to her observation, aloud; and nothing more was said about Mr Weston that day, by me or in my hearing. But next morning, soon after breakfast, Miss Murray came into the schoolroom where her sister was employed at her studies, or rather her lessons, for studies they were not, and said, 'Matilda, I want you to take a walk with me about eleven o'clock.'

'Oh, I can't Rosalie! I have to give orders about my new bridle and saddle-cloth, and speak to the rat-catcher about his dogs: Miss Grey must go with you.'

'No, I want *you*,' said Rosalie; and calling her sister to the window, she whispered an explanation in her ear; upon which the latter consented to go.

I remembered that eleven was the hour at which Mr Weston proposed to come to the porter's lodge; and remembering that I beheld the whole contrivance. Accordingly, at dinner, I was entertained with a long account of how Mr Weston had over-taken them as they were walking along the road; and how they had had a long walk and talk with him, and really found him quite an agreeable companion; and how he must have been, and evidently was, delighted with them and their amazing condescension, &c., &c.

CHAPTER 17

## Confessions

As I am in the way of confessions, I may as well acknowledge that, about this time, I paid more attention to dress than ever I had done before. This is not saying much; for hitherto I had been a little neglectful in that particular: but now, also, it was no uncommon thing to spend as much as two minutes in the con-templation of my own image in the glass; though I never could derive any consolation from such a study. I could discover no beauty in those marked features, that pale hollow cheek, and ordinary dark brown hair; there might be intellect in the fore-head, there might be expression in the dark grey eyes: but what of that? – a low Grecian brow and large black eyes devoid of sentiment would be esteemed far preferable. It is foolish to wish for beauty. Sensible people never either desire it for themselves, or care about it in others. If the mind be but well cultivated, and the heart well disposed, no one ever cares for the exterior. So said the teachers of our childhood; and so say we to the children of the present day. All very judicious and proper, no doubt; but are such assertions supported by actual experience?

We are naturally disposed to love what gives us pleasure, and what more pleasing than a beautiful face – when we know no harm of the possessor at least? A little girl loves her bird – why? Because it lives and feels; because it is helpless and harmless? A toad, likewise, lives and feels, and is equally helpless and harmless; but though she would not hurt a toad, she cannot love it like the bird, with its graceful form, soft feathers, and bright, speaking eyes. If a woman is fair and amiable, she is praised for both qualities, but especially the former, by the bulk of mankind: if, on the other hand, she is disagreeable in person and character, her plainness is commonly inveighed against as her greatest crime, because, to common observers, it gives the greatest offence; while, if she is plain and good, provided she is a person of retired manners and secluded life, no one ever knows of her goodness, except her immediate connections. Others, on the contrary, are disposed to form unfavourable opinions of her mind and disposition, if it be but to excuse themselves for their instinctive dislike of one so unfavoured by nature; and *vice versa* with her whose angel form conceals a vicious heart, or sheds a false deceitful charm over defects and foibles that would not be tolerated in another. They that have beauty, let them be thankful for it, and make a good use of it, like any other talent; they that have it not, let them console themselves, and do the best they can without it: certainly, though liable to be over-estimated, it is a gift of God, and not to be despised. Many will feel this who have felt that they could love, and whose hearts tell them that they are worthy to be loved again; while yet they are debarred by the lack of this or some such seeming trifle, from giving and receiving that happiness they seem almost made to feel and to impart. As well might the humble glow-worm despise that power of giving light without which the roving fly might pass her and repass her a thousand times, and never rest beside her: she might hear her winged darling buzzing over and around her; he vainly seeking her, she longing to be found, but with no power to make her presence known, no voice to call him, no wings to follow his flight; – the fly must seek another mate, the worm must live and die alone.

Such were some of my reflections about this period. I might go on prosing more and more, I might dive much deeper, and disclose other thoughts, propose questions the reader might be puzzled to answer, and deduce arguments that might startle his prejudices, or perhaps, provoke his ridicule, because he could not comprehend them; but I forbear.

Now, therefore, let us return to Miss Murray. She accompanied her mamma to the ball on Tuesday; of course splendidly attired, and delighted with her prospects and her charms. As Ashby Park was nearly ten miles distant from Horton Lodge, they had to set out pretty early, and I intended to have spent the evening with Nancy Brown, whom I had not seen for a long time; but my kind pupil took care I should spend it neither there nor anywhere else beyond the limits of the schoolroom, by giving me a piece of music to copy, which kept me closely occupied till bed-time. About eleven next morning, as soon as she had left her room, she came to tell me her news. Sir Thomas had indeed proposed to her at the ball: an event which reflected great credit on her mamma's sagacity, if not upon her skill in contrivance. I rather incline to the belief that she had first laid her plans, and then predicted their success. The offer had been accepted, of course, and the bridegroom-elect was coming that day to settle matters with Mr Murray.

Rosalie was pleased with the thoughts of becoming mistress of Ashby Park; she was elated with the prospect of the bridal ceremony and its attendant splendour and *éclat*, the honeymoon spent abroad, and the subsequent gaieties she expected to enjoy in London and elsewhere; she appeared pretty well pleased too, for the time being, with Sir Thomas himself, because she had so lately seen him, danced with him, and been flattered by him; but, after all, she seemed to shrink from the idea of being so soon united: she wished the ceremony to be delayed some months, at least; and I wished it too. It seemed a horrible thing to hurry on the inauspicious match, and not to give the poor creature time to think and reason on the irrevocable step she was about to take. I made no pretension to 'a mother's watchful, anxious care', but I was amazed and horrified at Mrs Murray's heartlessness, or want of thought for the real good of her child; and, by my unheeded warnings and exhortations, I vainly strove to remedy the evil. Miss Murray only laughed at what I said; and I soon found that her reluctance to an immediate union arose chiefly from a desire to do what execution she could among the young gentlemen of her acquaintance, before she was incapacitated from further mischief of the kind. It was for this cause that, before confiding to me the secret of her engagement, she had extracted a promise that I would not mention a word on the subject to any one. And when I saw this, and when I beheld her plunge more recklessly than ever into the depths of heartless coquetry, I had no more pity for her. 'Come what will,' I thought, 'she deserves it. Sir Thomas cannot be too bad for her; and the sooner she is incapacitated from deceiving and injuring others the better.'

The wedding was fixed for the 1st of June. Between that and the critical ball was little more than six weeks; but, with Rosalie's accomplished skill and resolute exertion, much might be done, even within that period: especially as Sir Thomas spent most of the interim in London; whither he went up, it was said, to settle affairs with his lawyer, and make other preparations for the approaching nuptials. He endeavoured to supply the want of his presence by a pretty constant fire of billets-doux; but these did not attract the neighbours' attention, and open their eyes, as personal visits would have done; and old Lady Ashby's haughty, sour spirit of reserve withheld her from spreading the news, while her indifferent health prevented her coming to visit her future daughter-in-law; so that, altogether, this affair was kept far closer than such things usually are.

Rosalie would sometimes show her lover's epistles to me, to convince me what a kind, devoted husband he would make. She showed me the letters of another individual, too, the unfortunate Mr Green, who had not the courage, or, as she expressed it, the 'spunk' to plead his cause in person, but whom one denial would not satisfy: he must write again and again. He would not have done so if he could have seen the grimaces his fair idol made over his moving appeals to her feelings, and heard her scornful laughter and the opprobrious epithets she heaped upon him for his perseverance.

'Why don't you tell him, at once, that you are engaged?' I asked.

'Oh, I don't want him to know that,' replied she. 'If he knew it, his sisters and everybody would know it, and then there would be an end of my – ahem! And, besides, if I told him that, he would think my engagement was the only obstacle, and that I would have him if I were free; which I could not bear that any man should think, and he, of all others, at least. Besides, I don't care for his letters,' she added contemptuously: 'he may write as often as he pleases, and look as great a calf as he likes when I meet him; it only amuses me.'

Meantime, young Meltham was pretty frequent in his visits to the house or transits past it: and, judging by Matilda's execrations and reproaches, her sister paid more attention to him than civility required: in other words, she carried on as animated a flirtation as the presence of her parents would admit. She made some attempts to bring Mr Hatfield once more to her feet; but finding them unsuccessful, she repaid his haughty indifference with still loftier scorn, and spoke of him with as much disdain and detestation as she had formerly done of his curate. But, amid all this, she never for a moment lost sight of Mr Weston. She embraced every opportunity of meeting him, tried every art to fascinate him, and pursued him with as much perseverance as if she really loved him and no other, and the happiness of her life depended upon eliciting a return of affection. Such conduct was completely beyond my comprehension. Had I seen it depicted in a novel, I should have thought it unnatural; had I heard it described by others, I should have deemed it a mistake or an exaggeration; but when I saw it with my own eyes, and suffered from it too, I could only conclude that excessive vanity, like drunkenness, hardens the heart, enslaves the faculties, and perverts the feelings; and that dogs are not the only creatures which, when gorged to the throat, will yet gloat over what they cannot devour, and grudge the smallest morsel to a starving brother.

She now became extremely beneficent to the poor cottagers. Her acquaintance among them was more widely extended, her visits to their humble dwellings were more frequent and excursive than they had ever been before. Hereby she earned among them the reputation of a condescending and very charitable young lady; and their encomiums were sure to be repeated to Mr Weston: whom also she had thus a daily chance of meeting in one or other of their abodes, or in her transits to and fro; and often, likewise, she could gather, through their gossip, to what places he was likely to go at such and such a time, whether to baptize a child, or to visit the aged, the sick, the sad, or the dying; and most skilfully she laid her plans accordingly. In these excursions she would sometimes go with her sister – whom, by some means, she had persuaded or bribed to enter into her schemes – sometimes alone, never, now, with me; so that I was debarred the pleasure of seeing Mr Weston, or hearing his voice even in conversation with another: which would certainly have been a very great pleasure, however hurtful or however fraught with pain. I could not even see him at church: for Miss Murray, under some trivial pretext, chose to take possession of that corner in the family pew which had been mine ever since I came; and, unless I had the presumption to station myself between Mr and Mrs Murray, I must sit with my back to the pulpit, which I accordingly did.

Now, also, I never walked home with my pupils: they said their mamma thought it did not look well to see three people out of the family walking, and only two going in the carriage; and, as they greatly preferred walking in fine weather, I should be honoured by going with the seniors. 'And, besides,' said they, 'you can't walk as fast as we do; you know you're always lagging behind.' I knew these were false excuses, but I made no objections, and never contradicted such assertions, well knowing the motives which dictated them. And in the afternoons, during those six memorable weeks, I never went to church at all. If I had a cold, or any slight indisposition, they took advantage of that to make me stay at home; and often they would tell me they were not going again that day, themselves, and then pretend to change their minds, and set off without telling me: so managing their departure that I never discovered the change of purpose till too late. Upon their return home, on one of these occasions, they entertained me with an animated account of a conversation they had had with Mr Weston as they came along. 'And he asked if you were ill, Miss Grey,' said Matilda; 'but we told him you were quite well, only you didn't want to come to church – so he'll think you're turned wicked.'

All chance meetings on week-days were likewise carefully prevented; for, lest I should go to see poor Nancy Brown or any other person, Miss Murray took good care to provide sufficient employment for all my leisure hours. There was always some drawing to finish, some music to copy, or some work to do, sufficient to incapacitate me from indulging in anything beyond a short walk about the grounds, however she or her sister might be occupied.

One morning, having sought and waylaid Mr Weston, they returned in high glee to give me an account of their interview. 'And he asked after you again,' said Matilda, in spite of her sister's silent but imperative intimation that she should hold her tongue. 'He wondered why you were never with us, and thought you must have delicate health, as you came out so seldom.'

'He didn't, Matilda – what nonsense you're talking!'

'Oh, Rosalie, what a lie! He did, you know; and you said – Don't Rosalie – hang it! – I won't be pinched so! And, Miss Grey, Rosalie told him you were quite well, but you were always so buried in your books that you had no pleasure in anything else.'

'What an idea he must have of me!' I thought.

'And,' I asked, 'does old Nancy ever inquire about me?'

'Yes; and we tell her you are so fond of reading and drawing that you can do nothing else.'

'That is not the case though; if you had told her I was so busy I *could* not come to see her, it would have been nearer the truth.'

'I don't think it would,' replied Miss Murray, suddenly kindling up; 'I'm sure you've plenty of time to yourself now, when you have so little teaching to do.'

It was no use beginning to dispute with such indulged, un-reasoning creatures: so I held my peace. I was accustomed, now, to keeping silence when things distasteful to my ear were uttered; and now, too, I was used to wearing a placid smiling countenance when my heart was bitter within me. Only those who have felt the like can imagine my feelings, as I sat with an assumption of smiling indifference, listening to the accounts of those meetings and interviews with Mr Weston, which they seemed to find such pleasure in describing to me; and hearing things asserted of him which, from the character of the man, I knew to be exaggerations and perversions of the truth, if not entirely false – things derogatory to him and flattering to them, especially to Miss Murray – which I burned to contradict, or, at least, to show my doubts about, but dared not; lest, in expressing my disbelief, I should display my interest too. Other things I heard, which I felt or feared were indeed too true: but I must still conceal my anxiety respecting him, in indignation against them, beneath a careless aspect; others, again, mere hints of something said or done, which I longed to hear more of, but could not venture to inquire. So passed the weary time. I could not even comfort myself with saying, 'She will soon be married; and then there may be hope.'

Soon after her marriage the holidays would come; and when I returned from home, most likely, Mr Weston would be gone, for I was told that he and the Rector could not agree (the Rector's fault, of course), and he was about to remove to another place.

No – besides my hope in God, my only consolation was in thinking that, though he knew it not, I was more worthy of his love than Rosalie Murray, charming and engaging as she was; for I could appreciate his exellence, which she could not: I would devote my life to the promotion of his happiness; she would destroy his happiness for the momentary gratification of her own vanity. 'Oh, if he could but know the difference!' I would earnestly exclaim. 'But no! I would not have him see my heart: yet, if he could but know her hollowness, her worthless, heartless frivolity, he would then be safe, and I should be – *almost* happy, though I might never see him more!'

I fear, by this time, the reader is well-nigh disgusted with the folly and weakness I have so freely laid before him. I never disclosed it then, and would not have done so had my own sister or my mother been with me in the house. I was a close and resolute dissembler – in this one case at least. My prayers, my tears, my wishes, fears, and lamentations, were witnessed by myself and Heaven alone.

When we are harrassed by sorrows or anxieties, or long oppressed by any powerful feelings which we must keep to ourselves, for which we can obtain and seek no sympathy from any living creature, and which yet we cannot or will not wholly crush, we often naturally seek relief in poetry – and often find it, too – whether in the effusions of others, which seem to harmonize with our existing case, or in our own attempts to give utterance to those thoughts and feelings in strains less musical, perchance, but more appropriate, and therefore more penetrating and sympathetic, and, for the time, more soothing, or more powerful to rouse and to unburden the oppressed and swollen heart. Before this time, at Wellwood House and here, when suffering from home-sick melancholy, I had sought relief twice or thrice at this secret source of consolation; and now I flew to it again, with greater avidity than ever, because I seemed to need it more. I still preserve those relics of past sufferings and experience, like pillars of witness set up in travelling through the vale of life, to mark particular occurrences. The footsteps are obliterated now; the face of the country may be changed; but the pillar is still there, to remind me how all things were when it was reared. Lest the reader should be curious to see any of these effusions, I will favour him with one short specimen: cold and languid as the lines may seem, it was almost a passion of grief to which they owed their being.

> Oh, they have robbed me of the hope
>     My spirit held so dear;
> They will not let me hear that voice
>     My soul delights to hear.
>
> They will not let me see that face
>     I so delight to see;
> And they have taken all thy smiles,
>     And all thy love from me.
>
> Well, let them seize on all they can; –
>     One treasure still is mine, –
> A heart that loves to think on thee,
>     And feels the worth of thine.

Yes, at least, they could not deprive me of that: I could think of him day and night; and I could feel that he was worthy to be thought of. Nobody knew him as I did; nobody could appreciate him as I did; nobody could love him as I – could, if I might: but there was the evil. What business had I to think so much of one that never thought of me? Was it not foolish? was it not wrong? Yet, if I found such deep delight in thinking of him, and if I kept those thoughts to myself, and troubled no one else with them, where was the harm of it? I would ask myself. And such reasoning prevented me from making any sufficient effort to shake off my fetters.

But, if those thoughts brought delight, it was a painful, troubled pleasure, too near akin to anguish; and one that did me more injury than I was aware of. It was an indulgence that a person of more wisdom or more experience would doubtless have denied herself. And yet, how dreary to turn my eyes from the contemplation of that bright object and force them to dwell on the dull, grey, desolate prospect around: the joyless, hopeless, solitary path that lay before me. It was wrong to be so joyless, so desponding; I should have made God my friend, and to do His will the pleasure and the business of my life; but faith was weak, and passion was too strong.

In this time of trouble I had two other causes of affliction. The first may seem a trifle, but it cost me many a tear: Snap, my little dumb, rough-visaged, but bright-eyed, warm-hearted companion, the only thing I had to love me, was taken away, and delivered over to the tender mercies of the village rat-catcher, a man notorious for his brutal treatment of his canine slaves. The other was serious enough: my letters from home gave intimation that my father's health was worse. No boding fears were expressed, but I was grown timid and despondent, and could not help fearing that some dreadful calamity awaited us there. I seemed to see the black clouds gathering round my native hills, and to hear the angry muttering of a storm that was about to burst and desolate our hearth.

## CHAPTER 18
### *Mirth and Mourning*

The 1st of June arrived at last: and Rosalie Murray was transmuted into Lady Ashby. Most splendidly beautiful she looked in her bridal costume. Upon her return from church, after the ceremony, she came flying into the schoolroom, flushed with excitement, and laughing, half in mirth and half in reckless desperation, as it seemed to me.

'Now, Miss Grey, I'm Lady Ashby!' she exclaimed. 'It's done, my fate is sealed: there's no drawing back now. I'm come to receive your congratulations and bid you good-bye; and then I'm off for Paris, Rome, Naples, Switzerland, London – oh, dear! what a deal I shall see and hear before I come back again. But don't forget me: I shan't forget you, though I've been a naughty girl. Come, why don't you congratulate me?'

'I cannot congratulate you,' I replied, ''till I know whether this change is really for the better: but I sincerely hope it is; and I wish you true happiness and the best of blessings.'

'Well, good-bye, the carriage is waiting, and they're calling me.'

She gave me a hasty kiss, and was hurrying away: but, suddenly returning, embraced me with more affection than I thought her capable of evincing, and departed with tears in her eyes. Poor girl! I really loved her then; and forgave her from my heart all the injury she had done me – and others also: she had not half known it, I was sure; and I prayed God to pardon her too.

During the remainder of that day of festal sadness I was left to my own devices. Being too much unhinged for any steady occupation, I wandered about with a book in my hand for several hours, more thinking than reading, for I had many things to think about. In the evening I made use of my liberty to go and see my old friend Nancy once again; to apologize for my long absence (which must have seemed so neglectful and unkind) by telling her how busy I had been; and to talk, or read, or work for her, whichever might be most acceptable, and also, of course, to tell her the news of this important day: and perhaps to obtain a little information from her in return, respecting Mr Weston's expected departure. But of this she seemed to know nothing, and I hoped, as she did, that it was all a false report. She was very glad to see me; but, happily, her eyes were now so nearly well that she was almost independent of my services. She was deeply interested in the wedding; but while I amused her with the details of the festive day, the splendours of the bridal party and of the bride herself, she often sighed and shook her head, and wished good might come of it; she seemed, like me, to regard it rather as a theme for sorrow than rejoicing. I sat a long time talking to her about that and other things – but *no one came*.

Shall I confess that I sometimes looked towards the door with a half-expectant wish to see it open and give entrance to Mr Weston as had happened once before? and that, returning through the lanes and fields, I often paused to look round me, and walked more slowly than was at all necessary – for, though a fine evening, it was not a hot one – and, finally, felt a sense of emptiness and disappointment at having reached the house without meeting or even catching a distant glimpse of any one, except a few labourers returning from their work?

Sunday, however, was approaching: I should see him then; for now that Miss Murray was gone, I could have my old corner again. I should see him, and by look, speech, and manner I might judge whether the circumstances of her marriage had very much afflicted him. Happily, I could perceive no shadow of a difference: he wore the same aspect as he had worn two months ago – voice, look, manner, all alike unchanged: there was the same keen-sighted, unclouded truthfulness in his discourse, the same forcible clearness in his style, the same earnest simplicity in all he said and did, that made itself not marked by the eye and ear, but felt upon the hearts of his audience.

I walked home with Miss Matilda; but *he did not join us*. Matilda was now sadly at a loss for amusement, and woefully in want of a companion: her brothers at school, her sister married and gone, she too young to be admitted into society; for which, from Rosalie's example, she was in some degree beginning to acquire a taste – a taste at least for the company of certain classes of gentlemen; at this dull time of year – no hunting going on, no shooting even – for, though she might not join in that, it was *something* to see her father or the gamekeeper go out with the dogs, and to talk with them on their return about the different birds they had bagged. Now, also, she was denied the solace which the companionship of the coachman, grooms, horses, greyhounds, and pointers might have afforded; for her mother having, notwithstanding the disadvantages of a country life, so satisfactorily disposed of her elder daughter, the pride of her heart, had begun seriously to turn her attention to the younger; and, being truly alarmed at the roughness of her manners, and thinking it high time to work a reform, had been roused at length to exert her authority, and prohibited entirely the yards, stables, kennels, and coach-house. Of course, she was not implicitly obeyed; but, indulgent as she had hitherto been, when once her spirit was roused, her temper was not so gentle as she required that of her governess to be, and her will was not to be thwarted with impunity. After many a scene of contention between mother and daughter, many a violent outbreak which I was ashamed to witness, in which the father's authority was often called in to confirm with oaths and threats the mother's slighted prohibitions – for even *he* could see that 'Tilly, though she would have made a fine lad, was not quite what a young lady ought to be' – Matilda at length found that her easiest plan was to keep clear of the forbidden regions; unless she could now and then steal a visit without her watchful mother's knowledge.

Amid all this, let it not be imagined that I escaped without many a reprimand and many an implied reproach, that lost none of its sting from not being openly worded; but rather wounded the more deeply, because, from that very reason, it seemed to preclude self-defence. Frequently I was told to amuse Miss Matilda with other things, and to *remind* her of her mother's precepts and prohibitions. I did so to the best of my power; but she could not be amused against her will, and could not against her taste; and though I went beyond mere reminding, such gentle remonstrances as I would use were utterly ineffectual.

'*Dear* Miss Grey! it is the *strangest* thing. I suppose you can't help it, if it's not in your nature – but I *wonder* you can't make win the confidence of that girl, and make your society at *least* as agreeable to her as that of Robert or Joseph!'

'They can talk the best about the things in which she is most interested,' I replied.

'Well! that is a strange confession, *however*, to come from her *governess*! Who is to form a young lady's tastes, I wonder, if the governess doesn't do it? I *have* known governesses who have so completely identified themselves with the reputation of their young ladies for elegance and propriety in mind and manners that they would *blush* to speak a word against them; and to hear the slightest blame imputed to their pupils was worse than to be censured in their own persons – and I really think it very natural, for my part.'

'Do you, ma'am?'

'Yes, of course: the young lady's proficiency and elegance is of more consequence to the governess than her own, as well as to the world. If she wishes to prosper in her vocation she must devote all her energies to her business: all her ideas and all her ambition will tend to the accomplishment of that one object. When we wish to decide upon the merits of a governess, we naturally look at the young ladies she professes to have educated, and judge accordingly. The *judicious* governess knows this: she knows that, while she lives in obscurity herself, her pupil's virtues and defects will be open to every eye; and that, unless she loses sight of herself in their cultivation, she need not hope for success. You see, Miss Grey, it is just the same as any other trade or profession: they that wish to prosper must devote themselves body and soul to their calling; and if they begin to yield to indolence or self-indulgence they are speedily distanced by wiser competitors: there is little to choose between a person that ruins her pupils by neglect, and one that corrupts them by her example. You will excuse my dropping these little hints; you know it is all for your own good. Many ladies would speak to you much more strongly; and many would not trouble themselves to speak at all, but quietly look out for a substitute. That, of course, would be the *easiest* plan: but I know the advantages of a place like this to a person in your situation; and I have no desire to part with you, as I am sure you would do very well if you will only think of these things and try to exert yourself a *little* more: then, I am convinced, you would *soon* acquire that delicate tact which alone is wanting to give you a proper influence over the mind of your pupil.'

I was about to give the lady some idea of the fallacy of her expectations; but she sailed away as soon as she had concluded her speech. Having said what she wished, it was no part of her plan to wait my answer: it was my business to hear, and not to speak.

However, as I have said, Matilda at length yielded in some degree to her mother's authority (pity it had not been exerted before); and being thus deprived of almost every source of amusement, there was nothing for it but to take long rides with the groom and long walks with the governess, and to visit the cottages and farmhouses on her father's estate, to kill time in chatting with the old men and women that inhabited them. In one of these walks, it was our chance to meet Mr Weston. This was what I had long desired; but now, for a moment, I wished either he or I were away: I felt my heart throb so violently that I dreaded lest some outward signs of emotion should appear; but I think he hardly glanced at me, and I was soon calm enough. After a brief salutation to both, he asked Matilda if she had lately heard from her sister.

'Yes,' replied she. 'She was at Paris when she wrote, and very well, and very happy.'

She spoke the last word emphatically, and with a glance impertinently sly. He did not seem to notice it, but replied, with equal emphasis, and very seriously –

'I hope she will continue to be so.'

'Do you think it likely?' I ventured to inquire: for Matilda had started off in pursuit of her dog, that was chasing a leveret.

'I cannot tell,' replied he. 'Sir Thomas may be a better man than I suppose; but, from all I have heard and seen, it seems a pity that one so young, and gay, and – and *interesting*, to express many things by one word – whose greatest, if not her only fault, appears to be thoughtlessness – no trifling fault to be sure, since it renders the possessor liable to almost every other, and exposes him to so many temptations: but it seems a pity that she should be thrown away on such a man. It was her mother's wish, I suppose?'

'Yes; and her own too, I think, for she always laughed at my attempts to dissuade her from the step.'

'You did attempt it? Then, at least, you will have the satisfaction of knowing that it is no fault of yours if any harm should come of it. As for Mrs Murray, I don't know how she can justify her conduct: if I had sufficient acquaintance with her, I'd ask her.'

'It seems unnatural: but some people think rank and wealth the chief good; and, if they can secure that for their children, they think they have done their duty.'

'True! but is it not strange that persons of experience, who have been married themselves, should judge so falsely?'

Matilda now came panting back, with the lacerated body of the young hare in her hand.

'Was it your intention to kill that hare, or to save it, Miss Murray?' asked Mr Weston, apparently puzzled at her gleeful countenance.

'I pretended to want to save it,' she answered, honestly enough, 'as it was so glaringly out of season; but I was better pleased to see it killed. However, you can both witness that I couldn't help it: Prince was determined to have her; and he clutched her by the back, and killed her in a minute! Wasn't it a noble chase?'

'Very! for a young lady after a leveret.'

There was a quiet sarcasm in the tone of his reply which was not lost upon her; she shrugged her shoulders, and, turning away with a significant 'Humph!' asked me how I had enjoyed the fun. I replied that I saw no fun in the matter; but admitted that I had not observed the transaction very narrowly.

'Didn't you see how it doubled – just like an old hare? and didn't you hear it scream?'

'I'm happy to say I did not.'

'It cried out just like a child.'

'Poor little thing! What will you do with it?'

'Come along – I shall leave it in the first house we come to. I don't want to take it home, for fear papa should scold me for letting the dog kill it.'

Mr Weston was now gone, and we too went on our way; but as we returned, after having deposited the hare in a farmhouse, and demolished some spice-cake and currant wine in exchange, we met him returning also from the execution of his mission, whatever it might be. He carried in his hand a cluster of beautiful bluebells which he offered to me; observing, with a smile, that though he had seen so little of me for the last two months, he had not forgotten that bluebells were numbered among my favourite flowers. It was done as a simple act of goodwill, without compliment or remarkable courtesy, or any look that could be construed into 'reverential, tender adoration' (*vide* Rosalie Murray); but still, it was something to find my unimportant saying so well remembered: it was something that he had noticed so accurately the time I had ceased to be visible.

'I was told,' said he, 'that you were a perfect bookworm, Miss Grey: so completely absorbed in your studies that you were lost to every other pleasure.'

'Yes, and it's quite true!' cried Matilda.

'No, Mr Weston; don't believe it: it's a scandalous libel. These young ladies are too fond of making random assertions at the expense of their friends; and you ought to be careful how you listen to them.'

'I hope *this* assertion is groundless, at any rate.'

'Why? Do you particularly object to ladies studying?'

'No; but I object to any one so devoting himself or herself to study as to lose sight of everything else. Except under peculiar circumstances, I consider very close and constant study as a waste of time, and an injury to the mind as well as the body.'

'Well, I have neither the time nor the inclination for such transgressions.'

We parted again.

Well! what is there remarkable in all this? Why have I recorded it? Because, reader, it was important enough to give me a cheerful evening, a night of pleasing dreams, and a morning of felicitous hopes. Shallow-brained cheerfulness, foolish dreams, unfounded hopes, you will say; and I will not venture to deny it: suspicions to that effect arose too frequently in my own mind. But our wishes are like tinder: the flint and steel of circumstances are continually striking out sparks, which vanish immediately, unless they chance to fall upon the tinder of our wishes; then they instantly ignite, and the flame of hope is kindled in a moment.

But alas! that very morning, my flickering flame of hope was dismally quenched by a letter from my mother, which spoke so seriously of my father's increasing illness that I feared there was little or no chance of his recovery; and, close at hand as the holidays were, I almost trembled lest they should come too late for me to meet him in this world. Two days after, a letter from Mary told me his life was despaired of, and his end seemed fast approaching. Then, immediately, I sought permission to anticipate the vacation, and go without delay. Mrs Murray stared, and wondered at the unwonted energy and boldness with which I urged the request, and thought there was no occasion to hurry; but finally gave me leave: stating, however, that there was 'no need to be in such agitation about the matter – it might prove a false alarm after all; and if not – why, it was only in the common course of nature: we must all die some time; and I was not to suppose myself the only afflicted person in the world'; and concluded with saying I might have the phaeton to take me to O——. 'And instead of *repining*, Miss Grey, be thankful for the *privileges* you enjoy. There's many a poor clergyman whose family would be plunged into ruin by the event of his death; but *you*, you see, have influential friends ready to continue their patronage, and to show you every consideration.'

I thanked her for her 'consideration', and flew to my room to make some hurried preparations for my departure. My bonnet and shawl being on, and a few things hastily crammed into my largest trunk, I descended. But I might have done the work more leisurely, for no one else was in a hurry; and I had still a considerable time to wait for the phaeton. At length it came to the door, and I was off: but, oh, what a dreary journey was that! how utterly different from my former passages homewards! Being too late for the last coach to ——, I had to hire a cab for ten miles, and then a car to take me over the rugged hills. It was half-past ten before I reached home. They were not in bed.

My mother and sister both met me in the passage – sad – silent
– pale! I was so much shocked and terror-stricken that I could
not speak, to ask the information I so much longed yet dreaded
to obtain.

'Agnes!' said my mother, struggling to repress some strong
emotion.

'Oh, Agnes!' cried Mary, and burst into tears.

'How is he?' I asked, gasping for the answer.

'Dead!'

It was the reply I had anticipated: but the shock seemed none
the less tremendous.

## Chapter 19
### *The Letter*

My father's mortal remains had been consigned to the tomb; and
we, with sad faces and sombre garments, sat lingering over the
frugal breakfast-table, revolving plans for our future life. My
mother's strong mind had not given way beneath even this
affliction: her spirit, though crushed, was not broken. Mary's
wish was that I should go back to Horton Lodge, and that our
mother should come and live with her and Mr Richardson at the
vicarage: she affirmed that he wished it no less than herself and
that such an arrangement could not fail to benefit all parties; for
my mother's society and experience would be of inestimable
value to them, and they would do all they could to make her
happy. But no arguments or entreaties could prevail; my mother
was determined not to go. Not that she questioned, for a
moment, the kind wishes and intentions of her daughter; but she
affirmed that so long as God spared her health and strength, she
would make use of them to earn her own livelihood, and be
chargeable to no one; whether her dependence would be felt as a
burden or not. If she could afford to reside as a lodger in ——
vicarage, she would choose that house before all others as the
place of her abode; but not being so circumstanced, she would
never come under its roof, except as an occasional visitor: unless

sickness or calamity should render her assistance really needful, or until age or infirmity made her incapable of maintaining herself.

'No, Mary,' said she, 'if Richardson and you have anything to spare, you must lay it aside for your family; and Agnes and I must gather honey for ourselves. Thanks to my having had daughters to educate, I have not forgotten my accomplishments. God willing, I will check this vain repining,' – she said, while the tears coursed one another down her cheeks in spite of her efforts; but she wiped them away, and resolutely shaking back her head, continued, 'I will exert myself, and look out for a small house, commodiously situated in some populous but healthy district, where we will take a few young ladies to board and educate – if we can get them – and as many day-pupils as will come, or as we can manage to instruct. Your father's relations and old friends will be able to send us some pupils, or to assist us with their recommendations, no doubt: I shall not apply to my own. What say you to it, Agnes? will you be willing to leave your present situation and try?'

'Quite willing, mamma: and the money I have saved will do to furnish the house. It shall be taken from the bank directly.'

'When it is wanted: we must get the house, and settle on preliminaries first.'

Mary offered to lend the little she possessed; but my mother declined it, saying that we must begin on an economical plan; and she hope that the whole or part of mine, added to what we could get by the sale of the furniture, and what little our dear papa had contrived to lay aside for her since the debts were paid, would be sufficient to last us till Christmas; when, it was hoped, something would accrue from our united labours. It was finally settled that this should be our plan; and that inquiries and preparations should immediately be set on foot; and while my mother busied herself with these, I should return to Horton Lodge at the close of my four weeks' vacation, and give notice for my final departure when things were in train for the speedy commencement of our school.

We were discussing these affairs on the morning I have mentioned, about a fortnight after my father's death, when a letter was brought in for my mother, on beholding which the colour mounted to her face – lately pale enough with anxious watchings and excessive sorrow. 'From my father!' murmured she, as she hastily tore off the cover. It was many years since she had heard from any of her own relations before. Naturally wondering what the letter might contain, I watched her countenance while she read it, and was somewhat surprised to see her bite her lip and knit her brows as if in anger. When she had done, she somewhat irreverently cast it on the table, saying with a scornful smile –

'Your grandpapa has been so kind as to write to me. He says he has no doubt I have long repented of my "unfortunate marriage", and if I will only acknowledge this, and confess I was wrong in neglecting his advice, and that I have justly suffered for it, he will make a lady of me once again – if that be possible after my long degradation – and remember my girls in his will. Get my desk, Agnes, and send these things away: I will answer the letter directly. But first, as I may be depriving you both of a legacy, it is just that I should tell you what I mean to say. I shall say that he is mistaken in supposing that I can regret the birth of my daughters (who have been the pride of my life, and are likely to be the comfort of my old age), or the thirty years I have passed in the company of my best and dearest friend; – that, had our misfortunes been three times as great as they were (unless they had been of my bringing on), I should still the more rejoice to have shared them with your father, and administered what consolation I was able; and, had his sufferings in illness been ten times what they were, I could not regret having watched over and laboured to relieve them; that, if he had married a richer wife, misfortunes and trials would no doubt have come upon him still; while I am egotist enough to imagine that no other woman could have cheered him through them so well: not that I am superior to the rest, but I was made for him, and he for me; and I can no more repent the hours, days, years of happiness we have spent together, and which neither could have had without the other, than I can the privilege of having been his nurse in sickness, and his comfort in affliction.

'Will this do, children? – or shall I say we are all very sorry for what has happened during the last thirty years, and my daughters wish they had never been born; but since they have had that misfortune, they will be thankful for any trifle their grandpapa will be kind enough to bestow?'

Of course, we both applauded our mother's resolution; Mary cleared away the breakfast things; I brought the desk; the letter was quickly written and despatched; and, from that day, we heard no more of our grandfather, till we saw his death announced in the newspaper a considerable time after – all his worldly possessions, of course, being left to our wealthy unknown cousins.

CHAPTER 20

## *The Farewell*

A house in A——, the fashionable watering-place, was hired for our seminary and a promise of two or three pupils was obtained to commence with. I returned to Horton Lodge about the middle of July, leaving my mother to conclude the bargain for the house, to obtain more pupils, to sell off the furniture of our old abode, and to fit out the new one.

We often pity the poor, because they have no leisure to mourn their departed relatives, and necessity obliges them to labour through their severest afflictions: but is not active employment the best remedy for overwhelming sorrow – the surest antidote for despair? It may be a rough comforter: it may seem hard to be harassed with the cares of life when we have no relish for its enjoyments; to be goaded to labour when the heart is ready to break, and the vexed spirit implores for rest only to weep in silence: but is not labour better than the rest we covet? and are not those petty, tormenting cares less hurtful than a continual brooding over the great affliction that oppresses us? Besides, we cannot have cares, and anxieties, and toil, without hope – if it be but the hope of fulfilling our joyless task, accomplishing some needful project, or escaping some further annoyance. At any rate, I was glad my mother had so much employment for every faculty of her action-loving frame. Our kind neighbours lamented that she, once so exalted in wealth and station, should be reduced to such extremity in her time of sorrow; but I am persuaded that she would have suffered thrice as much had she been left in affluence, with liberty to remain in that house, the scene of her early happiness and late affliction, and no stern necessity to prevent her from incessantly brooding over and lamenting her bereavement.

I will not dilate upon the feelings with which I left the old house, the well-known garden, the little village church – then doubly dear to me, because my father, who for thirty years had taught and prayed within its walls, lay slumbering now beneath its flags – and the old bare hills, delightful in their very desolation, with the narrow vales between, smiling in green wood and sparkling water – the house where I was born, the scene of all my early associations, the place where throughout life my earthly affections had been centred; – and left them to return no more! True, I was going back to Horton Lodge, where, amid many evils, one source of pleasure yet remained: but it was pleasure mingled with excessive pain; and my stay, alas! was limited to six weeks. And even of that precious time, day after day slipped by and I did not see him: except at church, I never saw him for a fortnight after my return. It seemed a long time to me: and, as I was often out with my rambling pupil, of course hopes would keep rising, and disappointments would ensue; and then I would say to my own heart, 'Here is a convincing proof – if you would but have the sense to see it, or the candour to acknowledge it – that he does not care for you. If he only thought *half* as much about you as you do about him, he would have contrived to meet you many times ere this: you must know that, by consulting your own feelings. Therefore, have done with this nonsense: you have no ground for hope: dismiss, at once, these hurtful thoughts and foolish wishes from your mind, and turn to your own duty, and the dull blank life that lies before you. You might have *known* such happiness was not for you.'

But I saw him at last. He came suddenly upon me as I was crossing a field in returning from a visit to Nancy Brown, which I had taken the opportunity of paying while Matilda Murray was riding her matchless mare. He must have heard of the heavy loss I had sustained: he expressed no sympathy, offered no condolence: but almost the first words he uttered were – 'How is your mother?' And this was no matter-of-course question, for I never told him that I *had* a mother: he must have learned the fact from others, if he knew it at all; and, besides, there was sincere goodwill, and even deep, touching, unobtrusive sympathy in the tone and manner of the inquiry. I thanked him with due civility, and told him she was as well as could be expected. 'What will she do?' was the next question. Many would have deemed it an impertinent one, and given an evasive reply; but such an idea never entered my head, and I gave a brief but plain statement of mother's plans and prospects.

'Then you will leave this place shortly?' said he.

'Yes, in a month.'

He paused a minute, as if in thought. When he spoke again, I hoped it would be to express his concern at my departure; but it was only to say – 'I should think you will be willing enough to go?'

'Yes – for some things,' I replied.

'For *some* things only – I wonder what should make you regret it!'

I *was* annoyed at this in some degree; because it embarrassed me: I had only one reason for regretting it; and that was a profound secret, which he had no business to trouble me about.

'Why,' said I – 'why should you suppose that I dislike the place?'

'You told me so yourself,' was the decisive reply. 'You said, at least, that you could not live contentedly without a friend; and that you had no friend here, and no possibility of making one – and besides, I know you *must* dislike it.'

'But if you remember rightly, I said, or meant to say, I could not live contentedly without a friend in the *world*: I was not so unreasonable as to require one always near me. I think I could be happy in a house full of enemies, if ' —— but no, that sentence must not be continued – I paused, and hastily added – 'And besides, we cannot well leave a place where we have lived for two or three years without some feeling of regret.'

'Will you regret to part with Miss Murray, your sole remaining pupil and companion?'

'I dare say I shall in some degree: it was not without sorrow I parted with her sister.'

'I can imagine that.'

'Well, Miss Matilda is quite as good – better, in one respect.'

'What is that?'

'She's honest.'

'And the other is not?'

'I should not call her *dis*honest; but it must be confessed she's a little artful.'

'*Artful* is she? – I saw she was giddy and vain – and now,' he added, after a pause, 'I can well believe she was artful too; but so excessively so as to assume an aspect of extreme simplicity and unguarded openness. Yes,' continued he musingly, 'that accounts for some little things that puzzled me a trifle before.'

After that, he turned the conversation to more general subjects. He did not leave me till we had nearly reached the park gates: he had certainly stepped a little out of his way to accompany me so far, for he now went back and disappeared down Moss Lane, the entrance of which we had passed some time before. Assuredly I did not regret this circumstance: if sorrow had any place in my heart, it was that he was gone at last – that he was no longer walking by my side, and that that short interval of delightful intercourse was at an end. He had not breathed a word of love, or dropped one hint of tenderness or affection, and yet I had been supremely happy. To be near him, to hear him talk as he did talk; and to feel that he thought me worthy to be so spoken to – capable of understanding and duly appreciating such discourse – was enough.

'Yes, Edward Weston, I could indeed be happy in a house full of enemies, if I had but one friend, who truly, deeply, and faithfully loved me; and if that friend were you – though we might be far apart – seldom to hear from each other, still more seldom to meet – though toil, and trouble, and vexation might surround me, still – it would be too much happiness for me to dream of! Yet who can tell,' said I within myself, as I proceeded up the park – 'who can tell what this one month may bring forth? I have lived nearly three-and-twenty years, and I have suffered much, and tasted little pleasure yet: is it likely my life all through will be so clouded? Is it not possible that God may hear my prayers, disperse these gloomy shadows, and grant me some beams of heaven's sunshine yet! Will He entirely deny to me those blessings which are so freely given to others, who neither ask them nor acknowledge them when received? May I not still hope and trust?' I did hope and trust for a while: but, alas, alas! the time ebbed away: one week followed another, and, excepting one distant glimpse and two transient meetings – during which scarcely anything was said – while I was walking with Miss Matilda, I saw nothing of him: except, of course, at church.

And now the last Sunday was come, and the last service. I was often on the point of melting into tears during the sermon – the last I was to hear from him: the best I should hear from any one, I was well assured. It was over – the congregation were departing; and I must follow. I had then seen him, and heard his voice, too, probably for the last time. In the churchyard, Matilda was pounced upon by the two Misses Green. They had many inquiries to make about her sister, and I know not what besides. I only wished they would have done, that we might hasten back to Horton Lodge: I longed to seek the retirement of my own room, or some sequestered nook in the grounds, that I might deliver myself up to my feelings – to weep my last farewell, and lament my false hopes and vain delusions. Only this once, and then adieu to fruitless dreaming – thenceforth, only sober, solid, sad reality should occupy my mind. But while I thus resolved, a low voice close beside me said – 'I suppose you are going this week, Miss Grey?' 'Yes,' I replied. I was very much startled; and had I been at all hysterically inclined, I certainly should have committed myself in some way then. Thank God, I was not.

'Well,' said Mr Weston, 'I want to bid you good-bye – it is not likely I shall see you again before you go.'

'Good-bye, Mr Weston,' I said. Oh, how I struggled to say it calmly! I gave him my hand. He retained it a few seconds in his.

'It is possible we may meet again,' said he; 'will it be of any consequence to you whether we do or not?'

'Yes, I should be very glad to see you again.'

I *could* say no less. He kindly pressed my hand, and went. Now I was happy again – though more inclined to burst into tears than ever. If I had been forced to speak at that moment, a succession of sobs would have inevitably ensued; and as it was, I could not keep the water out of my eyes. I walked along with Miss Murray, turning aside my face, and neglecting to notice several successive remarks, till she bawled out that I was either deaf or stupid; and then (having recovered my self-possession), as one awakened from a fit of abstraction, I suddenly looked up and asked what she had been saying.

CHAPTER 21
## *The School*

I left Horton Lodge, and went to join my mother in our new abode at A——. I found her well in health, resigned in spirit, and even cheerful, though subdued and sober, in her general demeanour. We had only three boarders and half a dozen day-pupils to commence with; but by due care and diligence we hoped ere long to increase the number of both.

I set myself with befitting energy to discharge the duties of this new mode of life. I call it *new*, for there was, indeed, a considerable difference between working with my mother in a school of our own, and working as a hireling among strangers, despised and trampled upon by old and young; and for the first few weeks I was by no means unhappy. 'It is possible we may meet again,' and 'will it be of any consequence to you whether we do or not?' – those words still rang in my ear and rested on my heart: they were my secret solace and support. 'I shall see him again. – He will come; or he will write.' No promise, in fact, was too bright or too extravagant for Hope to whisper in my ear. I did not believe half of what she told me: I pretended to laugh at it all; but I was far more credulous than I myself supposed; otherwise, why did my heart leap up when a knock was heard at the front door, and the maid, who opened it, came to tell my mother a gentleman wished to see her? and why was I out of humour for the rest of the day because it proved to be a music-master come to offer his services to our school? and what stopped my breath for a moment when, the postman having brought a couple of letters, my mother said, 'Here, Agnes, this is for you,' and threw one of them to me? and what made the hot blood rush into my face when I saw it was directed in a gentleman's hand? and why? – oh! why did that cold, sickening sense of disappointment fall upon me when I had torn open the cover and found it was *only* a letter from Mary, which, for some reason or other, her husband had directed for her?

Was it then come to this – that I should be *disappointed* to receive a letter from my only sister: and because it was not written by a comparative stranger? Dear Mary! and she had written it so kindly – and thinking I should be so pleased to have

it! – I was not worthy to read it! And I believe, in my indignation
against myself, I should have put it aside till I had schooled
myself into a better frame of mind, and was become more
deserving of the honour and privilege of its perusal: but there
was my mother looking on, and wishful to know what news it
contained; so I read it and delivered it to her, and then went into
the schoolroom to attend to the pupils: but amidst the cares of
copies and sums, in the intervals of correcting errors here, and
reproving derelictions of duty there, I was inwardly taking
myself to task with far sterner severity. 'What a fool you must
be,' said my head to my heart, or my sterner to my softer self; –
'how could you ever dream that he would write to *you*? What
grounds have you for such a hope – or that he will see you, or
give himself any trouble about you – or even think of you again?'
'What grounds?' – and then Hope set before me that last, short
interview, and repeated the words I had so faithfully treasured in
my memory. 'Well, and what was there in that? – Who ever
hung his hopes upon so frail a twig? What was there in those
words that any common acquaintance might not say to another?
Of course, it was possible you might meet again: he might have
said so if you had been going to New Zealand; but that did not
imply any *intention* of seeing you – and then, as to the question
that followed, any one might ask that: and how did you answer?
Merely with a stupid, commonplace reply, such as you would
have given to Master Murray, or any one else you had been on
tolerably civil terms with.' 'But then,' persisted Hope, 'the tone
and manner in which he spoke.' 'Oh, that is nonsense! he always
speaks impressively; and at that moment there were the Greens
and Miss Matilda just before, and other people passing by, and
he was obliged to stand close beside you, and to speak very low,
unless he wished everybody to hear what he said: which –
though it was nothing at all particular – of course, he would
rather not.' But then, above all, that emphatic yet gentle pressure
of the hand, which seemed to say, '*Trust me*'; and many other
things besides – too delightful, almost too flattering, to be repeated, even to oneself. 'Egregious folly – too absurd to require
contradiction – mere inventions of the imagination, which you
ought to be ashamed of. If you would but consider your own
unattractive exterior, your unamiable reserve, your foolish
diffidence – which must make you appear cold, dull, awkward,

and perhaps ill-tempered too; – if you had but rightly considered these from the beginning, you would never have harboured such presumptuous thoughts: and now that you have been so foolish, pray repent and amend, and let us have no more of it!'

I cannot say that I implicitly obeyed my own injunctions: but such reasoning as this became more and more effective as time wore on, and nothing was seen or heard of Mr Weston; until at last I gave up hoping, for even my heart acknowledged it was all in vain. But still, I would think of him: I would cherish his image in my mind; and treasure every word, look, and gesture that my memory could retain; and brood over his excellences and his peculiarities, and, in fact, all I had seen, heard, or imagined respecting him.

'Agnes, this sea air and change of scene do *you* no good, I think: I never saw you look so wretched. I must be that you sit too much, and allow the cares of the schoolroom to worry you. You must learn to take things easy, and to be more active and cheerful; you must take exercise whenever you can get it, and leave the most tiresome duties to me: they will only serve to exercise my patience, and, perhaps, try my temper a little.'

So said my mother, as we sat at work one morning during the Easter holidays. I assured her that my employments were not at all oppressive; that I was well; or, if there was anything amiss, it would be gone as soon as the trying months of spring were over: when summer came I should be as strong and hearty as she could wish to see me: but inwardly her observation startled me. I knew my strength was declining, my appetite had failed, and I was grown listless and desponding; – and if, indeed, he could never care for me, and I could never see him more – if I was forbidden to minister to his happiness – forbidden, for ever, to taste the joys of love, to bless and to be blessed – then, life must be a burden, and if my Heavenly Father would call me away, I should be glad to rest. But it would not do to die and leave my mother. Selfish, unworthy daughter, to forget her for a moment! Was not her happiness committed in a great measure to my charge? – and the welfare of our young pupils too? Should I shrink from the work that God had set before me, because it was not fitted to my taste? Did not He know best what I should do, and where I ought to labour? and should I long to quit His service before I had finished my task, and expect to enter into His rest without having laboured to earn it? 'No; by His help I will arise and address myself diligently to my appointed duty. If happiness in this world is not for me, I will endeavour to promote the welfare of those around me, and my reward shall be hereafter.' So said I in my heart; and from that hour I only permitted my thoughts to wander to Edward Weston – or at least to dwell upon him now and then – as a treat for rare occasions: and, whether it was really the approach of summer, or the effect of these good resolutions, or the lapse of time, or all together, tranquility of mind was soon restored; and bodily health and vigour began likewise, slowly but surely, to return.

Early in June I received a letter from Lady Ashby, late Miss Murray. She had written to me twice or thrice before, from the different stages of her bridal tour, always in good spirits, and professing to be very happy. I wondered every time that she had not forgotten me, in the midst of so much gaiety and variety of scene. At length, however, there was a pause; and it seemed she had forgotten me, for upwards of seven months passed away and no letter. Of course, I did not break my heart about *that*, though I often wondered how she was getting on; and when this last epistle so unexpectedly arrived, I was glad enough to receive it. It was dated from Ashby Park, where she was come to settle down at last, having previously divided her time between the Continent and the metropolis. She made many apologies for having neglected me so long, assured me she had not forgotten me, and had often intended to write, &c. &c., but had always been prevented by something. She acknowledged that she had been living a very dissipated life, and I should think her very wicked and very thoughtless; but, notwithstanding that, she thought a great deal, and, among other things, that she should vastly like to see me. 'We have been several days here already,' wrote she. 'We have not a single friend with us, and are likely to be very dull. You know I never had a fancy for living with my husband like two turtles in a nest, were he the most delightful creature that ever wore a coat; so do take pity upon me and come. I suppose your midsummer holidays commence in June, the same as other people's, therefore you cannot plead want of time; and you must and shall come – in fact, I shall die if you don't. I want you to visit me as a *friend*, and stay a long time. There is nobody with me, as I told you before, but Sir Thomas and old Lady

Ashby: but you needn't mind them – they'll trouble us but little with their company. And you shall have a room to yourself, whenever you like to retire to it, and plenty of books to read when my company is not sufficiently amusing. I forget whether you like babies; if you do, you may have the pleasure of seeing mine – the most charming child in the world, no doubt; and all the more so, that I am not troubled with nursing it – I was determined I wouldn't be bothered with that. Unfortunately, it is a girl, and Sir Thomas has never forgiven me: but, however, if you will only come, I promise you shall be its governess as soon as it can speak: and you shall bring it up in the way it should go, and make a better woman of it than its mamma. And you shall see my poodle, too: a splendid little charmer imported from Paris: and two fine Italian paintings of great value – I forget the artist. Doubtless you will be able to discover prodigious beauties in them, which you must point out to me, as I only admire by hearsay; and many elegant curiosities besides, which I purchased at Rome and elsewhere; and finally, you shall see my new home – the splendid house and grounds I used to covet so greatly. Alas! how far the promise of anticipation exceeds the pleasure of possession! There's a fine sentiment! I assure you I am becoming quite a grave old matron: pray come, if it be only to witness the wonderful change. Write by return of post, and tell me when your vacation commences, and say that you will come the day after, and stay till the day before it closes – in mercy to

> 'Yours affectionately,
> 'ROSALIE ASHBY.'

I showed this strange epistle to my mother, and consulted her on what I ought to do. She advised me to go; and I went – willing enough to see Lady Ashby, and her baby too, and to do anything I could to benefit her by consolation or advice; for I imagined she must be unhappy, or she would not have applied to me thus – but feeling, as may readily be conceived, that, in accepting the invitation, I made a great sacrifice for her, and did violence to my feelings in many ways, instead of being delighted with the honourable distinction of being entreated by the baronet's lady to visit her as a friend. However, I determined my visit should be only for a few days at most; and I will not deny that I derived some consolation from the idea that, as Ashby Park was not very far from Horton, I might possibly see Mr Weston, or, at least, hear something about him.

CHAPTER 22

# *The Visit*

Ashby Park was certainly a very delightful residence. The mansion was stately without, commodious and elegant within; the park was spacious and beautiful, chiefly on account of its magnifient old trees, its stately herds of deer, its broad sheet of water, and the ancient woods that stretched beyond it: for there was no broken ground to give variety to the landscape, and but very little of that undulating swell which adds so greatly to the charm of park scenery. And so, this was the place Rosalie Murray had so longed to call her own, that she must have a share of it, on whatever terms it might be offered – whatever price was to be paid for the title of mistress, and whoever was to be her partner in the honour and bliss of such a possession! Well! I am not disposed to censure her now.

She received me very kindly; and, though I was a poor clergyman's daughter, a governess, and a school-mistress, she welcomed me with unaffected pleasure to her home; and – what surprised me rather – took some pains to make my visit agreeable. I could see, it is true, that she expected me to be greatly struck with the magnificence that surrounded her; and, I confess, I was rather annoyed at her evident efforts to reassure me, and prevent me from being overwhelmed by so much grandeur – too much awed at the idea of encountering her husband and mother-in-law, or too much ashamed of my own humble appearance. I was not ashamed of it at all; for, though plain, I had taken good care not to be shabby or mean, and should have been pretty considerably at my ease if my condescending hostess had not taken such manifest pains to make me so; and as for the magnificence that surrounded her, nothing that met my eyes struck me or affected me half so much as her own altered appearance. Whether from the influence of fashionable dissipation, or some other evil, a space of little more than twelve months had had the effect that might be expected from as many years, in reducing the plumpness of her form, the freshness of her complexion, the vivacity of her movements, and the exuberance of her spirits.

I wished to know if she was unhappy; but I felt it was not my province to inquire: I might endeavour to win her confidence; but, if she chose to conceal her matrimonial cares from me, I would trouble her with no obtrusive questions. I therefore, at first, confined myself to a few general inquiries about her health and welfare, and a few commendations on the beauty of the park, and of the little girl that should have been a boy; a small delicate infant of seven or eight weeks old, whom its mother seemed to regard with no remarkable degree of interest or affection, though full as much as I expected her to show.

Shortly after my arrival, she commissioned her maid to conduct me to my room and see that I had everything I wanted: it was a small, unpretending, but sufficiently comfortable apartment. When I descended thence – having divested myself of all travelling encumbrances, and arranged my toilet with due consideration for the feelings of my lady hostess – she conducted me herself to the room I was to occupy when I chose to be alone, or when she was engaged with visitors, or obliged to be with her mother-in-law, or otherwise prevented, as she said, from enjoying the pleasure of my society. It was a quiet, tidy little sitting-room; and I was not sorry to be provided with such a harbour of refuge.

'And some time,' said she, 'I will show you the library: I never examined its shelves, but, I dare say, it is full of wise books; and you may go and burrow among them whenever you please. And now you shall have some tea – it will soon be dinner-time, but I thought, as you were accustomed to dine at one, you would perhaps like better to have a cup of tea about this time, and to dine when we lunch; and then, you know, you can have your tea in this room, and that will save you from having to dine with Lady Ashby and Sir Thomas: which would be rather awkward – at least, not awkward, but rather – a – you know what I mean. I thought you mightn't like it so well – especially as we may have other ladies and gentlemen to dine with us occasionally.'

'Certainly,' said I, 'I would much rather have it as you say; and, if you have no objections, I should prefer having all my meals in this room.'

'Why so?'

'Because, I imagine, it would be more agreeable to Lady Ashby and Sir Thomas.'

'Nothing of the kind.'

'At any rate, it would be more agreeable to me.'

She made some faint objections, but soon conceded; and I could see that the proposal was a considerable relief to her.

'Now, come into the drawing-room,' said she. 'There's the dressing bell; but I won't go yet: it's no use dressing when there's no one to see you; and I want to have a little discourse.'

The drawing-room was certainly an imposing apartment, and very elegantly furnished; but I saw its young mistress glance towards me as we entered, as if to notice how I was impressed by the spectacle, and accordingly I determined to preserve an aspect of stony indifference, as if I saw nothing at all remarkable. But this was only for a moment: immediately conscience whispered, 'Why should I disappoint her to save my pride? No – rather let me sacrifice my pride to give her a little innocent gratification.' And I honestly looked round, and told her it was a noble room, and very tastefully furnished. She said little, but I saw she was pleased.

She showed me her fat French poodle, that lay curled up on a silk cushion, and the two fine Italian paintings: which, however, she would not give me time to examine, but, saying I must look at them some other day, insisted upon my admiring the little jewelled watch she had purchased in Geneva; and then she took me round the room to point out sundry articles of *vertu* she had brought from Italy: an elegant little timepiece, and several busts, small graceful figures, and vases, all beautifully carved in white marble. She spoke of these with animation, and heard my admiring comments with a smile of pleasure: that soon, however, vanished, and was followed by a melancholy sigh; as if in consideration of the insufficiency of all such baubles to the happiness of the human heart, and their woeful inability to supply its insatiate demands.

Then, stretching herself upon a couch, she motioned me to a capacious easy-chair that stood opposite – not before the fire, but before a wide open window; for it was summer, be it remembered; a sweet, warm evening in the latter half of June. I sat for a moment in silence, enjoying the still, pure air, and the delightful prospect of the park that lay before me, rich in verdure and foliage, and basking in yellow sunshine, relieved by the long shadows of declining day. But I must take advantage of this pause: I had inquiries to make, and, like the substance of a lady's postscript, the most important must come last. So I began with asking after Mr and Mrs Murray, and Miss Matilda and the young gentlemen.

I was told that papa had the gout, which made him very ferocious; and that he would not give up his choice wines, and his substantial dinners and suppers, and had quarrelled with his physician because the latter had dared to say that no medicine could cure him while he lived so freely; that mamma and the rest were well. Matilda was still wild and reckless, but she had got a fashionable governess, and was considerably improved in her manners, and soon to be introduced to the world; and John and Charles (now at home for the holidays) were, by all accounts, 'fine, bold, unruly, mischievous boys'.

'And how are the other people getting on?' said I – 'the Greens, for instance?'

'Ah! Mr Green is heart-broken, you know,' replied she, with a languid smile: 'he hasn't got over his disappointment yet, and never will, I suppose. He's doomed to be an old bachelor; and his sisters are doing their best to get married.'

'And the Melthams?'

'Oh, they're jogging on as usual, I suppose: but I know very little about any of them – except Harry,' said she, blushing slightly, and smiling again. 'I saw a great deal of him while we were in London; for, as soon as he heard we were there, he came up under pretence of visiting his brother, and either followed me, like a shadow, wherever I went, or met me, like a reflection, at every turn. You needn't look so shocked, Miss Grey; I was very discreet, I assure you: but, you know, one can't help being admired. Poor fellow! He was not my only worshipper; though he was certainly the most conspicuous, and, I think, the most devoted among them all. And that detestable – ahem – and Sir Thomas chose to take offence at him – or my profuse expenditure, or something – I don't exactly know what – and hurried me down to the country at a moment's notice; where I'm to play the hermit, I suppose, for life.'

And she bit her lip, and frowned vindictively upon the fair domain she had once so coveted to call her own.

'And Mr Hatfield,' said I, 'what is become of him?'

Again she brightened up, and answered gaily –

'Oh! he made up to an elderly spinster and married her, not

long since; weighing her heavy purse against her faded charms, and expecting to find that solace in gold which was denied him in love, ha, ha!'

'Well, and I think that's all – except Mr Weston: what is he doing?'

'I don't know, I'm sure. He's gone from Horton.'

'How long since? and where is he gone to?'

'I know nothing about him,' replied she, yawning – 'except that he went about a month ago – I never asked where' (I would have asked whether it was to a living or merely another curacy, but thought it better not), 'and the people made a great rout about his leaving,' continued she, 'much to Mr Hatfield's displeasure: for Hatfield didn't like him, because he had too much influence with the common people, and because he was not sufficiently tractable and submissive to him – and for some other unpardonable sins, I don't know what. But now I positively must go and dress: the second bell will ring directly, and if I come to dinner in this guise, I shall never hear the end of it from Lady Ashby. It's a strange thing one can't be mistress in one's own house! Just ring the bell, and I'll send for my maid, and tell them to get you some tea. Only think of that intolerable woman'——

'Who – your maid?'

'No; my mother-in-law – and my unfortunate mistake! Instead of letting her take herself off to some other house, as she offered to do when I married, I was fool enough to ask her to live here still, and direct the affairs of the house for me; because, in the first place, I hoped we should spend the greater part of the year in town, and in the second place, being so young and inexperienced, I was frightened at the idea of having a houseful of servants to manage, and dinners to order, and parties to entertain, and all the rest of it, and I thought she might assist me with her experience; never dreaming she would prove a usurper, a tyrant, an incubus, a spy, and everything else that's detestable. I wish she was dead!'

She then turned to give her orders to the footman, who had been standing bolt upright within the door for the last half minute, and had heard the latter part of her animadversions; and, of course, made his own reflections upon them, notwithstanding the inflexible, wooden countenance he thought proper to preserve in the drawing-room. On my remarking afterwards that he must have heard her, she replied –

'Oh, no matter! I never care about the footmen; they're mere automatons: it's nothing to them what their superiors say or do; they won't dare to repeat it; and as to what they think – if they presume to think at all – of course, nobody cares for that. It would be a pretty thing indeed if we were to be tongue-tied by our servants!'

So saying, she ran off to make her hasty toilet, leaving me to pilot my way back to my sitting-room, where, in due time, I was served with a cup of tea. After that, I sat musing on Lady Ashby's past and present condition; and on what little information I had obtained respecting Mr Weston, and the small chance there was of ever seeing or hearing anything more of him throughout my quiet, drab-colour life: which, henceforth, seemed to offer no alternative between positive rainy days and days of dull grey clouds without downfall. At length, however, I began to weary of my thoughts, and to wish I knew where to find the library my hostess had spoken of; and to wonder whether I was to remain there doing nothing till bedtime.

As I was not rich enough to possess a watch, I could not tell how time was passing, except by observing the slowly lengthening shadows from the window; which presented a side view, including a corner of the park, a clump of trees, whose topmost branches had been colonized by an innumerable company of noisy rooks, and a high wall with a massive wooden gate: no doubt communicating with the stable-yard, as a broad carriage-road swept up to it from the park. The shadow of this wall soon took possession of the whole of the ground as far as I could see, forcing the golden sunlight to retreat inch by inch, and at last take refuge in the very tops of the trees. Ere long, even they were left in shadow – the shadow of the distant hills, or of the earth itself; and, in sympathy for the busy citizens of the rookery, I regretted to see their habitation, so lately bathed in glorious light, reduced to the sombre, work-a-day hue of the lower world, or of my own world within. For a moment, such birds as soared above the rest might still receive the lustre on their wings, which imparted to their sable plumage the hue and brilliance of deep red gold; at last, that too departed. Twilight came stealing on; the rooks became more quiet; I became more weary, and wished I were going home to-morrow. At length it grew dark; and I was thinking of ringing for a candle, and betaking myself to bed, when my hostess appeared, with many apologies for having neglected me so long, and laying all the blame upon that 'nasty old woman', as she called her mother-in-law.

'If I didn't sit with her in the drawing-room while Sir Thomas is taking his wine,' said she, 'she would never forgive me; and then, if I leave the room the instant he comes – as I have done once or twice – it is an unpardonable offence against her dear Thomas. *She* never showed such disrespect to *her* husband; and as for affection, wives never think of that nowadays, she supposes: but things were different in *her* time – as if there was any good to be done by staying in the room, when he does nothing but grumble and scold when he's in a bad humour, talk disgusting nonsense when he's in a good one, and go to sleep on the sofa when he's too stupid for either; which is most frequently the case now, when he has nothing to do but to sot over his wine.'

'But could you not try to occupy his mind with something better; and engage him to give up such habits? I'm sure you have powers of persuasion, and qualifications for amusing a gentleman, which many ladies would be glad to possess.'

'And so you think I would lay myself out for his amusement! No; that's not *my* idea of a wife. It's the husband's part to please the wife, not hers to please him; and if he isn't satisfied with her as she is – and thankful to possess her too – he isn't worthy of her, that's all. And as for persuasion, I assure you I shan't trouble myself with that: I've enough to do to bear with him as he is, without attempting to work a reform. But I'm sorry I left you so long alone, Miss Grey. How have you passed the time?'

'Chiefly in watching the rooks.'

'Mercy, how dull you must have been! I really must show you the library; and you must ring for everything you want, just as you would in an inn, and make yourself comfortable. I have selfish reasons for wishing to make you happy, because I want you to stay with me, and not fulfil your horrid threat of running away in a day or two.'

'Well, don't let me keep you out of the drawing-room any longer to-night, for at present I am tired, and wish to go to bed.'

CHAPTER 23
## *The Park*

I came down a little before eight next morning, as I knew by the striking of a distant clock. There was no appearance of breakfast. I waited above an hour before it came, still vainly longing for access to the library; and, after that lonely repast was concluded, I waited again about an hour and a half in great suspense and discomfort, uncertain what to do. At length Lady Ashby came to bid me good-morning. She informed me she had only just breakfasted, and now wanted me to take an early walk with her in the park. She asked how long I had been up, and on receiving my answer, expressed the deepest regret, and again promised to show me the library. I suggested she had better do so at once, and then there would be no further trouble either with remembering or forgetting. She complied, on condition that I would not think of reading, or bothering with the books now; for she wanted to show me the gardens, and take a walk in the park with me, before it became too hot for enjoyment: which, indeed, was nearly the case already. Of course, I readily assented; and we took our walk accordingly.

As we were strolling in the park, talking of what my companion had seen and heard during her travelling experience, a gentleman on horseback rode up and passed us. As he turned, in passing, and stared me full in the face, I had a good opportunity of seeing what he was like. He was tall, thin, and wasted, with a slight stoop in the shoulders, a pale face, but somewhat blotchy, and disagreeably red about the eyelids, plain features, and a general appearance of langour and flatness, relieved by a sinister expression in the mouth and the dull, soulless eyes.

'I detest that man!' whispered Lady Ashby, with bitter emphasis, as he slowly trotted by.

'Who is it?' I asked, unwilling to suppose that she should so speak of her husband.

'Sir Thomas Ashby,' she replied, with dreary composure.

'And do you *detest* him, Miss Murray?' said I, for I was too much shocked to remember her name at the moment.

'Yes, I do, Miss Grey, and despise him too; and if you knew him you would not blame me.'

'But you knew what he was before you married him.'

'No; I only thought so: I did not half know him really. I know you warned me against it, and I wish I had listened to you: but it's too late to regret that now. And besides, mamma ought to have known better than either of us, and she never said anything against it – quite the contrary. And then I thought he adored me, and would let me have my own way: he did pretend to do so at first, but now he does not care a bit about me. Yet I should not care for that: he might do as he pleased, if I might only be free to amuse myself and to stay in London, or have a few friends down here: but *he will* do as he pleases, and I must be a prisoner and a slave. The moment he saw I could enjoy myself without him, and that others knew my value better than himself, the selfish wretch began to accuse me of coquetry and extravagance; and to abuse Harry Meltham, whose shoes he was not worthy to clean. And then he must needs have me down in the country, to lead the life of a nun, lest I should dishonour him or bring him to ruin; as if he had not been ten times worse every way, with his betting-book, and his gaming-table, and his opera-girls, and his Lady This and Mrs That – yes, and his bottles of wine, and glasses of brandy and water too! Oh, I would give ten thousand worlds to be Miss Murray again! It is *too* bad to feel life, health, and beauty wasting away, unfelt and unenjoyed, for such a brute as that!' exclaimed she, fairly bursting into tears in the bitterness of her vexation.

Of course, I pitied her exceedingly; as well for her false idea of happiness and disregard of duty, as for the wretched partner with whom her fate was linked. I said what I could to comfort her, and offered such counsels as I thought she most required: advising her, first by gentle reasoning, by kindness, example, and persuasion, to try to ameliorate her husband; and then, when she had done all she could, if she still found him incorrigible, to endeavour to abstract herself from him – to wrap herself up in her own integrity, and trouble herself as little about him as possible. I exhorted her to seek consolation in doing her duty to God and man, to put her trust in Heaven, and solace herself with the care and nurture of her little daughter; assuring her she would be amply rewarded by witnessing its progress in strength and wisdom, and receiving its genuine affection.

'But I can't devote myself entirely to a child,' said she: 'it may die – which is not at all improbable.'

'But, with care, many a delicate infant has become a strong man or woman.'

'But it may grow so intolerably like its father that I shall hate it.'

'That is not likely; it is a little girl, and strongly resembles its mother.'

'No matter; I should like it better if it were a boy – only that its father will leave it no inheritance that he can possibly squander away. What pleasure can I have in seeing a girl grow up to eclipse me, and enjoy those pleasures that I am for ever debarred from? But supposing I could be so generous as to take delight in this, still it is *only* a child; and I can't centre all my hopes in a child: that is only one degree better than devoting oneself to a dog. And as for all the wisdom and goodness you have been trying to instil into me – that is all very right and proper I dare say, and if I were some twenty years older, I might fructify by it: but people must enjoy themselves when they are young; and if others won't let them – why, they must hate them for it!'

'The best way to enjoy yourself is to do what is right and hate nobody. The end of Religion is not to teach us how to die, but how to live; and the earlier you become wise and good, the more of happiness you secure. And now, Lady Ashby, I have one more piece of advice to offer you, which is that you will not make an enemy of your mother-in-law. Don't get into the way of holding her at arm's length, and regarding her with jealous distrust. I never saw her, but I have heard good as well as evil respecting her; and I imagine that, though cold and haughty in her general demeanour, and even exacting in her requirements, she has strong affections for those who can reach them; and, though so blindly attached to her son, she is not without good principles, or incapable of hearing reason. If you would but conciliate her a little, and adopt a friendly, open manner – and even confide your grievances to her – *real* grievances, such as you have a right to complain of – it is my firm belief that she would, in time, become your faithful friend, and a comfort and support to you, instead of the incubus you describe her.'

But I fear my advice had little effect upon the unfortunate young lady; and, finding I could render myself so little serviceable, my residence at Ashby Park became doubly painful.

But still, I must stay out that day and the following one, as I had promised to do so; though, resisting all entreaties and inducements to prolong my visit further, I insisted upon departing the next morning; affirming that my mother would be lonely without me, and that she impatiently expected my return. Nevertheless, it was with a heavy heart that I bade adieu to poor Lady Ashby, and left her in her princely home. It was no slight additional proof of her unhappiness that she should so cling to the consolation of my presence, and earnestly desire the company of one whose general tastes and ideas were so little congenial to her own – whom she had completely forgotten in her hours of prosperity, and whose presence would be rather a nuisance than a pleasure, if she could but have half her heart's desire.

## Chapter 24
## *The Sands*

Our school was not situated in the heart of the town: on entering A—— from the north-west there is a row of respectable-looking houses, on each side of the broad, white road, with narrow slips of garden-ground before them, Venetian blinds to the windows, and a flight of steps leading to each trim, brass-handled door. In one of the largest of these habitations dwelt my mother and I, with such young ladies as our friends and the public chose to commit to our charge. Consequently, we were a considerable distance from the sea, and divided from it by a labyrinth of streets and houses. But the sea was my delight; and I would often gladly pierce the town to obtain the pleasure of a walk beside it, whether with the pupils, or alone with my mother during the vacations. It was delightful to me at all times and seasons, but especially in the wild commotion of a rough sea-breeze, and in the brilliant freshness of a summer morning.

I awoke early on the third morning after my return from Ashby Park – the sun was shining through the blind, and I thought how pleasant it would be to pass through the quiet town and take a solitary ramble on the sands while half the world was in bed. I was not long in forming the resolution, nor slow to act upon it. Of course I would not disturb my mother, so I stole noiselessly downstairs, and quietly unfastened the door. I was dressed and out, when the church clock struck a quarter to six. There was a feeling of freshness and vigour in the very streets, and when I got free of the town, when my foot was on the sands and my face towards the broad, bright bay, no language can describe the effect of the deep, clear azure of the sky and ocean, the bright morning sunshine on the semi-circular barrier of craggy cliffs surmounted by green swelling hills, and on the smooth, wide sands, and the low rocks out at sea – looking, with their clothing of weeds and moss, like little grass-grown islands – and above all, on the brilliant, sparkling waves. And then, the unspeakable purity and freshness of the air! There was just enough heat to enhance the value of the breeze, and just enough wind to keep the whole sea in motion, to make the waves come bounding to the shore, foaming and sparkling, as if wild with glee. Nothing else was stirring – no living creature was visible besides myself. My footsteps were the first to press the firm, unbroken sands; – nothing before had trampled them since last night's flowing tide had obliterated the deepest marks of yesterday, and left it fair and even, except where the subsiding water had left behind it the traces of dimpled pools and little running streams.

Refreshed, delighted, invigorated, I walked along, forgetting all my cares, feeling as if I had wings to my feet, and could go at least forty miles without fatigue, and experiencing a sense of exhilaration to which I had been an entire stranger since the days of early youth. About half-past six, however, the grooms began to come down to air their masters' horses – first one, and then another, till there were some dozen horses and five or six riders: but that need not trouble me, for they would not come as far as the low rocks which I was now approaching. When I had reached these, and walked over the moist, slippery seaweed (at the risk of floundering into one of the numerous pools of clear, salt water that lay between them) to a little mossy promontory with the sea splashing round it, I looked back again to see who was next stirring. Still there were only the early grooms with their horses, and one gentleman with a little dark speck of a dog running before him, and one water-cart coming out of the town to get water for the baths. In another minute or two the distant bathing-machines would begin to move, and then the elderly gentlemen of regular habits and sober Quaker ladies would be coming to take their salutary morning walks. But however interesting such a scene might be, I could not wait to witness it, for the sun and the sea so dazzled my eyes in that direction, that I could but afford one glance; and then I turned again to delight myself with the sight and the sound of the sea dashing against my promontory – with no prodigious force, for the swell was broken by the tangled seaweed and the unseen rocks beneath; otherwise I should soon have been deluged with spray. But the tide was coming in; the water was rising; the gulfs and lakes were filling; the straits were widening, it was time to seek some safer footing; so I walked, skipped, and stumbled back to the smooth, wide sands, and resolved to proceed to a certain bold projection in the cliffs, and then return.

Presently, I heard a snuffling sound behind me, and then a dog came frisking and wriggling to my feet. It was my own Snap – the little, dark, wire-haired terrier! When I spoke his name, he leapt up in my face and yelled for joy. Almost as much delighted as himself, I caught the little creature in my arms, and kissed him repeatedly. But how came he to be there? He could not have dropped from the sky, or come all that way alone: it must be either his master, the rat-catcher, or somebody else that had brought him; so, repressing my extravagant caresses, and endeavouring to repress his likewise, I looked round, and beheld – Mr Weston!

'Your dog remembers you well, Miss Grey,' said he, warmly grasping the hand I offered him without clearly knowing what I was about. 'You rise early.'

'Not often so early as this,' I replied, with amazing composure, considering all the circumstances of the case.

'How far do you purpose to extend your walk?'

'I was thinking of returning – it must be almost time, I think.'

He consulted his watch – a gold one now – and told me it was only five minutes past seven.

'But, doubtless, you have had a long enough walk,' said he, turning towards the town, to which I now proceeded leisurely to retrace my steps; and he walked beside me.

'In what part of the town do you live?' asked he. 'I never could discover.'

Never could discover? Had he endeavoured to do so, then? I told him the place of our abode. He asked how we prospered in our affairs. I told him we were doing very well – that we had had a considerable addition to our pupils after the Christmas vacation, and expected a still further increase at the close of this.

'You must be an accomplished instructor,' he observed.

'No, it is my mother,' I replied; 'she manages things so well, and is so active, and clever, and kind.'

'I should like to know your mother. Will you introduce me to her some time, if I call?'

'Yes, willingly.'

'And will you allow me the privilege of an old friend, of looking in upon you now and then?'

'Yes, if – I suppose so.'

This was a very foolish answer, but the truth was, I considered that I had no right to invite any one to my mother's house without her knowledge; and if I had said, 'Yes, if my mother does not object,' it would appear as if by his question I understood more than was expected; so *supposing* she would not, I added, 'I suppose so': but of course I should have said something more sensible and more polite, if I had had my wits about me. We continued our walk for a minute in silence: which, however, was shortly relieved (no small relief to me) by Mr Weston commenting upon the brightness of the morning and the beauty of the bay, and then upon the advantages A—— possessed over many other fashionable places of resort.

'You don't ask what brings me to A——,' said he. 'You can't suppose I'm rich enough to come for my own pleasure.'

'I heard you had left Horton.'

'You didn't hear, then, that I had got the living of F——?' F——was a village about two miles distant from A——.

'No,' said I; 'we live so completely out of the world, even here, the news seldom reaches me through any quarter; except through the medium of the —— *Gazette*. But I hope you like your new parish, and that I may congratulate you on the acquisition.'

'I expect to like my parish better a year or two hence, when I have worked certain reforms I have set my heart upon – or, at least, progressed some steps towards such an achievement. But you may congratulate me now; for I find it very agreeable to *have* a parish all to myself, with nobody to interfere with me – to thwart my plans or cripple my exertions: and besides, I have a respectable house in a rather pleasant neighbourhood, and three hundred pounds a year; and in fact, I have nothing but solitude to complain of, and nothing but a companion to wish for.'

He looked at me as he concluded; and the flash of his dark eye seemed to set my face on fire: greatly to my own discomfiture, for to evince confusion at such a juncture was intolerable. I made an effort, therefore, to remedy the evil, and disclaim all personal application of the remark by a hasty, ill-expressed reply, to the effect that, if he waited till he was well known in the neighbourhood, he might have numerous opportunities for supplying his want among the residents of F—— and its vicinity, or the visitors of A——, if he required so ample a choice: not considering the compliment implied by such an assertion, till his answer made me aware of it.

'I am not so presumptuous as to believe that,' said he, 'though you tell it me; but if it were so, I am rather particular in my notions of a companion for life, and perhaps I might not find one to suit me among the ladies you mention.'

'If you require perfection, you never will.'

'I do not – I have no right to require it, as being so far from perfect myself.'

Here the conversation was interrupted by a water-cart lumbering past us, for we were now come to the busy part of the sands; and, for the next eight or ten minutes, between carts and horses, and asses, and men, there was little room for social intercourse, till we had turned our backs upon the sea, and began to ascend the precipitous road leading into the town. Here my companion offered me his arm, which I accepted, though not with the intention of using it as a support.

'You don't often come on to the sands, I think,' said he, 'for I have walked there many times, both morning and evening, since I came, and never seen you till now; and several times, in passing through the town, too, I have looked about for your school – but I did not think of the —— Road: and once or twice I made inquiries, but without obtaining the requisite information.'

When we had surmounted the acclivity, I was about to withdraw my arm from his, but by a slight tightening of the elbow was tacitly informed that such was not his will, and accordingly desisted. Discoursing on different subjects, we entered the town, and passed through several streets. I saw that he was going out of his way to accompany me, notwithstanding the long walk that was yet before him; and, fearing that he might be inconveniencing himself from motives of politeness, I observed –

'I fear I am taking you out of your way, Mr Weston – I believe the road to F—— lies quite in another direction.'

'I'll leave you at the end of the next street,' said he.

'And when will you come to see mamma?'

'To-morrow – God willing.'

The end of the next street was nearly the conclusion of my journey. He stopped there, however, bid me good-morning, and called Snap, who seemed a little doubtful whether to follow his old mistress or his new master, but trotted away upon being summoned by the latter.

'I won't offer to restore him to you, Miss Grey,' said Mr Weston, smiling, 'because I like him.'

'Oh, I don't want him,' replied I, 'now that he has a good master; I'm quite satisfied.'

'You take it for granted that I *am* a good one, then?'

The man and the dog departed, and I returned home, full of gratitude to Heaven for so much bliss, and praying that my hopes might not again be crushed.

## CHAPTER 25
### *Conclusion*

'Well, Agnes, you must not take such long walks again before breakfast,' said my mother, observing that I drank an extra cup of coffee and ate nothing – pleading the heat of the weather and the fatigue of my long walk as an excuse. I certainly did feel feverish and tired too.

'You always do things by extremes: now, if you had taken a *short* walk every morning, and would continue to do so, it would do you good.'

'Well, mamma, I will.'

'But this is worse than lying in bed or bending over your books: you have quite put yourself into a fever.'

'I won't do it again,' said I.

I was racking my brains with thinking how to tell her about Mr Weston, for she must know he was coming to-morrow. However, I waited till the breakfast things were removed, and I was more calm and cool; and then, having sat down to my drawing, I began –

'I met an old friend on the sands to-day, mamma.'

'An old friend! Who could it be?'

'Two old friends, indeed. One was a dog'; and then I reminded her of Snap, whose history I had recounted before, and related the incident of his sudden appearance and remarkable recognition; 'and the other,' continued I, 'was Mr Weston, the curate of Horton.'

'Mr Weston! I never heard of him before.'

'Yes, you have: I've mentioned him several times, I believe: but you don't remember.'

'I've heard you speak of Mr Hatfield.'

'Mr Hatfield was the rector, and Mr Weston the curate: I used to mention him sometimes in contradistinction to Mr Hatfield, as being a more efficient clergyman. However, he was on the sands this morning with the dog – he had bought it, I suppose, from the rat-catcher; and he knew me as well as it did – probably through its means: and I had a little conversation with him, in the course of which, as he asked about our school, I was led to say something about you and your good management; and he said he should like to know you, and asked if I would introduce him to you, if he should take the liberty of calling to-morrow; so I said I would. Was I right?'

'Of course. What kind of a man is he?'

'A very *respectable* man, I think: but you will see him to-morrow. He is the new vicar of F——, and as he has only been there a few weeks, I suppose he has made no friends yet, and wants a little society.'

The morrow came. What a fever of anxiety and expectation I was in from breakfast till noon – at which time he made his appearance! Having introduced him to my mother, I took my work to the window, and sat down to await the result of the interview. They got on extremely well together: greatly to my satisfaction, for I had felt very anxious about what my mother would think of him. He did not stay long that time: but when he rose to take leave, she said she should be happy to see him whenever he might find it convenient to call again; and when he was gone, I was gratified by hearing her say –

'Well! I think he's a very sensible man. But why did you sit back there, Agnes,' she added, 'and talk so little?'

'Because you talked so well, mamma, I thought you required no assistance from me: and, besides, he was your visitor, not mine.'

After that, he often called upon us – several times in the course of a week. He generally addressed most of his conversation to my mother: and no wonder, for she *could* converse. I almost envied the unfettered, vigorous fluency of her discourse, and the strong sense evinced by everything she said – and yet, I did not; for, though I occasionally regretted my own deficiencies for his sake, it gave me very great pleasure to sit and hear the two beings I loved and honoured above every one else in the world discoursing together so amicably, so wisely, and so well. I was not always silent, however: nor was I at all neglected. I was quite as much noticed as I would wish to be: there was no lack of kind words and kinder looks, no end of delicate attentions, too fine and subtle to be grasped by words, and therefore indescribable – but deeply felt at heart.

Ceremony was quickly dropped between us; Mr Weston came as an expected guest, welcome at all times, and never deranging the economy of our household affairs. He even called me 'Agnes': the name had been timidly spoken at first, but, finding it gave no offence in any quarter, he seemed greatly to prefer that appellation to 'Miss Grey'; and so did I. How tedious and gloomy were those days in which he did not come! And yet not miserable; for I had still the remembrance of the last visit and the hope of the next to cheer me. But when two or three days passed without my seeing him, I certainly felt very anxious – absurdly, unreasonably so; for, of course, he had his own business and the affairs of his parish to attend to. And I dreaded the close of the holidays, when *my* business also would begin, and I should be sometimes unable to see him, and sometimes – when my mother was in the schoolroom – obliged to be with him alone: a position

I did not at all desire, in the house; though to meet him out of doors, and walk beside him, had proved by no means disagreeable.

One evening, however, in the last week of the vacation, he arrived – unexpectedly: for a heavy and protracted thunder-shower during the afternoon had almost destroyed my hopes of seeing him that day; but now the storm was over, and the sun was shining brightly.

'A beautiful evening, Mrs Grey!' said he, as he entered. 'Agnes, I want you to take a walk with me to——' (he named a certain part of the coast – a bold hill on the land side, and towards the sea a steep precipice, from the summit of which a glorious view is to be had). 'The rain has laid the dust and cooled and cleared the air, and the prospect will be magnificent. Will you come?'

'Can I go, mamma?'

'Yes; to be sure.'

I went to get ready, and was down again in a few minutes; though, of course, I took a little more pains with my attire than if I had merely been going out on some shopping expedition alone. The thunder-shower had certainly had a most beneficial effect upon the weather, and the evening was most delightful. Mr Weston would have me to take his arm: he said little during our passage through the crowded streets, but walked very fast, and appeared grave and abstracted. I wondered what was the matter, and felt an indefinite dread that something unpleasant was on his mind; and vague surmises concerning what it might be troubled me not a little, and made me grave and silent enough. But these fantasies vanished upon reaching the quiet outskirts of the town: for as soon as we came within sight of the venerable old church, and the —— hill, with the deep blue sea beyond it, I found my companion was cheerful enough.

'I'm afraid I've been walking too fast for you, Agnes,' said he: 'in my impatience to be rid of the town, I forgot to consult your convenience; but now, we'll walk as slowly as you please. I see, by those light clouds in the west, there will be a brilliant sunset, and we shall be in time to witness its effect upon the sea, at the most moderate rate of progression.'

When we had got about half-way up the hill, we fell into silence again; which, as usual, he was the first to break.

'My house is desolate yet, Miss Grey,' he smilingly observed, 'and I am acquainted now with all the ladies in my parish, and several in this town too; and many others I know by sight and by report; but not one of them will suit me for a companion: in fact, there is only one person in the world that will: and that is yourself; and I want to know your decision.'

'Are you in earnest, Mr Weston?'

'In earnest! How could you think I should jest on such a subject?'

He laid his hand on mine that rested on his arm: he must have felt it tremble – but it was no great matter now.

'I hope I have not been too precipitate,' he said, in a serious tone. 'You must have known that it was not my way to flatter and talk soft nonsense, or even to speak the admiration that I felt; and that a single word or glance of mine meant more than the honied phrases and fervent protestations of most other men.'

I said something about not liking to leave my mother, and doing nothing without her consent.

'I settled everything with Mrs Grey, while you were putting on your bonnet,' replied he. 'She said I might have her consent, if I could obtain yours; and I asked her, in case I should be so happy, to come and live with us – for I was sure you would like it better. But she refused, saying she could now afford to employ an assistant, and would continue the school till she could purchase an annuity sufficient to maintain her in comfortable lodgings; and, meantime, she would spend her vacations alternately with us and your sister, and should be quite contented if you were happy. And so now I have overruled your objections on her account. Have you any other?'

'No – none.'

'You love me then?' said he, fervently pressing my hand.

'Yes.'

---

Here I pause. My diary, from which I have compiled these pages, goes but little further. I could go on for years; but I will content myself with adding that I shall never forget that glorious summer evening, and always remember with delight that steep hill, and the edge of the precipice where we stood together, watching the splendid sunset mirrored in the restless world of waters at our feet – with hearts filled with gratitude to Heaven, and happiness, and love – almost too full for speech.

A few weeks after that, when my mother had supplied herself with an assistant, I became the wife of Edward Weston; and never have found cause to repent it, and am certain that I never shall. We have had trials, and we know that we must have them again; but we bear them well together, and endeavour to fortify ourselves and each other against the final separation – that greatest of all afflictions to the survivor. But, if we keep in mind the glorious heaven beyond, where both may meet again, and sin and sorrow are unknown, surely that too may be borne; and, meantime, we endeavour to live to the glory of Him who has scattered so many blessings in our path.

Edward, by his strenuous exertions, has worked surprising reforms in his parish, and is esteemed and loved by its inhabitants – as he deserves; for whatever his faults may be as a man (and no one is entirely without), I defy anybody to blame him as a pastor, a husband, or a father.

Our children, Edward, Agnes, and little Mary, promise well; their education, for the time being, is chiefly committed to me; and they shall want no good thing that a mother's care can give. Our modest income is amply sufficient for our requirements: and by practising the economy we learnt in harder times, and never attempting to imitate our richer neighbours, we manage not only to enjoy comfort and contentment ourselves, but to have every year something to lay by for our children, and something to give to those who need it.

And now I think I have said sufficient.

**FINIS**

# POEMS BY ANNE BRONTË

## The North Wind

That wind is from the North: I know it well;
No other breeze could have so wild a swell.
Now deep and loud it thunders round my cell,
   Then faintly dies, and softly sighs,
And moans and murmurs mournfully.
I know its language: thus it speaks to me:

'I have passed over thy own mountains dear,
   Thy northern mountains, and they still are free;
Still lonely, wild, majestic, bleak, and drear,
   And stern, and lovely, as they used to be

   'When thou, a young enthusiast,
     As wild and free as they,
O'er rocks, and glens, and snowy heights,
     Didst often love to stray.

'I've blown the pure, untrodden snows
In whirling eddies from their brows;
And I have howled in caverns wild,
Where thou, a joyous mountain-child,
   Didst dearly love to be.
The sweet world is not changed, but thou
Art pining in a dungeon now,
   Where thou must ever be.

'No voice but mine can reach thy ear,
And Heaven has kindly sent me here
   To mourn and sigh with thee,
And tell thee of the cherished land
   Of thy nativity.'

Blow on, wild wind; thy solemn voice,
    However sad and drear,
Is nothing to the gloomy silence
    I have had to bear.

Hot tears are streaming from my eyes,
    But these are better far
Than that dull, gnawing, tearless time,
    The stupor of despair.

Confined and hopeless as I am,
    Oh, speak of liberty!
Oh, tell me of my mountain home,
    And I will welcome thee!


### The Bluebell

A fine and subtle spirit dwells
    In every little flower,
Each one its own sweet feeling breathes
    With more or less of power.

There is a silent eloquence
    In every wild bluebell,
That fills my softened heart with bliss
    That words could never tell.

Yet I recall, not long ago,
    A bright and sunny day:
'Twas when I led a toilsome life
    So many leagues away.

That day along a sunny road
    All carelessly I strayed
Between two banks where smiling flowers
    Their varied hues displayed.

Before me rose a lofty hill,
 Behind me lay the sea;
My heart was not so heavy then
 As it was wont to be.

Less harassed than at other times
 I saw the scene was fair,
And spoke and laughed to those around,
 As if I knew no care.

But as I looked upon the bank,
 My wandering glances fell
Upon a little trembling flower,
 A single sweet bluebell.

Whence came that rising in my throat,
 That dimness in my eyes?
Why did those burning drops distil,
 Those bitter feelings rise?

Oh, that lone flower recalled to me
 My happy childhood's hours,
When bluebells seemed like fairy gifts,
 A prize among the flowers.

Those sunny days of merriment
 When heart and soul were free,
And when I dwelt with kindred hearts
 That loved and cared for me.

I had not then mid heartless crowds
 To spend a thankless life,
In seeking after others' weal
 With anxious toil and strife.

'Sad wanderer, weep those blissful times
 That never may return!'
The lovely floweret seemed to say,
 And thus it made me mourn.

## Appeal

Oh, I am very weary,
   Though tears no longer flow;
My eyes are tired of weeping,
   My heart is sick of woe;

My life is very lonely,
   My days pass heavily,
I'm weary of repining;
   Wilt thou not come to me?

Oh, didst thou know my longings
   For thee, from day to day,
My hopes, so often blighted,
   Thou wouldst not thus delay!

## Lines Written at Thorp Green

That summer sun, whose genial glow
Now cheers my drooping spirit so,
   Must cold and silent be,
And only light our northern clime
With feeble ray, before the time
   I long so much to see.

And this soft, whispering breeze, that now
So gently cools my fevered brow,
   This too, alas! must turn
To a wild blast, whose icy dart
Pierces and chills me to the heart,
   Before I cease to mourn.

And these bright flowers I love so well,
Verbena, rose, and sweet bluebell,
   Must droop and die away;
Those thick, green leaves, with all their shade
And rustling music, they must fade,
   And every one decay.

But if the sunny, summer time,
And woods and meadows in their prime,
   Are sweet to them that roam;
Far sweeter is the winter bare,
With long, dark nights, and landscape drear,
   To them that are at Home!


### Despondency

I have gone backward in the work,
   The labour has not sped;
Drowsy and dark my spirit lies,
   Heavy and dull as lead.

How can I rouse my sinking soul
   From such a lethargy?
How can I break these iron chains
   And set my spirit free?

There have been times when I have mourned
   In anguish o'er the past,
And raised my suppliant hands on high,
   While tears fell thick and fast;

And prayed to have my sins forgiven,
   With such a fervent zeal,
An earnest grief, a strong desire,
   As now I cannot feel.

And vowed to trample on my sins,
   And called on Heaven to aid
My spirit in her firm resolves
   And hear the vows I made.

And I have felt so full of love,
   So strong in spirit then,
As if my heart would never cool,
   Or wander back again.

And yet, alas! how many times
  My feet have gone astray!
How oft have I forgot my God!
  How greatly fallen away!

My sins increase, my love grows cold,
  And Hope within me dies:
Even Faith itself is wavering now;
  Oh, how shall I arise?

I cannot weep, but I can pray,
  Then let me not despair;
Lord Jesus, save me, lest I die;
  And hear a wretch's prayer!

### Lines Composed in a Wood on a Windy Day

My soul is awakened, my spirit is soaring
  And carried aloft on the wings of the breeze;
For above and around me the wild wind is roaring,
  Arousing to rapture the earth and the seas.

The long withered grass in the sunshine is glancing
  The bare trees are tossing their branches on high;
The dead leaves beneath them are merrily dancing,
  The white clouds are scudding across the blue sky.

I wish I could see how the ocean is lashing
  The foam of its billows to whirlwinds of spray;
I wish I could see how its proud waves are dashing,
  And hear the wild roar of their thunder to-day!

*The Captive Dove*

Poor restless dove, I pity thee;
    And when I hear thy plaintive moan,
I mourn for thy captivity,
    And in thy woes forget mine own.

To see thee stand prepared to fly,
    And flap those useless wings of thine,
And gaze into the distant sky,
    Would melt a harder heart than mine.

In vain – in vain! Thou canst not rise:
    Thy prison roof confines thee there;
Its slender wires delude thine eyes,
    And quench thy longings with despair.

Oh, thou wert made to wander free
    In sunny mead and shady grove,
And far beyond the rolling sea,
    In distant climes, at will to rove!

Yet, hadst thou but one gentle mate
    Thy little drooping heart to cheer,
And share with thee thy captive state,
    Thou couldst be happy even there.

Yes, even there, if, listening by,
    One faithful dear companion stood;
While gazing on her full bright eye,
    Thou mightst forget thy native wood.

But thou, poor solitary dove,
    Must make, unheard, thy joyless moan;
The heart that Nature formed to love
    Must pine, neglected, and alone.

## The Consolation

Though bleak these woods, and damp the ground
    With fallen leaves so thickly strown,
And cold the wind that wanders round
    With wild and melancholy moan;

There *is* a friendly roof I know,
    Might shield me from the wintry blast;
There is a fire, whose ruddy glow
    Will cheer me for my wanderings past.

And so, though still, where'er I go,
    Cold stranger-glances meet my eye;
Though, when my spirit sinks in woe,
    Unheeded swells the unbidden sigh;

Though solitude, endured too long,
    Bids youthful joys too soon decay,
Makes mirth a stranger to my tongue,
    And overclouds my noon of day;

When kindly thoughts that would have way,
    Flow back discouraged to my breast;
I know there *is*, though far away,
    A home where heart and soul may rest.

Warm hands are there, that, clasped in mine,
    The warmer heart will not belie;
While mirth, and truth, and friendship shine
    In smiling lip and earnest eye.

The ice that gathers round my heart
    May there be thawed; and sweetly, then,
The joys of youth, that now depart,
    Will come to cheer my soul again,

Though far I roam, that thought shall be
    My hope, my comfort, everywhere;
While such a home remains to me,
    My heart shall never know despair!

## Past Days

'Tis strange to think there *was* a time
   When mirth was not an empty name,
When laughter really cheered the heart,
   And frequent smiles unbidden came,
And tears of grief would only flow
In sympathy for others' woe;

When speech expressed the inward thought,
   And heart to kindred heart was bare,
And summer days were far too short
   For all the pleasures crowded there;
And silence, solitude, and rest, –
Now welcome to the weary breast –

Were all unprized, uncourted then;
   And all the joy one spirit showed,
The other deeply felt again;
   And friendship like a river flowed,
Constant and strong its silent course,
For nought withstood its gentle force:

When night, the holy time of peace,
   Was dreaded as the parting hour;
When speech and mirth at once must cease,
   And silence must resume her power;
Though ever free from pains and woes,
She only brought us calm repose.

And when the blessèd dawn again
   Brought daylight to the blushing skies,
We woke, and not *reluctant* then,
   To joyless *labour* did we rise;
But full of hope, and glad and gay,
We welcomed the returning day.

## A Reminiscence

Yes, thou art gone! and never more
    Thy sunny smile shall gladden me;
But I may pass the old church door,
    And pace the floor that covers thee,

May stand upon the cold, damp stone,
    And think that, frozen, lies below
The lightest heart that I have known,
    The kindest I shall ever know.

Yet, though I cannot see thee more,
    'Tis still a comfort to have seen;
And though thy transient life is o'er,
    'Tis sweet to think that thou hast been;

To think a soul so near divine,
    Within a form so angel fair,
United to a heart like thine,
    Has gladdened once our humble sphere.


## Music on Christmas Morning

Music I love – but never strain
    Could kindle raptures so divine,
So grief assuage, so conquer pain,
    And rouse this pensive heart of mine –
As that we hear on Christmas morn
Upon the wintry breezes borne.

Though Darkness still her empire keep,
    And hours must pass, ere morning break;
From troubled dreams, or slumbers deep,
    That music *kindly* bids us wake:
It calls us, with an angel's voice,
To wake, and worship, and rejoice;

To greet with joy the glorious morn,
　　Which angels welcomed long ago,
When our redeeming Lord was born,
　　To bring the light of Heaven below;
The Powers of Darkness to dispel,
And rescue Earth from Death and Hell.

While listening to that sacred strain,
　　My raptured spirit soars on high;
I seem to hear those songs again
　　Resounding through the open sky,
That kindled such divine delight,
In those who watched their flocks by night.

With them, I celebrate His birth –
　　Glory to God in highest Heaven,
Good-will to men, and peace on earth,
　　To us a Saviour-king is given;
Our God is come to claim His own,
and Satan's power is overthrown!

A sinless God, for sinful men,
　　Descends to suffer and to bleed;
Hell *must* renounce its empire then;
　　The price is paid, the world is free,
And Satan's self must now confess
That Christ has earned a *Right* to bless:

Now holy Peace may smile from Heaven,
　　And heavenly Truth from earth shall spring:
The captive's galling bonds are riven,
　　For our Redeemer is our King;
And He that gave His blood for men
Will lead us home to God again.

## Night

I love the silent hour of night,
    For blissful dreams may then arise,
Revealing to my charmèd sight
    What may not bless my waking eyes.

And then a voice may meet my ear,
    That death has silenced long ago;
And hope and rapture may appear
    Instead of solitude and woe.

Cold in the grave for years has lain
    The form it was my bliss to see;
And only dreams can bring again
    The darling of my heart to me.

## Home

How brightly glistening in the sun
    The woodland ivy plays!
While yonder beeches from their barks
    Reflect his silver rays.

That sun surveys a lovely scene
    From softly smiling skies;
And wildly through unnumbered trees
    The wind of winter sighs:

Now loud, it thunders o'er my head,
    And now in distance dies.
But give me back my barren hills
    Where colder breezes rise;

Where scarce the scattered, stunted trees
    Can yield an answering swell,
But where a wilderness of heath
    Returns the sound as well.

For yonder garden, fair and wide,
　With groves of evergreen,
Long winding walks, and borders trim,
　And velvet lawns between –

Restore to me that little spot,
　With grey walls compassed round,
Where knotted grass neglected lies,
　And weeds usurp the ground.

Though all around this mansion high
　Invites the foot to roam.
And though its halls are fair within –
　Oh, give me back my HOME!


## If This Be All

O God! if this indeed be all
　That Life can show to me;
If on my aching brow may fall
　No freshening dew from Thee;

If with no brighter light than this
　The lamp of hope may glow
And I may only *dream* of bliss,
　And wake to weary woe;

If friendship's solace must decay,
　When other joys are gone,
And love must keep so far away,
　While I go wandering on, –

Wandering and toiling without gain,
　The slave of others' will
With constant care and frequent pain,
　Despised, forgotten still;

Grieving to look on vice and sin,
    Yet powerless to quell
The silent current from within,
    The outward torrent's swell;

While all the good I would impart,
    The feelings I would share,
Are driven backward to my heart,
    And turned to wormwood there;

If clouds must *ever* keep from sight
    The glories of the Sun,
And I must suffer Winter's blight,
    Ere Summer is begun:

If Life must be so full of care –
    Then call me soon to Thee;
Or give me strength enough to bear
    My load of misery.


### 'Oh, they have robbed me of the hope'

Oh, they have robbed me of the hope
    My spirit held so dear;
They will not let me hear that voice
    My soul delights to hear.

They will not let me see that face
    I so delight to see;
And they have taken all thy smiles,
    And all thy love from me.

Well, let them seize on all they can; –
    One treasure still is mine, –
A heart that loves to think on thee,
    And feels the worth of thine.

## 'Farewell to thee'

Farewell to thee! but not farewell
  To all my fondest thoughts of thee:
Within my heart they still shall dwell;
  And they shall cheer and comfort me.

O beautiful, and full of grace!
  If thou hadst never met mine eye,
I had not dreamed a living face
  Could fancied charms so far outvie.

If I may ne'er behold again
  That form and face so dear to me,
Nor hear thy voice, still would I fain
  Preserve for aye their memory.

That voice, the magic of whose tone
  Could wake an echo in my breast,
Creating feelings that, alone,
  Can make my trancèd spirit blest.

That laughing eye, whose sunny beam
  My memory would not cherish less; –
And oh, that smile! whose joyous gleam
  No mortal language can express.

Adieu! but let me cherish still
  The hope with which I cannot part.
Contempt may wound, and coldness chill,
  But still it lingers in my heart.

And who can tell but Heaven, at last,
  May answer all my thousand prayers,
And bid the future pay the past
  With joy for anguish, smiles for tears.

## The Narrow Way

Believe not those who say
    The upward path is smooth,
Lest thou shouldst stumble in the way,
    And faint before the truth.

It is the only road
    Unto the realms of joy;
But he who seeks that blest abode
    Must all his powers employ.

Bright hopes and pure delights
    Upon his course may beam,
And there, amid the sternest heights,
    The sweetest flowerets gleam.

On all her breezes borne,
    Earth yields no scents like those;
But he that dares not grasp the thorn
    Should never crave the rose.

Arm – arm thee for the fight!
    Cast useless loads away;
Watch through the darkest hours of night,
    Toil through the hottest day.

Crush pride into the dust,
    Or thou must needs be slack;
And trample down rebellious lust,
    Or it will hold thee back.

Seek not thy honour here;
    Waive pleasure and renown;
The world's dread scoff undaunted bear,
    And face its deadliest frown.

To labour and to love,
    To pardon and endure,
To lift thy heart to God above,
    And keep thy conscience pure;

Be this thy constant aim,
   Thy hope, thy chief delight;
What matter who should whisper blame,
   Or who should scorn or slight?

What matter, if thy God approve,
   And if, within thy breast,
Thou feel the comfort of His love,
   The earnest of His rest?

### Last Lines

A dreadful darkness closes in
   On my bewildered mind;
O let me suffer and not sin,
   Be tortured yet resigned.

Through all this world of blinding mist
   Still let me look to thee,
And give me courage to resist
   The Tempter, till he flee.

Weary I am – O give me strength,
   And leave me not to faint:
Say thou wilt comfort me at length
   And pity my complaint.

I've begged to serve thee heart and soul,
   To sacrifice to Thee
No niggard portion, but the whole
   Of my identity.

I hoped amid the brave and strong
   My portioned task might lie,
To toil amid the labouring throng
   With purpose keen and high;

But thou hast fixed another part,
    And thou hast fixed it well;
I said so with my breaking heart
    When first the anguish fell.

O thou hast taken my delight
    And hope of life away,
And bid me watch the painful night
    And wait the weary day.

The hope and the delight were thine:
    I bless thee for their loan;
I gave thee while I deemed them mine
    Too little thanks, I own.

Shall I with joy thy blessings share
    And not endure their loss;
Or hope the martyr's crown to wear
    And cast away the cross?

These weary hours will not be lost,
    These days of passive misery,
These nights of darkness, anguish-tost,
    If I can fix my heart on thee.

The wretch that weak and weary lies
    Crushed with sorrow, worn with pain,
Still to Heaven may lift his eyes
    And strive and labour not in vain;

Weak and weary though I lie
    Crushed with sorrow, worn with pain,
I may lift to Heaven mine eye
    And strive and labour not in vain;

That inward strife against the sins
    That ever wait on suffering
To strike wherever first begins
    Each ill that would corruption bring;

That secret labour to sustain
    With humble patience every blow;
To gather fortitude from pain
    And hope and holiness from woe.

Thus let me serve thee from my heart
  Whate'er may be my written fate,
Whether thus early to depart
  Or yet a while to wait.

If thou shouldst bring me back to life,
  More humbled I should be,
More wise, more strengthened for the strife,
  More apt to lean on thee.

Should Death be standing at the gate,
  Thus should I keep my vow;
But hard whate'er my future fate,
  So let me serve thee now.